The Domestic Diversifying Acquisition Decision

by
John P. Dory

umi
RESEARCH PRESS

.347848

658.16
D721

Text first published as a typescript facsimile in 1976

Library of Congress Cataloging in Publication Data

Dory, John Paul, 1943-
The domestic diversifying acquisition decision.

(Research for business decisions ; no. 2)
Bibliography: p.
Includes index.
1. Conglomerate corporations—United States.
2. Diversification in industry—United States.
3. Consolidation and merger of corporations—United
States. I. Title. II. Series.

HD2756.U5D67   658.1'6   78-24529
ISBN 0-8357-0954-X
ISBN 0-8357-0955-8 pbk.

The Domestic Diversifying
Acquisition Decision

Research for Business Decisions, No. 2

Other Titles in This Series

CONTENTS

CONTENTS

EXHIBITS

CHAPTER I

INTRODUCTION TO SCANNING FOR DOMESTIC
DIVERSIFYING ACQUISITIONS

This treatise describes and analyzes the process with which firms gathering information for their domestic diversifying acquisition decisions. The analysis attempts to relate the process of scanning in a selected variety of industrial firms to a number of relevant characteristics of these firms, particularly their objectives and strategies for diversification. Managers of firms which are planning or engaging in diversification through acquisition should find an understanding of these relationships useful.

The subject of the research is important because during the 1948-1972 period, the diversity of major U.S. corporations had increased substantially.[1] During this same period, the value of corporate acquisitions increased annually at a more rapid rate than total corporate expenditures for new plant and equipment.[2] Also during this period, the number and value of diversifying acquisitions increased as a portion of all acquisitions.[3] However, between 15% and 20% of all acquisitions were complete failures and only about 20% were completely successful in attaining the objectives set for them.[4] The failure rate for diversifying acquisitions was greater. Although there is some risk inherent in acquisition decisions, this low success rate suggests some ineffective decision-making. One way to improve acquisition decisions would be to improve the information upon which they are based.[5] Chapters VI and VII suggest appropriate approaches to gathering more useful information.

Guidance for gathering information about domestic diversifying acquisitions is not available to firms in published form. Many researchers, consultants, and managers have analyzed acquisitions from their own specialized points of view, for example, accounting, economics, finance, or law.[6] Although they acknowledged the importance of information to the acquisition decision, none appear to have systematically examined the process and problems of information gathering. Formal studies of information theory, information systems, and decision theory have not addressed the problems of locating and gathering information from sources external to an organization.[7] Yet, by their nature, diversifying acquisition decisions required information gathered from external sources. Research about scanning the business environment provided insight on the general problems of information gathering, but did not provide a framework for describing and analyzing formalized information scanning processes for the domestic diversifying acquisition decision.[8]

This study covers new ground by its focus on scanning for information related to acquisition decisions which diversify a firm's product-market scope. Each of these central concepts - acquisitions, diversification, and scanning - are discussed briefly in the remainder of this chapter.

Acquisitions

An acquisition is the combining together of two companies, based in the United States, but competing in different markets, to form one economic unit. It includes all legal forms of combination[9] whether they are mergers, consolidations, or parent-subsidiary formations. It also includes these legal forms regardless of whether the financial accountant treats them as purchases or as poolings of interests. It also includes these legal forms regardless of the tax implications for the owners of the previously separate corporations. These different treatments may have substantial effect on the price and conditions of an acquisition contract. However, they have no effect on the acquisition scanning process.

The research focused on the acquisition decision from the point of view of the acquiring firm. Usually the firm is larger than the acquired company and retains its corporate identity following the acquisition. Also, the acquired company's management is usually subordinated to the acquiring firm's management following the acquisition. In assuming responsibility for the future performance of an acquired company, the firm's management needs different types and amounts of information than is needed by the acquired company's owners or managers. To provide it with appropriate information, the acquiring firm's management requires a considerably different scanning process than the acquired company's management. To simplify terminology throughout the subsequent chapters, the term "firm" refers to the acquiring firm and the term "company" refers to the acquired company.

The beginning or end of the formal acquisition scanning process is difficult to define. For this research, the process begins when the firm expresses a willingness to commit resources to search for acquisition alternatives or to gather information about them. Many possible stimuli can motivate this willingness. Often these stimuli reach top management while its members are informally scanning the environment for other purposes.

Technically, the acquisition scanning process ends when the acquisition contract is signed and ratified by the boards of directors of both corporations. However, the firm's management continues to gather information about the company and its markets after this time. For this research, the acquisition scanning process ends when the firm accepts an "agreement in principle" with a company on the terms of acquisition. Symbolically, the agreement represents a stage in the decision process when the firm stops gathering information to determine its commitment to a particular acquisition alternative.

Diversification

A firm diversifies when it enters a market in which it did not previously compete and with which it did not previously have a buyer/seller relationship. In this sense, a market is a set of suppliers offering similar products to a set of customers with a common need. Firms enter new markets through either acquisition or internal development. The choice between these alternatives receives little managerial consideration after the acquisition scanning process has begun.[10]

Conceptually, a diversifying acquisition alters the scope of the firm's relevant environment and the potential impact of parts of that environment on the firm. Although some trends and conditions in the economic, governmental, social and technological environment affect all domestic firms, others affect only certain markets or certain competitors within some markets. Therefore, entering a new market through acquisition, or internal development, increases the number and type of environmental trends and conditions which can have an impact on the firm. Simultaneously, entry into a new market may reduce the impact of trends and conditions which affect only some of the markets in which a firm competes.

It also alters the scope, configuration, and value of the resources available to the firm. These resources include not only the firm's physical and financial assets, but also its established manufacturing, marketing, purchasing, and research capabilities; the talents of managerial, technical, and operating personnel; the organization structure and process; and the reputation or image of the firm to its various publics. To the extent that the firm and the company it acquires have developed different resources, the acquisition increases the scope of resources available to the firm. The way in which the firm structures, develops, and deploys these resources usually changes their configuration and value over time.

Finally, a diversifying acquisition may change the attitudes, aspirations, and composition of the firm's top management group. By changing the relevant environment and available resources, as well as introducing new managers into the hierarchy, an acquisition causes, or reflects, a change in the aspirations of the top management group. In addition, changes in the organization structure and processes of the firm usually tend to change the attitudes and composition of the top management group.

In essence, this concept of diversification requires that the management of a firm acquire or develop new skills to compete successfully in the markets it enters. These skills relate to various functional areas and to the coordination of various areas. Furthermore, they require management to understand the needs of the customers, the product and process technology, and their relationships sufficiently to determine what skills will be needed in the future.[11]

Scanning Problems

The major managerial problems of domestic diversifying acquisition decision processes are:[12]

1. Planning for an acquisition, especially establishing diversification objectives, determining the resources available for acquisitions, defining criteria for markets to enter and companies to acquire, and organizing those to be involved in the scanning process.

2. Identifying markets for entry and prospects for acquisitions, especially determining the sources of leads and defining the firm's relationships with those sources.

3. Evaluating acquisition prospects, especially gathering information about markets and prospects, learning why prospects are for sale, and determining an acceptable price to pay for a prospect.

4. Approaching the acquisition prospect, especially determining who should approach the prospect and who should be approached within the prospect's organization, preparing the manner and content of the approach, and negotiating a deal.

5. Integrating the prospect into the firm's organization, especially arranging for personnel orientations, establishing management controls, and implementing appropriate operational changes.

These problems are not encountered sequentially; they are interrelated. As a common denominator, they all require information.

Information about the firm's environment, resources, and management values influences the quality of its domestic diversifying acquisition decisions. Information determines the alternatives which the firm identifies and considers. Also, it determines the criteria which the firm applies in selecting among alternatives. Finally, it determines what results the firm expects from selecting particular alternatives. The quantity, accuracy, and relevance of information considered in making the decision reduces the uncertainty about expected results.

Much of the information required for the acquisition decision is not readily available to the managers of the firm. Managers usually have information about the firm's resources and managerial values. Also, they tend to have information about environmental trends and conditions which directly affect their firm or its markets. However, they usually do not have adequate information about potential markets for entry or companies to acquire at the beginning of the acquisition decision process.

Furthermore, this information is difficult to gather because it is about businesses which are unfamiliar to managers. Thus, when they begin to plan diversifying acquisitions for their firms, they may not have adequate knowledge to make quality decisions. They may also lack access to sources of information or knowledge to comprehend information. They may not be able to locate sources of adequate information.

This treatise addresses these problems systematically and describes how some firms with considerable domestic diversifying acquisition experience have dealt with them. Analysis of these descriptions indicates that some information gathering processes are more likely to result in quality acquisition decisions than others. Furthermore, analysis of the major factors which influenced those processes indicates that not all firms should adopt the same acquisition scanning process and concludes what factors should help to determine the choice among available processes.

Plan of Remaining Chapters

The next chapter develops a set of concepts and a systematic approach for gathering information to describe the acquisition scanning processes in six firms. The concepts indicate what information should be gathered about the processes and the factors which influence them. They form the basis for developing the research program which was used to gather the information. The research program includes a structure for selecting research subjects and a methodology for gathering information about them.

Chapters III, IV, and V present the information gathered on the basis of this research methodology. Each chapter has four parts. The first part is an overview of a specific business environment, such as the abrasives industry. The second and third parts each describe the acquisition histories, programs, and scanning processes employed by a firm in that environment. The final part of each chapter compares the scanning processes of the two firms and the major factors which influenced similarities and differences between them.

Chapter VI evaluates and analyzes the acquisition scanning processes of all the firms in the study. The chapter begins with an evaluation of the scanning processes using several different criteria. This evaluation indicates which firms had relatively more or less appropriate acquisition scanning processes. The chapter concludes with a descriptive model of the processes based on the experience of firms with more appropriate processes. The model describes the interaction between the variables which describe the acquisition scanning process and the variables which influenced that process.

Chapter VII concludes the treatise by extending the model to firms not included in the study. In this generalized form, the model has important implications for how other firms should scan for the domestic diversifying acquisition decision.

NOTES

[1] Richard P. Rumelt, *Strategy, Structure, and Economic Performance* (Division of Research, Graduate School of Business Administration, Harvard University, Boston, MA, 1974).

[2] Bureau of Economics, Federal Trade Commission, *Economic Report of the President* (U.S. Government Printing Office, Washington, D.C., 1972), p. 239.

[3] Bureau of Economics, Federal Trade Commission, *Current Trends in Merger Activity* (U.S. Government Printing Office, Washington, D.C. 1971).

[4] H. Igor Ansoff, et al., *Acquisition Behavior of U.S. Manufacturing Firms, 1946-1965* (Vanderbilt University Press, Nashville, TN, 1971), Chap. 2, and John Kitching, "Why do Mergers Miscarry?" *Harvard Business Review* (November-December 1967), pp. 84-101.

[5] Herbert A. Simon, *The New Science of Management Decision* (Harper and Row, New York, NY, 1960), Chap. 1, defines decision making as the process of gathering information, searching for alternatives, and selecting among alternatives.

[6] Representative works are: William W. Albers and Joel E. Segall, eds., (economists), *The Corporate Merger* (University of Chicago Press, Chicago, IL, 1966); William H. Baumer and Leo J. Northart (managers), *Buy, Sell, Merge; How To Do It* (Prentice-Hall, Englewood Cliffs, NJ, 1971); Allen D. Choka (attorney), *Buying, Selling and Merging Businesses* (Joint Committee on Continuing Legal Education, Philadelphia, PA, 1969); John J. Hennessy, Jr. (Consultant), *Acquiring and Merging Businesses* (Prentice-Hall, Englewood Cliffs, NJ, 1966); George D. McCarthy (accountant), *Acquisitions and Mergers* (Ronald Press, NY, 1963); Uwe E. Reinhardt (finance professor), *Mergers and Consolidations; A Corporate Finance Approach* (General Learning Press, Morristown, NJ, 1972); and Arthur Wyatt and Donald Kiesco (financial accountants), *Business Consolidations: Planning and Action* (International Textbook, Scranton, PA, 1969).

[7] James C. Emery, *Organizational Planning and Control Systems* (Macmillan, New York, NY, 1969; David I. Cleland and William R. King, *Management: A Systems Approach* (McGraw-Hill, New York, NY, 1972); and Herman Chernoff and Lincoln Moses, *Elementary Decision Theory* (John Wiley and Sons, New York, NY, 1959).

[8] Francis J. Aguilar, *Scanning the Business Environment* (Macmillan, New York, NY, 1967).

[9] Joseph R. Guardino, *Accounting, Legal and Tax Aspects of Corporate Acquisitions* (Prentice-Hall, Englewood Cliffs, NJ, 1973).

[10] Jesse W. Markham, *Conglomerate Enterprise and Public Policy* (Division of Research, Graduate School of Business Administration, Harvard University, Boston, MA, 1973).

[11] Leonard Wrigley, *Diversification and Divisional Autonomy* (Unpublished doctoral dissertation deposited in Baker Library, Graduate School of Business Administration, Harvard University, Boston, MA, 1969).

[12]Myles L. Mace and George C. Montgomery, Jr. *Management Problems of Corporate Acquisitions* (Division of Research, Graduate School of Business Administration, Harvard University, Boston, MA, 1962).

CHAPTER II

CONCEPTUAL DEVELOPMENT OF THE RESEARCH DESIGN

The chapter explains the research design for selecting and collecting the data needed to describe and to analyze the process by which firms gather information for their domestic diversifying acquisition decisions. The first section of the chapter develops a set of variables which collectively describe an acquisition scanning process. The second section then attempts to identify some of the major factors which likely influence scanning effectiveness. Based on these variables and factors, the final section describes the design of the research study.

Defining the Scanning Process For Diversifying Acquisitions

Scanning is defined here as the activity of gathering information about a firm's environment.[1] The purpose of scanning is to improve decision making by improving the information upon which decisions are based. Some scanning does not have an explicit focus; its purpose may be to detect problems or issues for consideration. Other scanning is clearly intended to provide information for a specific decision or kind of decision. An acquisition scanning process is of this latter type. Its purpose is to gather information about a firm's environment which will assist management in identifying and selecting appropriate companies to acquire.

A firm's acquisition scanning process can usefully be described in terms of six characteristics: (1) types of information gathered, (2) sources of information about markets to enter, (3) sources of information about prospects to acquire, (4) types of information processing, (5) participants in the process, and (6) the sequence of scanning activities.

Types of Information Gathered

The first characteristic is the type and amount of information gathered by the scanning process. This includes the information necessary to identify companies which the firm might acquire and markets which the firm might enter. These companies become acquisition alternatives. This also includes the information used to select among the identified alternatives. This information may pertain either to prospective companies or to the markets in which they compete.

Sources of Market Information

The second characteristic is the sources from which markets for entry are identified and evaluated.   However, most sources of identification may also supply some information which is useful for evaluating the alternatives which they identify. In addition, sources may be different for market information than for prospect information. Distinguishing between these two types of sources is useful because of the sequence in which they may be consulted by various firms.

Sources of Prospect Information

The third characteristic is the sources from which prospective companies for acquisition are identified and evaluated. One important source of prospect information is intermediaries. These are finders, brokers, or other agents that assist a firm in locating companies which are willing to be acquired. These companies are called candidates in this research. Many firms use intermediaries to identify candidates as an approach to scanning. However, information about candidates and other kinds of prospects can also be gathered from many other kinds of sources.

Types of Information Processing

The fourth characteristic is the type and amount of information processing performed by the firm, particularly the use of formal analytical tools or procedures. This is important because it indicates the types of knowledge and skills which the firm includes in its scanning activity.   Also, it indicates the extent to which the firm processes information internally rather than relying on its sources to process it.

Participants in the Process

The fifth characteristic is the participants in the scanning process; particularly, their backgrounds, experience, and organizational positions. The background of a participant is primarily concerned with education and functional specialty. It indicates the range and type of knowledge and analytical capability available to a participant based on his background. Experience is primarily in terms of work in particular companies, industries, or geographic areas. It indicates the range of knowledge and access to information which the participant has accumulated through his prior work experience. Organizational position indicates the perspective a participant has about his own firm.

Sequence of Scanning Activities

The final characteristic is the sequence in which scanning activities are performed. This sequence distinguishes various patterns of search and decision-making. Some firms may identify markets before they identify prospects. Some firms may identify both before they begin to gather information about either. Some firms may gather information about many candidates at the same time and others will gather it sequentially. Although many different sequences are possible, these dominant patterns seem most important in terms of distinguishing among the scanning processes of various firms.

The research program outlined in the final section of this chapter must be capable of describing an acquisition scanning process in these terms.

The Factors Which Influence
The Acquisition Scanning Process

Since domestic diversifying acquisitions affect the environment, resources, and management values of a firm, many factors can potentially influence the acquisition scanning process. Identifying all of them is neither necessary nor desirable. Rather, it is important to identify those which have the greatest influence. Evidence from previous researchers suggests two factors which likely have a major influence on the process. These factors are the diversification objectives of the firm and the diversification strategy used to achieve them. Treating these factors in some detail does not indicate that they are the only important factors. Rather, since they are easily identified, they are used to provide a structure for the research program.

Acquisition Objectives ✓

Researchers and managers have identified many different reasons why firms diversify through acquisition or through internal development.[2] These reasons all suggest that managers became aware of changes in their environments or resources which required a response by their firms. The initial response was to develop explicity or implicity, one or more objectives which the diversifying acquisition program was intended to accomplish. Conceptually, most of these objectives can be represented on a continuum ranging from aggressive to defensive.

Acquisition objectives are typically aggressive when the firm faces its environment with more resources than it can utilize efficiently within its current markets. Often this resource is a cash flow which can more than cover the asset needs of the firm's various businesses.[3] However, these resources need not be financial. The firm may have superior technology, manufacturing capacity, or strong distribution channels which could effectively be applied to other products or customers through diversification while improving the firm's performance.

Acquisition objectives are typically defensive when the firm faces threats or risks within its markets and diversifies to escape the threats or reduce the risks. For example, many firms during the post World War II era diversified to reduce the risk of technological obsolescence within their markets.[4] Other firms faced impending legislation which threatened to restructure their markets or drastically reduce demand for their products. Often these firms would deliberately forego some investments in the resources for their existing markets to permit more rapid diversification.

These two kinds of diversification objectives are the extremes of a continuum. Firms in mature markets face the eventual prospect of sales decline and increasing concentration so that investment requirements are reduced, future performance is threatened.[5] Such a firm may have objectives which are partially aggressive and partially defensive. However, unless market decline is imminent or concentration is likely to occur quickly to the detriment of the firm's market share, the primary objective is often more aggressive than defensive. Precise measurement of such objectives is often both difficult and unnecessary.

In general, firms with defensive objectives are under greater pressure to rapidly achieve diversity. The implication is not that defensively postured firms plan more poorly or hastily, but that their plans often cannot afford the long delays and uncertainty associated with random search or extensive information gathering. Although no firm wants to acquire an unsuitable company, the firm with defensive diversification objectives can less afford to risk an acquisition failure than the firm with more aggressive objectives. The former may therefore tend to utilize more limited sources of information or may rely on external information processing capabilities to insure that the information they gathered is used or interpreted properly. Such firms may also be less adventurous in seeking acquisition prospects. One hypothesis then is that firms with defensive diversification objectives tend to adopt different acquisition scanning processes than firms with aggressive diversification objectives.

Diversification Strategies

A second major factor which may influence the acquisition scanning process is the choice of diversification strategy; that is, a firm's commitment to diversity and the resources which span that diversity as evidenced by the way discrete business units are related to one another.[6] Two different kinds of diversification strategies are of interest. The distinction between the two is in terms of the relationships among the markets which the firm enters. Two markets are related when they utilize the same customers, channels, product and process technologies, raw materials, vendors, or managerial conventions. A firm which has diversified in a way that each of its businesses is related to at least one other business follows a related business strategy. Firms which follow this strategy tend to have more limited market scopes than firms following unrelated business strategies.

Firms following related business strategies should have better access to more reliable sources of information than firms following unrelated business strategies. The relationship between acquisition prospects and existing businesses usually provides managers of the firm with personal or professional associates who become valuable sources of information. Often the relationship between markets includes a common set of customers or vendors from which information can be gathered. Furthermore, related markets often are within a common industry for which published and unpublished information is accessible to the firm. Often consultants who specialize in the industry and who have been retained by the firm for other reasons can provide substantial information. Also, many firms following related business strategies maintain large corporate staff groups which can gather information about many potential related markets for entry.[7] By comparison, a firm following an unrelated business strategy may have considerably less access to sources of information and less staff resources to gather and process it. A second hypothesis then is that firms which follow unrelated business strategies tend to adopt different acquisition scanning processes than firms which follow related business strategies.

Designing the Research Program

The previous sections of this chapter developed concepts and hypotheses about the acquisition scanning process which form a basis for the design of the research program to fulfill the purpose of this treatise. The first section identified characteristics which describe an acquisition scanning process for a firm. The research program must be capable of gathering the information necessary to describe each of these for a firm.

In addition, and to the extent possible, the research program should gather data which could be used to evaluate a firm's acquisition scanning process. The second section identified two important factors which can assist in the construction of the research program. The research program must permit the gathering of information to identify and describe other factors which significantly influence the acquisition scanning process.

The remainder of the chapter is a detailed description of the research program. The program has three distinct but interrelated elements. The first is the structure of the research, which indicates the number and types of firms to be included in the research program. The second is the selection of firms to participate in the research. The third is the methodology for gathering data about each of the firms participating in the research.

The research is exploratory and analytically descriptive in nature and the subjects are large, United States based, profit-oriented business firms which have completed domestic diversifying acquisitions since 1960. Furthermore, the focus of the research is from the point of view of the top managements of the acquiring firms.

Research Structure

The structure of the research reflects the expected influences of the acquisition objectives and diversification strategies on the acquisition scanning process. Therefore, the study included three settings. One pair of firms followed a related business strategy and attempted to achieve aggressive acquisition objectives. A second pair followed a related business strategy and attempted to achieve defensive acquisition objectives. A third pair followed an unrelated business strategy.

Matched pairs of firms were studied in order to distinguish between scanning differences attributable to the influences of hypothesized factors and those attributable to factors unique to the particular firms or industries included in the research. While additional firms in each category could have improved the validity and reliability of the findings, only two firms were used because the in-depth nature of the data gathering methodology permitted the researcher to distinguish between these two types of factors adequately.

This structure facilitated the analysis of the research findings. If all six firms had adopted the same acquisition scanning process, then the researcher could conclude that the hypothesized factors did not significantly influence the process. If the four firms with related business strategies adopted the same process and the two firms with unrelated business strategies followed a different process, then he could conclude that diversification strategy but not acquisition objectives influenced the process. Similarly, if the two firms with aggressive objectives adopted different processes than the two firms with defensive objectives, then he could conclude that acquisition objectives did influence the acquisition scanning process. Finally, if the paired firms generally adopted different processes, then the researcher could conclude that other factors also influence the acquisition scanning process. The research methodology permitted the gathering of information to determine what these other factors might be. It also permitted the gathering of information to determine what factors, if any, had a common influence on all of the scanning processes.

Research Participants

To select industries and firms for inclusion in the research, general patterns of diversification were observed in several industries. Evidence presented in Chapter III suggested that firms within the abrasives industry diversified with aggressive acquisition objectives. Their products were maturing and during years when capital goods production was high, these firms had adequate cash flow to support acquisition programs. The three major competitors in this industry were diversifying. Evidence presented in Chapter IV indicated that firms in the tobacco industry diversified with defensive acquisition objectives. The major threat was a possible sharp decrease in the demand for cigarettes precipitated by mounting medical evidence supporting the claim that smoking was dangerous to human health. While the tobacco firms publicly eschewed the evidence, they all diversified. Most of the firms which followed unrelated business strategies and maintained active acquisition programs were conglomerates. These were easily identified.

The selection of individual firms of each type was not a difficult process. In the abrasives industry, the Norton Company and the Carborundum Company had active acquisition programs, whereas Minnesota Mining and Manufacturing, Inc., the third major competitor in the industry, had acquired most of its diversity during the 1950s. Within the tobacco industry, any of the five major competitors qualified for study. Philip Morris, Inc., and American Brands, Inc., were selected partially because they had considerably different market share performance records. International Telephone and Telegraph and Textron were selected as conglomerate firms because they were both well known as managed conglomerates rather than holding companies. They did not acquire and divest many companies as did some other conglomerates.

Research Methodology

The methodology used to gather research data was a combination of library research and field interviews. Through preliminary library research, the researcher familiarized himself with the acquisitions and activities of the firms in the research before visiting them. Interviews were conducted with the managers responsible for the acquisition scanning process. These managers identified others in their firms who were also involved in the scanning process and arranged separate interviews with each of them. This involved a total of at least three interviews.

The interview process was selected rather than either survey questionnaires or direct observation of the acquisition process for several reasons. The exploratory nature of the research required that the researcher obtain information in more descriptive detail than would have been possible with questionnaires. Furthermore, the factors which influenced acquisition scanning processes could not be determined through written statements. The questions to obtain such information would be too ambiguous and would require a dialogue between the researcher and the manager to insure the proper understanding of the factors and their relationship to the scanning system. This information would also be difficult to obtain solely through observation of the process in more than one firm, since the scanning process for a particular acquisition involved many people gathering and communicating information over several months or years. Therefore, interview provided an opportunity to describe and analyze the acquisition decision process in more than one firm while maintaining some of the richness of detail necessary for the descriptions to be useful. Interview also permitted the researcher to investigate several acquisitions consummated by each research subject.

The format of the interviews appeared unstructured, but had a planned sequence. Early questions allowed the interviewee to describe the acquisition scanning process in his own words with the researcher noting which of the process characteristics were used and which were not. In the second phase of each interview, the researcher asked specifically about any characteristics which the interviewee did not mention. During the third phase of the interview, the researcher asked why the scanning process was designed or organized as it was and what factors influenced that design. In the fourth phase the researcher asked the interviewee to comment on the evolution of the design of the acquisition scanning process over time, indicating what factors influenced changes in the design and how these changes influenced the effectiveness of the process.

This interview format, repeated with several managers in a firm, provided a reasonably complete description of the acquisition scanning process, and helped to avoid the biased notions of any one participant. The open nature of the questions in the interviews minimized the effect of the researcher's biases.   The historical question at the end of the interview not only permitted more detailed analysis of the factors influencing the process, but often provided an opportunity for the researcher to learn about the process during periods when the firm followed other diversification strategies. The findings of the research for each firm are presented in analytical case format in Chapters III, IV, and V.

NOTES

[1]Francis J. Aguilar, *Scanning the Business Environment* (Macmillan, New York, NY, 1967).

[2]See Exhibit II-1 for a partial list of reasons why firms diversify as reported by Thomas A. Staudt, "Program for Product Diversification," *Harvard Business Review*, November-December 1954, pp. 122-123.

[3]Bruce D. Henderson, "Why The (Smart) Rich Get Richer," *Forbes*, May 15, 1974, pp. 90-92.

[4]Alfred D. Chandler, *Strategy and Structure* (M.I.T. Press, Cambridge, MA, 1962).

[5]George A. Field, "Do Products Really Have Life Cycles?" *California Management Review*, Autumn, 1971, pp. 92-95; Rolando Polli and Victor Cook, "Validity of the Product Life Cycle," *Journal of Business*, October 1969, pp. 385-400; and Theodore Levitt, "Exploit The Product Life Cycle," *Harvard Business Review*, November-December 1965, pp. 81-94.

[6]Leonard Wrigley, *Divisional Autonomy and Diversification* (unpublished doctoral dissertation deposited in Baker Library, Graduate School of Business Administration, Harvard University, Boston, MA, 1970), and Richard R. Rumelt, *Strategy, Structure, and Economic Performance*, (Division of Research, Graduate School of Business Administration, Harvard University, Boston, MA, 1974).

[7]Norman A. Berg, "What's Different About Conglomerate Management," *Harvard Business Review*, November-December 1969, pp. 112-120.

EXHIBIT II-1

Reasons Why Firms Diversify

Survival

To offset a declining or vanishing market.
To compensate for technological obsolescence.
To offset obsolete facilities.
To offset declining profit margins.
To offset an unfavorable geographic location brought about by changing economic factors.

Stability

To eliminate or offset seasonal slumps.
To offset cyclical fluctuations.
To maintain employment of the labor force.
To provide balance between high-margin and low-margin products.
To provide balance between old and new products.
To maintain share of market.
To meet new products of competitors.
To tie customers to the firm.
To distribute risk by serving several markets.
To maintain an assured source of supply.
To assure an outlet for the sale of the product.
To develop a strong competitive supply position by offering several close substitute products.

Productive Utilization of Resources

To utilize waste or by-products.
To maintain balance in vertical integration.
To make use of basic raw material.
To utilize excess productive capacity.
To make use of product innovations from internal technical research.
To capitalize distinctive know-how.
To make full use of management resources.
To utilize excess marketing capacity.
To exploit the value of an established market posiion, trade name, or prestige.
To keep pace with an ever-increasing rate of technology.
To capitalize on company research and existing techniques as well as its advances in technology.
To capitalize on a firm's market contacts.

Adaptation to Changing Customer Needs

To meet the demands or convenience of diversified dealers.
To meet the specific requests of important individuals and/or groups of customers.

To meet government requests for national security.

To improve performance of existing products (equipment) through adding accessories or complementary products.

Growth

To counter market saturation on present products.

To reinvest earnings.

To take advantage of unusually attractive merger or acquisition opportunities.

To stimulate the sale of basic products.

To encourage growth for its own sake or to satisfy the ambitions of management or owners.

Miscellaneous

To realize maximum advantage from the tax structure.

To salvage or make the best of previously acquired companies or products.

To maintain a reputation for industrial leadership.

To comply with the desires (or whims) of owners or executives.

To strengthen the firm by obtaining new management and abilities.

Source: Thomas A. Staudt, "Program for Product Diversification," *Harvard Business Review,* November-December 1954, pp. 122-123.

CHAPTER III

DOMESTIC DIVERSIFYING ACQUISITIONS
IN THE ABRASIVES INDUSTRY

This is the first of three data chapters which describe and analyze the domestic diversifying acquisition scanning processes of two companies within an industry. This chapter begins with a short note on the abrasives industry describing some of the major issues which confronted the companies in the industry as they planned and executed their acquisitions. The second and third sections of this chapter describe the acquisition scanning processes of the Norton Company and the Carborundum Company. These sections conclude with analyses of the major factors which influenced the processes. The final section of the chapter compares and contrasts the processes of these two companies, with particular emphasis on the causes of major similarities and differences.

The Abrasives Industry

Although not large, the abrasives industry contributed greatly to the growth and development of the United States as an industrial leader. Many industries use abrasives to produce close tolerances and precision surfaces, both of which facilitate mechanization and automation. Following a brief description of the products and customers of the abrasives industry, this note reviews the growth and profitability performance and expectations for the industry, the price, cost and competitive structures of the industry, and the major problems and opportunities which faced the major competitors in the industry.

Product Description and Use

Abrasives are substances which form, clean, or dress the surfaces of other solid materials or comminute other materials by friction or percussion. Abrasives are used in three basic forms: granular, coated, and bonded. Granular abrasives are particles of abrasive material usually either tumbled with the material to be abraded or projected at high velocity at the surfaces to be abraded. Coated abrasives are abrasive grains adhered to paper, cloth, fiber, or other flexible backings with various adhesives. Bonded abrasives are abrasive grains molded into solid or rigid forms by bonding agents such as ceramic materials, organic resins, shellac, and rubber. During use the bonding agent maintains the position of the abrasive grains and constantly presents new grains or cutting edges to the surface being abraded. Bonded and coated abrasives are usually mounted on machines which move them against the surface to be abraded.

Each form of abrasive has properties which are advantageous for some applications and inappropriate for other. For some applications more than one form might be appropriate. Switching from one form to another usually requires capital investment in new abrasives machinery and therefore limits the amount and rate of customer switching from one form to another. Nevertheless, the demand for coated abrasives has been smaller but growing more rapidly than that of bonded abrasives.

Although available supplies of natural abrasive materials have been adequate, about 90% of all industrial and commercial applications use artificial abrasives, principally aluminum oxide and silicon carbide. Artificial abrasives supplanted natural materials because they can be manufactured in wide ranges of hardness and with great uniformity and accuracy of particle size. High speed and high pressure automated equipment requires the uniformity inherent in artificial abrasives. Extensive research and development efforts have improved artificial abrasives and the process by which they are produced; however, progress was gradual and few new materials have been generally accepted for continued use.

Abrasives are important in producing and finishing parts for a wide variety of products composed of many different materials. Although woodworking and metal working are the major uses of abrasives, stone, plastic, rubber, leather, and glass are also formed and finished by abrasives. Firms in many industries purchase abrasives, particularly those which manufacture nonelectrical machinery, primary metals, transportation equipment, fabricated metal products, electrical machinery, furniture, and other wood products.

To supply abrasives to such a wide variety of customers, most of the major abrasives manufacturers sold through regional or local independent distributors, each of which maintained inventories of over 300,000 different abrasives products, including variations in size, shape, hardness, grain size, material, and media (bonding agent, adhesive, and backing material). Successful competition in abrasives markets required that both the distributors and the abrasives manufacturers maintain intimate knowledge of the peculiar problems which arose from the abrasives applications in each market. To meet this requirement, abrasives manufacturers maintained field technical representatives specializing by industry or application.

Thus, in addition to the product and production technology common to all abrasives markets, a separate and sophisticated applications technology was required for competing in each abrasives market. The development of this technology, and the entry into any of these markets, represents a substantial investment over an extended period of time in the required applications technology.

Forecasts and Trends of Abrasives Industry

Forecasts of future abrasive consumption varied. Major variations resulted from different emphases on technological and economic trends. Optimistic growth estimates relied on extrapolations of past industry growth trends which resulted from extensive investment in research and development by the major abrasives manufacturers over many years. Past research and development resulted in more durable abrasive products and more efficient abrasive systems. For many applications, this reduced the cost of removing material by abrasion relative to the cost of removing material by conventional cutting tools. Thus, optimistic forecasters projected an increasing substitution of abrasives for other cutting tools. They also assumed a continued increase in the volume of activities which used abrasives.

The more pessimistic forecasters, whose judgments recently had been more accurate, extrapolated a second developing trend toward the increasing substitution of plastic parts for metal parts in many industries and products, especially mechanical systems and their housings. This trend developed because the material costs favored the use of plastics wherever they could function effectively, and because most plastic parts could be molded with the desired shape and surface finish, eliminating the need for subsequent machining operations, including abrasion. Therefore, the forecasters of slow growth for abrasives demand expected the reduction in parts requiring subsequent machining to more than offset the increase in number of new applications of abrasives.

Furthermore, abrasives industry dollar sales volume could not be increased by major price increases, without sacrificing the cost advantage abrasives had achieved over cutting tools. Abrasives customers could easily determine the total cost to them of using new abrasives or abrasives machinery relative to their previous machining methods. Therefore, product improvements not only limited price increases, but usually also reduced the volume of abrasives required for a particular application. Thus in the short term, price was relatively inelastic, although in the long term they were constrained by prices of alternative production methods.

Trends within specific abrasives markets had little impact on the overall demand for abrasives since the customer base was broad with no one market representing a large portion of all abrasives sold. However, the nature of the customers across all abrasives markets and the products which they manufacture using abrasives dictated that the demand for abrasives responded strongly to changes in the capital goods production levels; therefore the abrasives industry sales varied directly with the capital goods cycle.

Industry Structure

This strong dependence on the capital goods cycle created problems for the abrasives manufacturers, which were exacerbated by the slow growth of the industry. A large portion of the abrasives manufacturing costs were fixed, rather than variable, so that changes in demand had a major impact on changes in profits. The portion of fixed costs was greater for the large abrasives firms which had integrated backwards to produce their own abrasives materials. These abrasives manufacturers also sold abrasives materials to many of the smaller abrasives manufacturers, which converted them to coated or bonded products. These smaller abrasives manufacturers did not have sufficient volume to achieve economies of scale for producing artificial abrasive materials.

The economies of scale were not limited to the production of abrasives materials, however. Larger sales volume could support larger research and development expenditures and spread production start-up costs over more sales. The manufacturing technology also had some economies of scale which improved efficiency with size. Finally, larger sales volume allowed for more efficient and effective distribution methods and stronger relationships with distributors.

The economies of scale for abrasives manufacture were only one factor contributing to the high concentration of sales in a few firms. According to published government statistics, the sales of the four largest abrasives manufacturers represented over half of the sales of the entire industry, a concentration ratio which had remained relatively stable over a long period of time. The concentration ratios were higher for each of the major types of abrasives. Furthermore, industry experts attributed most of these sales to the three largest companies in the industry: The Carborundum Company, Minnesota Mining and Manufacturing Company, and The Norton Company. Each of these firms manufactured and sold a full line of abrasives products in a large number of the abrasives markets.

Although market share data was not available, the share of market for each of these competitors was believed to vary with the type of abrasive. The number of minor competitors also varied by the form of abrasives: about 20 firms produced abrasive grains, about 40 produced coated abrasives, and about 250 produced bonded abrasives. Most of these smaller competitors produced only one form of abrasive products and participated in only a few markets. Many had regional rather than national distribution, and many serviced only low volume customers. Few, if any, of the smaller competitors produced their own artificial abrasives materials.

During the early history of the industry, technology provided the major barrier to the entrance of new competitors into the abrasive markets. As the applications of abrasives became more sophisticated, the barriers also included specific marketing knowledge and technological understanding of the abrasives customers' real production requirements. Although these barriers have continued to exist, few firms were interested in entering the industry because of the low growth prospects, highly variable profits, and the strong competitive advantage of the three large competitors. This competitive advantage effectively prevented the smaller competitors from gaining market share.

Although this competitive advantage included economies of scale and technological leadership, it also included several other factors. Abrasives costs were an insignificant portion of the total manufacturing cost for most abrasives users, but their failure or unavailability could cause major production problems. Therefore, product reliability and availability became important considerations in purchasing abrasives. The three major abrasives companies could control product availability effectively because they had developed superior inventory control systems for their distributors and had sufficiently large sales volumes to control the inventories and activities of those distributors. Furthermore, they had the resources to deal effectively and efficiently with unexpected supply problems. Product reliability was not only a result of the superior technological expertise of the three competitors, but also of tighter quality control systems, more controlled development of new applications, and many technical field representatives to more quickly define, solve and rectify customer problems. Furthermore, in some purchasing decisions, the availability of all of a customer's abrasive needs from a single supplier could be important by simplifying the ordering procedures for abrasives. This was an advantage primarily to major volume users of abrasives.

Within this industry structure with strong evidence of market maturation, the major competitors had no viable options for continued growth in the abrasives industry. It was difficult and unprofitable to gain market share by attempting to service the low-volume, widely dispersed customers of the smaller competitors. It was legally impossible to acquire such competitors. The prospect of major technological change was small and the evolutionary technological change which the major competitors controlled would therefore not have a major impact on the future forecasted demand. Yet, without some prospect of future growth and stability, the stock prices of these competitors would erode. The undesirable consequences of low prices and strong cash flow would be possible acquisition by more aggressive firms.

Two major alternatives appeared viable: first, the large abrasives manufacturers could attempt to enter the foreign markets where the demand growth for abrasives would be significantly greater than in the United States; and second, they could attempt to diversify. All of the major competitors in the abrasives industry pursued both of these alternatives. It is against this background that the following sections explore the diversification efforts and activities of two of the three major competitors, the Norton Company and the Carborundum Company.

The Norton Company

In 1972, the Norton Company was a multiproduct, multimarket, multinational corporation with $14.5 million in profits and $374 million in sales, of which about 25% was from non-abrasive products. Since 1962, the compound annual sales growth rate of the Norton Company was about 6.5%. Between 1958 and 1962 the earnings per share increased 11.8% although there were wide fluctuations within this period. Since 1962, Norton acquired 20 companies, 8 of which were based in the United States. All of the 8 were diversifying acquisitions.[1] During this same period, Norton also obtained partial ownership of several overseas companies, established licensing agreements with others, established operations in other countries, and divested 15 product lines. Norton maintained an active research and development program focused primarily on abrasives and ceramics technology.

Virtually all corporate diversification occurred after 1962, at which time the company first sold stock to the general public. By 1972, over 65% of the stock was still held by members of the company or members of the founding family. Until 1962, the principal business of Norton was the manufacture and sale of abrasive products, including a line of abrasives machinery. The abrasive products included granular, coated, and bonded abrasives, as well as refractory products for industrial furnace applications. In addition, the company produced a line of pressure-sensitive tapes. All of these products were produced in 12 plants in the United States and Canada and 12 plants operated by subsidiaries throughout the remainder of the world. Primarily through acquisition, Norton had diversified into a wide variety of products serving customers in many industries by 1973.[2]

Program History and Participants

Early diversification efforts were planned primarily by Messrs. Milton P. Higgins, Chairman of the Board, and Ralph F. Gow, President, with inputs from Mr. Richard Harris, who was appointed Director of Corporate Development in 1963. During 1966, the same year that Norton acquired U.S. Stoneware and its subsidiary Chamberlin Engineering, the management began to institute a formal planning system. Apparently, operating problems and problems with the formal planning system diverted management's attention from the diversifying acquisition program. Since acquisitions prior to 1966 enjoyed considerable post-acquisition autonomy, it also appeared that one reason for introducing a formal planning system was to gain some control over these acquisitions through a better understanding of their businesses. In 1967, Mr. John Jeppson was elected President and Chief Executive Officer of Norton and subsequently appointed Vice President Mr. Robert Cushman to chair a committee to evaluate Norton's product lines. The work of this committee led to the fifteen divestitures which occurred between 1969 and 1972. In 1972, Mr. Cushman succeeded to the Presidency.

After Mr. Jeppson was elected President in 1967, Mr. Donald Melville joined Norton as the Marketing Vice President and served on Mr. Cushman's product line review committee, after having been marketing director for Continental Can Company. In early 1969, Mr. Melville became Group Vice President for the advanced materials operations and in 1971 became Executive Vice President for diversified products (non-abrasives).

Two men reporting to Mr. Melville in 1972 had primary responsibility for Norton's acquisition program: Mr. Richard Griffin, Director of Corporate Planning, and Mr. Norman Johnson,[3] Director of Business Planning. Mr. Johnson had served Norton for over 21 years in a variety of both manufacturing and marketing positions. Although his basic function was to help the non-abrasive divisions of Norton formulate strategic plans, he in fact devoted over 60% of his time to scanning for new acquisition prospects. Mr. Griffin joined Norton in early 1972 with an extensive background and experience in mergers, acquisitions and diversification. Prior to joining Norton, Mr. Griffin managed his own consulting firm which specialized in mergers and acquisitions. Before that he worked a total of seven years with two firms, helping them formulate and implement diversification programs. Messrs. Melville, Johnson, and Griffin worked in contiguous offices at the Norton Headquarters. Mr. Griffin also worked closely with two other Norton employees: one a financial analyst who spent over half of his time analyzing acquisition possibilities, and a market researcher who devoted a small part of his time to market surveys for acquisitions possibilities.

The acquisition activity of the Norton Company evolved through a series of stages of programs, each of which represented a different approach to the objectives and scanning process for acquisitions. The 1963 acquisition of National Research and 1964 acquisition of Clipper Manufacturing were the first stage. They were not the result of a formally established acquisition program designed to achieve corporate diversification objectives. National Research was acquired primarily as an opportunity for Norton to obtain a listing on the New York Stock Exchange. The Norton management also felt that National Research would provide entry into some relatively high technology areas, but this was only a secondary consideration. Prior to learning about the National Research acquisition possibility, Norton management had not been searching for a high technology opportunity. Clipper Manufacturing, whose products used abrasives, also became a prospect before management planned to enter the paving machinery industry. Most of the product lines acquired through these two acquisitions were divested during the 1970-1972 period as part of Norton's attempt to realign its corporate strategy.

The 1966 acquisition of U.S. Stoneware and its subsidiary, Chamberlin Engineering, was the first to result from strategic planning. These marked the beginning of the second program. Through them, Norton sought to increase its industrial ceramics business by participating in additional markets, including the chemical process products field in which U.S. Stoneware competed. Also about 1966, in conjunction with the initiation of Norton's formal planning system, management sought to plan its diversifying activity more completely than it had in the past. The planning staff generated studies of numerous possible markets which Norton might enter through acquisition. However, the only two acquisitions during this period, Koebel Diamond Tool and Sandon, were both very closely related to Norton's traditional product lines. Norton had distributed Sandon's products for several years prior to the acquisition.

In mid-1973, Norton had a somewhat more aggressive acquisition program in progress, even though it had acquired only two companies to date under this program. These acquisitions were Newton Glove and Lakeville Plastics. Through this third acquisition program Norton planned to acquire companies with aggregate sales of about $20 million per year so that by 1980, 40% of Norton's sales would be derived from non-abrasive products, compared with 25% in 1972. Although management expected to conclude one or two large acquisitions by 1980, in anticipated that the major part of Norton's non-abrasives growth would result from many smaller acquisitions. The acquisition program did not focus on major corporate problems in 1972, but on major problems which might arise after 1980 if the acquisition program were not successful in achieving a greater balance within the company. However, management felt that the goals of the program were quite modest and their achievement would not be difficult. Apparently because of the relatively long time horizon for the program, management generally perceived it more as capitalizing on an opportunity than as a response to eminent environmental threat.

This program included three separate types of domestic diversifying acquisitions. First, Norton sought to acquire companies which would broaden its participation in the several non-abrasive product lines[4] which remained after the divestment program of 1970-1972. These "Type I" acquisitions would relate to existing product lines by providing more products for current or similar customers or by providing current product lines to new types of customers. Second, Norton sought to acquire a few large companies which would each have a substantial impact on the portion of Norton's sales derived from non-abrasive products. These "Type II" acquisitions would most likely be unrelated to the markets in which Norton previously competed. Third, Norton sought to acquire small companies whose individual impact on Norton's sales would be marginal. These "Type III" acquisitions would provide a basis for further related diversification through Type I acquisitions to form major Norton divisions.[5] In addition to these three types of domestic diversifying acquisitions, Norton also sought to acquire abrasives companies in overseas markets which would enhance its participation in the worldwide abrasives markets. The thrust of these acquisitions would be in countries in which Norton's present market position was weak or nonexistent but in which substantial growth was expected.

Acquisition Criteria

The criteria for domestic diversifying acquisitions resulted primarily from the product line review committee's extensive analysis of Norton's resources. Management asserted that acquisitions which conformed to the criteria would utilize Norton's major strengths to overcome or reduce its major weaknesses. One major strength was Norton's financial position (the average current ratio between 1969 and 1972 was about 3.6) and a low debt level (the long term debt was about 17% of capitalization in 1972 and had been decreasing over the past several years). Furthermore, Norton had a relatively high positive cash flow (about $6 million in 1972) generated primarily by its abrasives businesses.

A second major strength was Norton's extensive industrial distribution system. Although the system was developed to sell abrasives, management felt it could provide a channel for almost any consumable industrial product which would be used repeatedly by many large and small customers. The system was particularly appropriate for products whose customers demanded prompt delivery. A part of this strength was also skill in managing and servicing distribution channels with that characteristic. Management felt that a major strength was its own capability to manage businesses which produced consumable industrial products although some managers recognized that Norton did not have the quality or quantity of managerial talent required to adequately improve companies with poor performance.

Management perceived Norton's major weaknesses in both market and financial terms. Its major commitment to domestic abrasives markets would provide a sales growth rate considerably slower than management's aspirations in the foreseeable future. Since Norton perceived no course of action to substantially increase its share of these markets whose growth rate had declined over the past 20 years, management planned to use its cash flow and debt capacity to finance its entry into markets with higher expected growth rates.

Norton's second major weakness was an inadequate research and development capability to design products for markets it might otherwise choose to enter. This weakness, coupled with the lead time required to design products and enter these markets, focused management's attention on entering growth markets through acquisition.

A third weakness was Norton's fluctuating non-growth earnings per share and declining return on equity which decreased the attractiveness of its common stock (Norton's price/earnings ratio was about 6, compared with the Dow-Jones average of about 15). This relatively low price earnings ratio prevented Norton from exchanging its stock to acquire companies with expected higher future growth rates and related higher price/earnings ratios. However, acquiring companies for cash limited the size of those companies which Norton could afford to finance with its projected cash flows.

From these major strengths and weaknesses, Norton derived criteria for the industries it would be willing to enter through acquisition. Some criteria applied to all domestic diversifying acquisitions. (1) In general Norton sought to enter markets for industrial consumable products. Although recognizing the value of a consumer goods franchise, management felt it did not have the requisite skills in advertising and related distribution to compete effectively. (2) The preference for consumable supply products related to a second criterion, that potential markets not have a cyclical demand and profitability coincident with the capital goods cycle upon which abrasives depended. (3) Norton required that the projected growth rate of a potential market be greater than that of the abrasives markets. The growth rate criterion was stated more explicitly for the various types of acquisitions. Management expected that acquired companies would finance their growth with the positive cash flow from Norton's abrasives businesses. (4) Norton sought to enter markets which were not heavily concentrated, unless it could acquire one of the three largest competitors in such a market. Management had observed the difficulties and disadvantages of minor competitors within its own highly concentrated abrasives markets and did not want to compete under such handicaps. (5) Norton sought markets with return on invested capital in excess of its own average 5.5%. Entering such markets would increase the value of Norton's common stock, even if entry had little affect on Norton's price/earnings ratio. (6) Norton sought to enter markets which were not highly capital intensive. Management felt entry into such markets would unduly restrict Norton's future diversity and mobility. Norton specified additional criteria for each type of acquisition.

For Type I acquisitions (small acquisitions related to Norton's current nonabrasives businesses), major criteria were that the acquisitions be obtained for cash rather than for stock and that the expected future performance be equal to Norton's performance in nonabrasive markets. Market criteria for these acquisitions were different for each nonabrasives market. For example, management believed Norton's technological skills in industrial ceramics were superior to all other firms, but felt its marketing could not serve new kinds of customers. Therefore, acquisitions in this industry would only be to broaden its marketing capability. An acquisition would be particularly attractive to Norton if its own superior product design and manufacturing capabilities could also be used to improve the company's competitive position. In contrast, for the chemical processing products markets, Norton felt its marketing capabilities were strong, but its technological capability could not easily design or manufacture new products to enter new markets. Hence a criterion for potential markets in this industry stressed new products rather than new customer relations.

For Type II acquisitions (large acquisitions, unrelated to Norton's current product lines), one criterion was an expected sustainable annual market growth rate between 5% and 10%. Although Norton preferred higher projected growth rates, it believed that prospects with projected growth rates greater than 10% would also have price/earnings ratios substantially higher than Norton's and would cause excessive dilution. Since Type II acquisitions would be managed as separate operating divisions of the Norton Company, another criterion for these acquisitions was that they have competent management willing to remain with Norton and operate the acquired businesses. A third criterion for these prospects was that the price be between $30 million and $120 million, payable in Norton stock. A fourth and related criterion was that the prospect have a significant market position. Management hoped to consummate at least two Type II acquisitions before 1980.

For Type III acquisitions (small related acquisitions which could become a nucleus from which to form significant Norton divisions), one criterion was that Norton expect their annual market growth rate to exceed 10%. This criterion was necessary to insure that these small acquisitions would provide the base for Norton's future growth. Since Norton would acquire prospects of this type for cash, the high price/earnings ratio normally associated with high growth companies would not cause a dilution of Norton's earnings per share.

A second criterion for potential markets for Type III acquisitions was that a sufficient number of acceptable candidates existed in the group of related markets to have a significant collective impact on Norton's size. This not only would assure an adequate impact on Norton's future growth, but also would permit groups of these acquisitions in related markets to be managed as separate divisions of Norton.

As a third criterion, Norton sought markets or groups of related markets in which it believed it could develop a proprietary capability or economy of scale which would act as an effective competitive advantage. This would help Norton achieve future market position. Some examples management cited of proprietary capabilities were Norton's ability to foresee capital needs and make timely investments, economies of research or manufacturing through wider geographic coverage than competitors, and marketing skills or distributor relations unavailable to competitors.

Related to prospect availabilities and expected proprietary position, Norton's fourth criterion called for a reasonable probability of achieving an adequate size and position within a short period of time, usually envisioned as about four years. Norton felt these criteria would be most easily met by small, fragmented markets. The criteria which Norton applied to individual prospects for Type III acquisitions included their having annual sales greater than $1 million but less than $20 million. Although Norton also preferred to acquire these companies for cash, it was willing to issue stock or other securities when necessary.

Acquisition Scanning Process

Just as the information requirements or criteria differed for each of the acquisition types at Norton, so also did the acquisition scanning processes vary. For Type I acquisitions, intermediaries and divisional management gathered information. For Type II acquisitions, Mr. Griffin and intermediaries identified prospects and corporate management gathered information from published sources and management consultants about the prospects and the markets in which they competed. For Type III acquisitions, Messrs. Melville, Griffin and Johnson all attempted to identify markets for entry and prospects for acquisition. The sources of information on markets for entry and prospects for Type III acquisitions also varied.

Type I Acquisitions. Management began its search for Type I acquisitions by announcing its interest to over 300 intermediaries. These interests were defined in terms of product-market areas which related to Norton's diversified products. When these announcements were made, management had not been aware of the small number of prospects within these areas which were available for acquisition. For example, most of the industrial ceramics companies had been acquired over a period of several years by conglomerate companies because of their relatively high expected growth rates in the future. Therefore, candidates would arise only if a conglomerate desired to spin-off its industrial ceramics division. In such a case, Norton management would not be willing to acquire the division unless it could determine the reason for the spin-off and felt that reason would not be a barrier to Norton's success in operating the division. Also, within the chemical process products area, the four prospects most closely related to Norton's activities did not wish to be acquired.

Mr. Griffin noted that searching for Type I acquisition prospects was a responsibility of the division managements as well as a corporate management activity. However, he felt that division management had not been sufficiently aggressive in this endeavor. For most Type I prospects, the divisional management was asked to provide some information about a prospect to supplement the information provided by intermediaries. However, the corporate management generally permitted the divisional management to accept or reject acquisition prospects after information had been gathered and initial contacts concluded. Mr. Griffin felt that corporate management should exert more influence on these divisions to accept candidates approved by the corporate management and to plan for diversification.

Type II Acquisitions. The acquisition decision process for Type II acquisitions was considerably different from that for Type I acquisition. Markets for entry through Type II acquisitions were not selected prior to identifying acquisition prospects. Mr. Griffin explained that only a few large companies competed in any of the markets which Norton might enter through acquisition. A detailed study of one of these markets would require excessive amounts of time and money which would not be productive unless Norton could locate an acceptable acquisition prospect competing in that market. Rather, Norton studied markets in detail only after an acquisition candidate was identified and negotiations were begun. Norton identified Type II acquisition candidates in two ways. First, Norton notified over 300 intermediaries of its interest in consummating a large acquisition in the industrial consumable products area. Second, Mr. Griffin searched for possible acquisition candidates himself.

To begin this search, he compiled a list of Standard Industrial Classification codes which represented all non-consumer goods, non-capital goods industries at the three-digit level. Using these and a price-earnings ratio criterion to determine if acquisitions by Norton at the market price would cause an excessive dilution of earnings, Mr. Griffin screened all the companies listed on the New York Stock Exchange and the American Stock Exchange by computer. From this screening, he obtained a list of approximately 350 companies which Norton could consider in more detail. The computer screen used the Standard and Poor's *Compustat* data, which also provided a ten-year financial summary and other numerical information on each of the 350 companies which passed the screen. Based on a review of this data and his own personal knowledge of some of these companies, Mr. Griffin was able to eliminate all but about 200 of these. The financial data from *Compustat* provided the basis for an active data file which Mr. Griffin maintained on each of these 200 prospects. He added annual reports, SEC 10-K reports, Standard and Poor's reports, security analysts reports, institutional reports, and copies of published articles cited in Funk and Scott and kept these files up to date.

These files served two major purposes. First, Mr. Griffin hoped to be able to respond quickly to any indication that one of these prospects was interested in being acquired by having a nucleus of information readily available in the file. Second, on the basis of this information, Mr. Griffin ranked these prospects in terms of their desirability as acquisitions and of their likely interest in being acquired. He then began approaching these prospects in the order he ranked them. He felt that any prospect which did not refuse to discuss being acquired was a possible candidate, and he began a dialogue concerning areas of mutual interest. Because of the low likelihood of consummating an acquisition, Mr. Griffin deemed it desirable to have discussions with 10 or 12 large firms in progress at once. These discussions often terminated because of lacking mutual interest at that time. However, discontinuing active discussion did not always imply Norton's future disinterest. Rather, Mr. Griffin reaffirmed Norton's interest with many by contacting them about every six months to determine if any of the impediments to earlier discussion had subsided. In terms of both the initial approach and subsequent discussion, Morton's reputation as an ethical company with competent management and quality products was a definite advantage. This reputation was strongest with prospects who used the same distributors as did Norton.

Mr. Griffin had also gathered and analyzed some information concerning the likely effect on Norton's stock price of consummating a large acquisition within the next two years. He identified ten mergers in which the acquirer's assets exceeded $100 million and the acquired company's assets were at least half of the acquirer's assets. He then compared the price/earnings ratio of the stock of each of the companies before the merger with the price/earnings ratio of the stock of the successor company after the merger. In each case, Mr. Griffin noted that the price/earnings ratio after the merger was about equal to the lower of the two premerger company price/earnings ratios. This study not only indicated that the immediate effect of a large acquisition on Norton's price/earnings ratio would be negligible, but also provided a basis for estimating the expected dilution of earnings which might be caused by the consummation of a large acquisition. Mr. Griffin explained that these were all short-term effects of a large acquisition, since in the longer run, the stabilization of Norton's earnings caused by a large acquisition would favorably affect Norton's price/earnings ratio.

Type III Acquisitions. Type III acquisitions posed the most complex scanning problems. Not only did Norton management have the tasks of screening both markets and prospects, but also management had the task of creating and formulating a concept of how to relate a series of acquisitions to form a viable operating division. Furthermore, published information about prospects for Type III acquisitions was generally not available, since they were usually small, privately-owned, regionally-based companies. In addition, the fragmented nature of most of these markets caused difficulties in identifying many of the competitors in these industries. Finally, the nature of the concept which related a series of Type III acquisitions influenced the design of the scanning process. Three different approaches were typified by entry into the safety products industry, entry into the precision plastic parts industry, and possible entry into a distribution market.

Safety Products Industry. Norton's interest in the safety products industry began casually when Mr. Griffin received a cursory report on the industry from a general management consulting firm. The report described the expected growth of the industry and some of its major sectors, the major factors which might influence that growth, the major competitors by sector of the industry, and a few numerical statistics on the major competitors. Messrs. Griffin and Melville met with the author of the report to discuss some of the findings and then they commissioned a market research firm to identify all of the competitors in each market of the industry. Mr. Griffin commented that there was no reason to employ the management consulting firm to provide more detail since the consultant had already provided most of the information he had compiled. By comparison, the market research firm could provide a list of competitors at less cost than the management consultant and this independent assessment of the industry improved the reliability of the data upon which Norton made its decision. Because many safety products manufacturers were small, privately owned companies, data about most of the individual competitors was scant.

The consultant's report predicted substantial growth in the safety products industry. The prediction was based on expected demand generated by federal legislation, particularly the Occupational Safety and Health Act. "Over the next several years, much greater emphasis will be placed on engineering out hazards -- and utilizing sophisticated new technology to reduce losses when a problem occurs," stated the report, and yet, "these changes will take time." Based on the report, management felt that the safety products industry was an established opportunity rather than a gamble on future developments; therefore, Norton's entry should be "as quick as possible." The consultant also verified that the industry was highly fragmented and needed to be rationalized.

Based on this information, Mr. Griffin formulated the concept for a series of acquisitions of small, low technology companies, each producing a different product, which could be assembled and given a central marketing thrust and national distribution through Norton's established abrasives distribution channels. Implementation of the concept required sufficient availability of safety products candidates to insure a series of acquisitions. Mr. Griffin noted that he might never have formulated the concept, except that the next piece of mail he opened after the consultant's report was from a major Wall Street financial institution, identifying the Newton Glove Company as an acquisition candidate. Newton's major product was industrial safety gloves. This coincidence focused Mr. Griffin's attention on the industry and prompted him to present the opportunity to Mr. Melville. Less than two weeks later, Mr. Melville notified over 300 intermediaries of Norton's interest in the safety products field and several other acquisition opportunities were soon presented.

Based on the apparent soundness of the consultant's report and the availability of candidates, Mr. Griffin commissioned the market research study to facilitate the search process. For each market in the industry, the study identified and ranked the competitors, so Mr. Griffin could begin approaching them. Because of the large number of competitors in the industry and the lack of published information, screening became a process of judgmentally ranking the desirability of the various markets and approaching the competitors. Norton began with the largest and ended when the largest 3 to 8 competitors in each market were eliminated from consideration. Some were not interested in being acquired at a reasonable price, while others supplied information which deterred Norton's further interest in the candidate. Also, during this process of screening the competitors in the safety products industry, Norton gathered additional information about the industry and its markets. An acquisition agreement with Newton Glove was not signed until it was apparent that Norton could acquire several other desirable safety products firms.

Mr. Melville indicated that he would not have expected the major Wall Street financial institution to identify any acquisition candidates suitable for Norton. In his experience, investment and commercial bankers generally had not been sensitive to Norton's needs and apparently did not actively search for candidates in its interest. The sequence of events prior to the Newton acquisition would suggest that the major Wall Street financial institution had not attempted to respond to Norton's stated acquisition criteria. Although Norton had indicated interest in consumable products for industrial markets, it had limited that interest to candidates with annual sales of at least $20 million; Newton Glove was less than half that size. By comparison, Mr. Melville felt business brokers worked very hard at locating appropriate candidates since consummating acquisitions was their livelihood.

Plastics Products Industry. Norton's interest in specialty molded plastics markets developed quite independently of and differently from its interest in the safety products industry. In response to the product planning committee's decision to retain and expand Norton's plastic tubing business, Mr. Johnson began studying the plastics industry as part of his job to help the tubing division formulate its strategy. Although he did not identify opportunities to which Norton could effectively apply the skills of its plastic tubing business, Mr. Johnson did discover an opportunity for Norton to develop through Type III acquisitions. The opportunity was in the high production technology (hard to produce precision parts) segment of the industry, where few competitors had adequate skill to compete and none had access to national distribution. The concept he formulated was to combine through acquisition a series of geographically dispersed plastic molding operations with high production technology, to design and produce a product line which required that technology, and to market the product line through national distribution channels. National markets would afford adequate volume to justify design and tooling investments for the product line.

Mr. Johnson began gathering information on the plastics industry by reading trade journal (e.g., *Modern Plastics*) articles and advertisements.   To provide some framework for his new information, Mr. Johnson used the seven-digit Standard Industrial Classification of products within the four-digit "Miscellaneous Plastic Products" industry. In addition, Mr. Johnson attended many different types of trade shows, attempting to determine a class of plastic products, a market or set of related markets, in which Norton could develop a competitive advantage. He wrote for relevant literature, asked many questions, and obtained a directory from the Society for Plastics, which listed about 2,500 members, and many resin suppliers.   Mr. Johnson began visiting with representatives of the resin suppliers to discuss his ideas and learn about possible acquisition prospects.   He noted that many suppliers were cooperative, providing relatively detailed information about both products and their markets as well as about their customers who might be acceptable prospects.   While accumulating this information, Mr. Johnson determined that the high technology segment of the industry was not only less competitive, but also provided higher growth and profitability potentials than others.   He recognized that Norton could gain a competitive advantage in these segments by developing a superior distribution capability and by the timely anticipation and provision of capital investments.   Based on his study of the plastics industry, Mr. Johnson believed that Norton could enter the precision plastics molding field gradually and still achieve a major market position, since the field was still in an early stage of its development.   In addition to custom molding, Mr. Johnson believed Norton could also successfully design, develop, manufacture, and market a product line of standardized plastic parts (e.g., pulleys, bearings, and gears) once it had entered the field.

Mr. Johnson not only notified Norton's intermediaries of his interest in plastic molding companies, but also began his own search. This search was through several plastic resin suppliers who provided him with both lists of their customers (plastic molders) and information on their products and production facilities and capabilities.   Mr. Johnson attributed their propensity to help him to their own self interest.   They foresaw the possibility that Norton might acquire and significantly expand a small plastics operation.   Supplying the resin to such an expanding customer would contribute to their own sales and profitability. Mr. Johnson wrote to those prospects which particularly interested him requesting brochures and other information about their products and capabilities.   As of mid 1973, Norton had not acquired any prospects identified by the resin suppliers.   Rather, Lakeville, Norton's first acquisition in the precision plastics field, was a candidate presented to Norton by an intermediary.

Messrs. Melville and Johnson noted that as plastics acquisitions were consummated the criteria or types of information required about prospects changed, although geographical expansion would continue to be important. For example, Lakeville did not have the strong cost control system which would be required to operate a geographically dispersed manufacturing operation. Therefore, Norton was particularly interested in acquiring a precision plastics molder with a superior cost control system. Also, since Norton hoped to be able to produce its line of standardized parts in more than one plant, the interchangeability of molds among the equipment of various acquired plants would be an important consideration. If possible, the managements of future plastics acquisitions should also be compatible with the manager of Lakeville. Finally, Messrs. Melville and Johnson felt that after several plastics acquisitions had been completed, Norton would need a company with some superior marketing capability to begin to form the nucleus of a national marketing and distributions system.

Since the number of prospects was large, but the size of each was small, and production capability was an important consideration in appraising prospects, plant visits were a major means of gathering information about a prospect. Mr. Johnson had visited most of the candidates, but Mr. Melville had also visited several. Mr. Johnson noted that a major problem was making intuitive judgments about which opportunities to pursue further and invest the time in visiting. Mr. Johnson felt that the former owner and general manager of Lakeville would provide important insights for the assessment of future acquisition candidates. Distance of a candidate from Norton's headquarters was not a major issue.

Product X. A third example of how Norton scanned for Type III acquisitions was in the area of the industrial distribution throughout the United States of Product "X" (an industrial component disguised because negotiations were in progress). The industry, the acquisitions, and the concept for combining them were all provided by a former executive of a firm which distributed Product X. He approached the Norton management with a detailed description of the industry, its markets, their customers, their needs, its major competitors, their strengths and weaknesses, its expected growth, its major strategic problems, etc. Acting as a broker, this former executive suggested that Norton could acquire a series of small distributors with local geographic markets and combine them to form an efficient national distribution system for Product X. As proof that the concept was feasible, the broker noted that the only national distributor for Product X was formed using the same concept. He also demonstrated that enough available competitors with sufficient combined market share existed to duplicate the original formation.

Mr. Melville expressed considerable interest in the proposal and felt the broker's report was sufficiently accurate and complete to begin approaching prospects. Based on the report, the first company acquired should have had a success record with a computer-based system for inventory control, order processing, and purchasing. The prospect which the broker felt best met this criteria was willing to discuss merger with Norton, but not at a price low enough to interest Mr. Melville: and without that key acquisition, he felt the success of the concept was in jeopardy. So for this third example of a Type III acquisition scanning process, a former industry executive was the major source of information and prospect identification. Mr. Melville noted that Norton was still interested in acquiring the company if the owner ever agrees to a lower price.

Summary. Searching for industries and markets to enter through Type III acquisitions tended to be a sequential process at Norton. Messrs. Melville, Griffin, and Johnson identified concepts while reviewing acquisition proposals or gathering relatively general environmental information. Thus, when conceiving and presenting a concept, they already had obtained some information about the industry around which the concept was formulated--e.g., concentration, estimated size, expected growth, and profitability. Additional information was secured from various sources, as the safety products and precision plastics examples demonstrate. The sequence in which concepts were studied was the sequence in which they were identified.

At Norton, the more an industry was studied, the more management became committed to its concept. Also, once management began searching for prospects within a concept industry, the search would continue uninterrupted until either the search proved fruitless or Norton had consummated a sufficient number of acquisitions to assure the success of the concept. Thus, while Messrs. Griffin and Johnson were searching for acquisitions in the safety products and precision plastics industries, they were not actively studying industries related to other concepts, although Mr. Griffin did concurrently pursue Type II prospects and Mr. Johnson did pursue some Type I prospects for the plastic tubing business.

Factors Influencing the Acquisition Process

Norton's acquisition scanning process was influenced by many factors, including the board of directors, the firm's resources and organization, the backgrounds of the scanners, and strategy and environment of the firm. Several of these influences were acknowledged earlier and are repeated or amplified here to recognize these factors explicitly and indicate the nature and importance of their influence.

Board of Directors. Tracing the history of domestic diversifying acquisition programs at the Norton Company highlighted the influence of the board of directors on the acquisition scanning process in 1972. The recommendations of the product line review committee implied that Norton's first acquisition program was unsuccessful. Top management generally attributed this failure to gathering inadequate information about the markets Norton entered. Thus, the second program, lasting from 1966 to 1972, stressed information gathering and analysis while deferring decision-making. However, the board did not formulate and articulate a clear set of objectives for this second acquisition program. Therefore, the director of corporate development had neither guidance nor direction to focus his search for markets to enter or prospects to acquire. The second acquisition program failed partially because the board desired to avoid acquisition failures like those of the first program. For the first program the board emphasized locating candidates and negotiating acquisitions without adequate information or criteria. For the second, it emphasized information gathering without concern for candidate availability. The first program produced poor performance acquisitions while the second produced no significant acquisitions. These problems inevitably contributed to a skepticism of diversification by some members of the board of directors.

At Mr. Cushman's request, the board appointed Mr. Melville to expand non-abrasives activities through acquisition and internal development. To help design and implement the new acquisition program, Mr. Melville needed certain kinds of expertise, both to further strengthen the board's confidence in the program and to complement his own expertise. Mr. Johnson had skills in planning and implementing business strategy, and had a thorough knowledge of the company accumulated over many years. His attention to the integration and realignment of new acquisitions improved both the likelihood of successful acquisitions as well as the board's perception of that likelihood. Mr. Griffin had an impressive record of successfully engineering diversification programs for several other companies and an intimate knowledge of the mechanics and process of acquisition. His record of success, as well as the knowledge upon which it was founded, became valuable resources for Mr. Melville's acquisition program both in substantive contribution and in an image projected to the board.

Recognizing the problem of inadequate direction which plagued the two previous diversifying acquisition programs, Mr. Melville formulated the objectives for the new program and obtained the approval of the board for these objectives to encourage its support. Mr. Griffin then designed an acquisition process which sought to achieve the program objectives and avoid the problems of previous programs. An important process design specification was that the acquisition staff not gather extensive information about markets for entry until it determined that several competitors in that market were willing to be acquired. Similarly, the staff would not gather detailed information about acquisition candidates before it determined that entry into the markets in which they participated would further the objectives of the program. To facilitate this process, the acquisition staff obtained the permission of the board of directors to initiate communication with prospects prior to board approval.

Resources. Although these process design innovations improved the likelihood of a successful acquisition program, they did not eliminate all of the major problems. For example, the board was more willing to approve small acquisitions for three reasons. First, they would be smaller initial investments by the board. Second, they would be a lower risk to the company, and thereby more acceptable. Third, Norton's low price/earnings ratio would discourage the use of stock necessary to consummate large acquisitions. Mr. Melville favored Type I acquisitions over Type III acquisitions because he felt the board would be more receptive to acquisition proposals which related to the product line review committee recommendations. In addition, he felt the risk of failure of Type I acquisitions was lower because Norton had access to information about Type I acquisitions and had an understanding of the major problems of some of the markets to be entered through Type I acquisitions.

The limited resources available for the program not only influenced the program priorities, but also the scanning process. For example, Norton determined the availability of candidates in a market before gathering extensive information about that market. This increased the likelihood that scanning could lead to acquisition proposals quickly. It also quickly rejected industries which were inappropriate for entry through Type III acquisitions. Similarly, using intermediaries to determine the availability of competitors within particular markets required no unnecessary expenditure of resources because intermediaries only received payment when candidates were actually acquired. Although obtaining information from recognized and impartial experts and relying on multiple sources of information where possible increased the cost of scanning, it also increased the credibility of proposals. These costs were incurred only after the acquisition staff felt reasonably confident that a proposal would be appropriate for Norton.

Because Type III acquisition prospects were small, the acquisition staff felt it had adequate resources to gather information directly from the candidates by commencing with negotiations. The acquisition staff felt the board would rely on this internally developed expertise because the individual acquisitions represented relatively small investments;

whereas market expertise was more necessary because the commitment to a series of acquisitions represented more substantial cumulative investment.

Organization. Historically, the managers of Norton's non-abrasives division had great autonomy from the corporate management. Not until 1971 were these non-abrasives businesses organized into a single group under the direction of Mr. Melville. By the end of 1972, Norton was beginning to exert some managerial influence over the remaining non-abrasives divisions. These division managers had little experience, or interest, in growth through diversifying acquisition. Generally, they did not actively search for prospects which might add to the growth of their own divisions. Thus, the organization limited the involvement of divisional managements in the acquisition scanning process.

Organization could also influence Type III acquisitions. Because they were small, they would lack depth of management, yet the successful integration of these acquisitions with subsequent Type I acquisitions would require greater depth of management than Norton had readily available. Since the precision plastics industry was still early in its developmental stage, recruiting capable divisional management outside Norton's current management team would be difficult. Mr. Johnson also noted the need for a sophisticated cost control system for the precision plastics division as it expanded through acquisition, but felt acquiring a company with such a system was the only way to develop it since Norton did not have appropriate expertise within the corporate organization. Similar problems would likely exist in the development of the safety products division but with no one in the Norton organization familiar with all phases of the safety products industry. Furthermore, the past organization of the Norton Company had not encouraged the development of general management skills and expertise, particularly in the development of new businesses. These skills had not been needed in the mature single-product abrasives industry although they would be needed for the diversification strategy.

Organization also created a problem of skill transference which was not reflected in the scanning process. Part of the competitive strategy intended for both precision plastics and safety products was the development of strong industrial distribution systems which would benefit from the skills of the abrasives division management. However, the abrasives business was isolated from the non-abrasives businesses. This complicated the transfer of individuals with appropriate skills.

Background of Scanners. The three members of the acquisition staff also influenced the design of the acquisition process at Norton. Mr.

Griffin had employed a similar scanning process for engineering the diversifying acquisition programs of his previous employers. Because of this background, Mr. Griffin preferred intermediaries and recognized experts as sources of information. He felt that a company research staff would not be able to respond quickly with information about acquisition opportunities. Based on his experience, timely responses and decisions were important for a successful acquisition program. Mr. Griffin felt that information gathered from primary sources about a market or a prospect would be no more reliable and possibly less reliable than information gathered from recognized experts.

By comparison, Mr. Johnson's background was that of a division manager. He was more comfortable making decisions about matters in businesses about which he had developed his own expertise. To encourage the divisions to grow through Type I acquisition, Mr. Johnson felt compelled to be able to support his point of view from personal exposure to primary sources of information both within the divisions and within the markets of the acquisition prospects. Mr. Johnson did not prefer searching for acquisition candidates and gathering information about them over managing a division. His interest was not only in planning, but also in action or implementation and in building long-term associations with people and problems. This interest was not adequately satisfied in acquisition scanning activity unless it was coupled with the development of a business which required acquisitions for growth. In his approach to acquisitions, Mr. Johnson corroborated Mr. Griffin's contention that building expertise in an industry from primary sources of information and observation required a long learning period. However, his approach to scanning improved the integration and management of acquired companies.

Mr. Melville's own ability to assign his subordinates to jobs which met their skills and interests was also a major factor in the design of the acquisition process at Norton. Furthermore, his experience permitted him to select an acceptable balance between exerting too much pressure on the staff, which could result in ill-conceived acquisitions, and too little pressure, which could result in an inadequate number of acquisitions.

Other Factors. Two other influences affected the acquisition process. First, the strategy of the Norton Company provided a basis for the acquisition program objectives and the acquisition criteria. Second, the environment of Norton not only influenced the strategy of the firm, but also the scanning process directly by providing and limiting both the opportunities available for acquisition and information about those opportunities.

Summary.   Norton's acquisition program and process was influenced by many factors, including: the company environment, strategy, organization, and board of directors, and the backgrounds and experiences of the members of the acquisition staff.   Although no one factor appeared to dominate the design of the acquisition program at Norton, the board of directors, the organization, and the participants were the most important.

The Carborundum Company

In 1972, the Carborundum Company was a multiproduct, multimarket, multinational corporation with $16.3 million in profits and $340 million in sales, of which about 38% represented sales of companies acquired since 1960, including post-acquisition growth.   Since 1960, the compound annual sales growth rate of Carborundum was about 7.5% and the earnings per share growth rate was about 6.2%.   During this period, the firm acquired 35 companies, 11 of which were based in the United States.   Only one of the 11 was not a diversifying acquisition,[6] and only one of the overseas acquisitions represented diversification.   During this same period, Carborundum also obtained partial ownership of an additional eight overseas companies, established licensing arrangements with several overseas companies, and established operations in other countries.   Carborundum also maintained an active research and development department which had developed several successful products for diversification as well as for areas in which the firm was active.

Virtually all corporate diversification had occurred since 1953, at which time the principal business of the Company was the production and sale of crude silicon carbide and crude aluminum oxide and the manufacture and sale of a wide range of products fabricated from these manufactured abrasives.   These products were manufactured in 10 plants in the United States and Canada and 5 plants operated by subsidiaries in Europe.   Through both acquisition and internal development, Carborundum had diversified by 1973 into a wide variety of products serving customers in many industries.[7]

Program History and Participants

A corporate Policy and Planning Council, formed in 1969, planned for diversification and scanned for acquisitions.   The Council had four members: the president, two senior vice presidents, and the vice president for corporate development.   According to Mr. William H. Wendel, the president, the authority of the Council spanned business planning, acquisitions and divestment, systems expansion, licensing, adequacy of management control, strategic planning and resource allocation. Each Council member had expertise in certain areas, which enabled the group to counsel, audit, criticize and guide all activities of Carborundum. This Council superseded a Policy Group formed in 1964 which included the same executives and performed the same general functions; however, members of the Policy Group also had general management responsibility for operations.

Regretfully, Mr. Donald Sturges, Vice President for Corporate Development, acquisition scanning coordinator from 1967, died while this research was in progress. Other Policy and Planning Council members were intimately familiar with Mr. Sturges' activity, and Mr. Leon Patt, Senior Vice President, assumed his duties on an interim basis in late 1972. Mr. Patt, a Vice President and Director of Carborundum since 1959, had general management responsibility for coated abrasive products until 1962, and then for international operations until 1969. In March 1973, Mr. Paul Eisenhardt[8] became the Manager of Acquisition Analysis, reporting directly to Mr. Wendel. Prior to this appointment, Mr. Eisenhardt had been with Carborundum for about one year as a financial analyst. He formerly taught finance and related courses at the U.S. Naval Post Graduate School after receiving his MBA degree from the Harvard Business School. Mr. Eisenhardt had no prior acquisitions experience, except some financial analysis he had performed for Mr. Sturges. However, his major function was the collection and presentation of information about prospects.

Acquisition Criteria

Carborundum based its diversification strategy on several concepts, the most important of which was *fit*: The company and the acquisition must each contribute something to one another, besides money or management. Fit could be contributions on any of several dimensions or vectors, particularly: technological expertise, manufacturing methodology, marketing experience, or raw material requirements.

The concept of *vectored growth* referred to selecting the vectors of fit which Carborundum desired to extend either to enhance a corporate strength or overcome a weakness. For example, expertise in selling to a particular industry leads to a new business for the same market, which in turn provides new technological capabilities around which additional businesses may then be built around the new vector.

A concept which helped the Council to select vectors for growth was the *systems concept*, a set of interrelated products which could be combined to provide more creative approaches and comprehensive solutions to customers' problems; for example, pollution control systems rather than filter media or table-top systems rather than chinaware. Mr. Wendel first applied this concept to the Curtis Machine Company acquisition in 1955, when he was vice president for the coated abrasives division. The acquisition of Curtis, and later of Tysaman and Pangborn, provided Carborundum with an integrated product line of abrasive systems rather than just abrasive material for many of the markets it served.

A final concept, applied more to research and development decisions, but also evident in the acquisition program, was the *breakthrough strategy*, a planned course of action, which if successful within a specified period of time, would have a significant impact on the company's sales and profits. Applying this concept, Carborundum selected a limited number of new product-market niches for entry, rather than trying to develop new businesses from all possible fit vectors simultaneously. Mr. Wendel observed that using these concepts, Carborundum could go almost anywhere as long as it went in a correct sequence.

Fit and vectored growth were primary criteria for selecting markets for entry. Carborundum's diversifying acquisitions through 1963 emphasized developing the marketing experience growth vector. However, beginning with the Basic Carbon and Falls Industries acquisitions in 1964, Carborundum shifted its emphasis to the technological expertise or manufacturing methodology growth vectors. Prior to the acquisition program, Carborundum's technological expertise and manufacturing methodology for abrasives matched any competitor in the abrasives industry. Furthermore, Carborundum sold to customers in every industry, including retail, which used abrasives in any significant quantity. However, Carborundum could not improve its market penetration easily because one of its major competitors, the Norton Company, had the competitive advantage of designing, manufacturing, and selling a relatively complete line of abrasive machinery as well as consumable abrasives. Norton could provide a more complete customer service and develop customer loyalty because of its abrasive systems capability.

Seeking to achieve a growth rate above the average of the industry and to remain competitive in its abrasive markets, Carborundum began to develop its own abrasive systems capability. Carborundum lacked the technological expertise in machine design and manufacturing methodology in mechanical assembly necessary to support the sale of abrasive machinery. However, it did have the marketing experience necessary to establish customer relations and solve customer problems. Since internally developing the technological expertise and manufacturing methodology would have involved considerable expense and time delays,

Carborundum tried to obtain these capabilities through acquisition. In return, the acquired companies gained the superior marketing experience of Carborundum. Through the 1964 carbon company acquisitions, Carborundum gained new technological expertise and marketing experience for the design and sale of carbon electrodes and annodes for continuous steel casting, and tried to apply this expertise to new markets.

Another criterion affecting the selection of markets for entry remained largely intuitive during the acquisition program through 1967. This was management's concern for a balanced mix of business along the dimensions of growth, profitability, and risk. Management had observed that fast growing businesses generally required a rapid increase of capital investment and working capital. It also observed that rapidly growing products tended to be higher risk investments early in their life cycles. However, the acquisition of a developing company with such products was less risky than internal development or joint venture. Carborundum counterbalanced all of these risks with the relative stability of the more mature but profitable abrasives business.

Carborundum also felt that heavy dependence on fluctuations of the domestic capital goods cycle was an undesirable risk. Through the acquisition of Copeland and other "table-top" companies, Carborundum sought to hedge against its exposure to the capital goods cycle, and thereby improve its image in the financial community. Carborundum's entry into the pollution control industry reduced its exposure to the capital goods cycle and also provided participation in a high-potential industry. Management felt that legislated pollution standards would support the demand for pollution control equipment and supplies even during capital goods cycle downturns.

As another protection against the domestic capital goods cycle, Carborundum acquired many overseas companies in the abrasives business, to protect the firm against cyclical fluctuations felt more in the United States than in the world economy. Also, beginning in about 1969, Carborundum started several joint ventures with Japanese firms. These ventures attempted to exploit new products generated by Carborundum's research and development department. Since these joint ventures represented products for which new markets were not developed, they were not viewed as alternatives to acquiring competitors in the same markets. However, they did represent another attempt to reduce Carborundum's risk. Thus, although domestic diversifying acquisitions were not the only form of growth and risk reduction employed by Carborundum, they were an important form.

Other criteria which affected market selection included rejection of industries controlled by government or similar factors which limited the latitude and influence of Carborundum's management over performance. Although government contract research produced a substantial portion of Tem-Pres' revenues, these represented a minute portion of Carborundum's total revenues. Furthermore, Carborundum sought these government contracts less for their revenues than for the potential transfers of developed technological expertise to other products. This criterion was partially a residual effect of Carborundum's entry into the nuclear metals industry in 1952. A change in government requirements and contracting terms transformed the profitable venture into an unprofitable operation which was eventually divested. Although the pollution control industry depended on future government legislation for its growth and development, Carborundum's management felt this legislation was forthcoming and compliance would stimulate demand and insure future growth. Furthermore, Carborundum's management felt it could influence the profitability and growth of its own pollution control activities by the choice and timing of technological development. Also, Carborundum purposed to be a high technology materials and systems company, and therefore did not, through either acquisition or internal development, select non-manufacturing markets.

Carborundum also applied the concepts of fit and vectored growth to screening and ranking acquisition prospects. For example, both Curtis and Tysaman not only provided the machine design and manufacturing capability Carborundum sought to obtain through acquisition, but also improved its position in some markets. Based on Curtis' familiarity with the purchasing patterns in the wood-working industry, Carborundum completely revised its sales approach for coated abrasives to the wood-working industry and substantially increased its market penetration. Other machinery design and manufacturing firms were also screened but many designed machinery primarily for Carborundum's existing customers and could not have affected penetration into the wood-working industry. Similarly, Tysaman provided improved relations and marketing approaches to the stone cutting trade, which other grinding machine prospects could not. For both of these acquisitions Carborundum defined the growth vector it sought to obtain and utilize through acquisition, but had not defined the markets of the companies to be acquired until after prospects were identified and screened. This was not true of the Lockport Felt and Copeland acquisitions, for which Carborundum had well defined its target markets before identifying and screening prospects.

Although fit and participation in a selected market were initial screening criteria applied to acquisition prospects, Carborundum implicitly applied other criteria. For example, Carborundum only acquired prospects with high-quality product images. The heritage of quality was part of the Carborundum strategy in the abrasives business prior to 1954 when diversification began. Management felt that to associate the name of a lower quality product with that of Carborundum through acquisition (or any other means) could deteriorate the value of Carborundum's trademarks and weaken its strategy for abrasives. For example, Copeland had a reputation of high quality in the consumer chinaware market whereas several other china companies were eliminated because they did not.

Also, Carborundum preferred prospects located geographically near its corporate headquarters in Niagara Falls, New York. Carborundum's management style relied on close personal interaction between corporate and divisional management and often among divisional managements. Geographic proximity also facilitated integration of an acquisition into the total operations of Carborundum, and successful integration was necessary to insure the benefits implied by the fit relationship. Copeland violated this geographic proximity criterion demonstrating that this criterion aided more in ranking than eliminating prospects. Carborundum approached Copeland only after it determined that it could not acquire a quality consumer chinaware company in the Northeastern United States. Although a British firm, Copeland made products which were well known and respected in the United States. Neither Copeland's product line nor its distribution facilities could closely integrate with Carborundum's. Rather, Carborundum temporarily transferred managers to England to help Copeland upgrade its manufacturing facilities and to install a complex computerized inventory system similar to the one Carborundum used for its abrasives distribution.

Financial criteria did not dominate the screening or ranking of acquisition prospects; however, they did influence the process. One acquisition candidate Carborundum investigated and decided not to pursue because the fit was good but the prospect was well managed and Carborundum felt it could make no improvements to increase profitability. This contrasted to the Copeland acquisition where the fit was good and the Policy Group felt Carborundum's technological expertise and manufacturing methodology in ceramics could improve product uniformity, process quality, and profitability. This feeling was sustained after the acquisition. Previous financial performance was not a criterion, but rather the expected future performance of a prospect based on the contributions which Carborundum could make to its operations and the benefit which the prospect could bestow on Carborundum.

As other examples of financial criteria, Messrs. Patt and Eisenhardt both noted that Carborundum did not acquire companies which would significantly dilute its earning per share. Similarly, through 1967, Carborundum acquired no company with book value exceeding $10 million, although Commercial Filters approached that value. Also, Carborundum generally considered only prospects which could provide a return on invested capital at least equal to its own and preferred prospects in less capital intensive industries than abrasives. These criteria largely reflected the conservative financial policies which Carborundum traditionally maintained to cope easily with fluctuations of its sales volume with the capital goods cycle. High growth potential acquisitions generally commanded high price/earnings multiples and therefore were necessarily small to avoid earnings dilution. Furthermore management wanted small growth companies because it knew how to nurture them.

Mr. Eisenhardt noted that since 1972, the company had adopted a more systematic procedure for financial analysis of acquisition prospects as part of the screening procedure. This included the use of discounted cash flow and other sophisticated techniques, but these procedures were only used for prospects which passed an initial screening based on fit and very elementary financial ratios. Also, by 1972, the company was willing to consider a few acquisitions in mature and profitable segments of their life cycles. Such acquisitions would necessarily have economic cycles counter to those of Carborundum's abrasives business. Through such acquisitions, Carborundum might provide a more consistent cash flow to support the growth of both acquired and internally generated businesses.

Thus, Carborundum's criteria for screening a market for entry were the fit between Carborundum and competitors in the industry, the growth potential of the industry, the cyclicality and predictability of demand in the market, and the risk of failure in the market. For screening acquisition prospects Carborundum's criteria included not only the criteria applied to markets for entry, but also fit (in a more detailed sense), product quality image and reputation, geographic location, size, and predicted financial performance. The information about markets and prospects needed to apply these criteria varied, but generally could be described as one of four types: financial characteristics, marketing experience, manufacturing methodology, and technological expertise. The sources of each type of information varied depending on the market or the prospect.

The Acquisition Scanning Process

The acquisition process at the Carborundum Company developed around the conceptual underpinnings of fit, vectored growth, and systems. The fit criterion assured that some member of the Carborundum management would be at least partially familiar with some aspect of a market for entry. If Carborundum shared marketing experience with competitors in the market, then some members of a Carborundum divisional marketing department or of the corporate market research department would have some information about that market and would often have access to additional sources of information about both marketing and competitors in that market. The abrasives machinery acquisitions were facilitated by such sources of information. If manufacturing methodology were the growth vector, then usually some member of the Carborundum management had a personal or professional relationship with an expert in the industry and the capability of understanding the particular manufacturing needs and problems of it.

Sources of Information. Information sources of this kind were particularly useful for the acquisition of the carbon companies.   If technological expertise were the growth vector, then members of the Carborundum corporate research and development department had some experience with the base technology of a market for entry and could provide some information on that aspect of the industry.[9]   Also, for most acquisitions, published data and trade associations often provided some limited information.   Although none of these sources guaranteed complete and reliable information about a market, they often provided sufficient information or additional sources of information for Carborundum's management to determine if it had further interest in investigating the market.   If additional information were desired, Carborundum's management generally sought to locate an executive with many years of experience in the market who could provide a more detailed and integrated description of that market. If such an executive could not be located, Carborundum usually located a consultant who specifically served clients within that market.

Locating sources of information about individual prospects often involved quite different problems. For example, financial information was readily available for publicly owned prospects, but generally not available for privately held companies. For a privately held company, the only real source of financial data was the company itself, or an intermediary which represented it.   Information about the marketing experience of a prospect was usually easy to obtain if Carborundum shared any of its customers and therefore could solicit much information directly from those customers.   Otherwise, the market research department at Carborundum could either conduct a limited market survey to learn something about the prospect or could identify a market research firm which had the experience and capability to provide a reliable study.

However, these sources required time to locate and then often could not provide information immediately.   From a market study, Carborundum's management could begin to gather some information about the manufacturing methodology and technological expertise of the prospect as manifested in comments from customers and in the prospect's marketing strategy.   Information relating directly to these aspects of a prospect's operations was difficult to obtain from any source except industry experts or the prospect itself.   As one useful source of information on some prospects, Carborundum maintained a continuing relationship with an "acquisition consultant." This consultant maintained both files on many companies and sources on many more.   If Carborundum supplied him with a list of prospects, he would provide Carborundum with the information he had.   Mr. Patt noted that Carborundum probably could have derived similar information by its own study but that it probably would have been more costly and certainly more time consuming.

Identifying Markets. Carborundum usually applied the concepts of fit and vectored growth to selecting markets for entry through acquisition   before   evaluating   acquisition   prospects.   Although Carborundum could have screened all markets to determine which would be consistent with the vectored growth concept, management did not follow this approach in practice.   Rather, information about events internal and external to the firm stimulated members of the Policy and Planning Council to consider certain markets for entry.   In more recent years, information that a candidate in a particular market was interested in being acquired often stimulated management to consider that market for entry.   After some initial discussion, the Council felt that some of these   markets   merited   further   investigation   and   sought   other Carborundum managers whose responsibilities or experience might have exposed them to information about these markets.   In discussions about a market, the Council usually included the manager responsible for activities which appeared to relate Carborundum with each market. Gaining the concurrence and support of such a manager was almost essential since he would later have responsibility for the profitability of the   acquired   operation.

Published data and personal contacts of the Council members also provided useful information about each market. If the Council still favored entering a market after gathering and analyzing this cursory information, it gathered additional information on a more formal basis through three separate types of studies. First, managers responsible for the activities which appeared to relate Carborundum with the market prepared detailed reports further examining the appropriateness of the fit. Second, the Marketing Research department either prepared studies of market structure and competitor profiles or located independent market research firms who had conducted or would conduct such studies. Third, the Council sometimes engaged a market expert, often a former executive of a firm that competed in the market, to describe the nature and significance of the new skills Carborundum would need to compete in   the   proposed   market.

The importance of the expert's role depended on Carborundum's growth vectors. When the vector was primarily marketing experience,

Carborundum managers had access to sources of information, particularly the customers of the market, which could provide large quantities of relevant and useful information. Carborundum's good relationship with its customers generally facilitated this information gathering process. The information inputs of the expert were less valuable to Carborundum in this case and if employed at all, his relationship was usually temporary. However, if the growth vector were in technological expertise or manufacturing methodology, then Carborundum had more limited access to sources of information about the market and therefore had greater need for an expert. Although Carborundum had occasionally employed consultants to prepare industry studies, the Council members generally felt that a former executive could provide more reliable and comprehensive information about the market and could better aid Carborundum's technical or manufacturing managers. Furthermore, the expert often had better access to sources of the information requested by the Council. Carborundum often initially retained an expert on a temporary basis. If this market remained desirable and if the expert appeared compatible and effective, he usually became a permanent employee to help identify and screen prospects and to help integrate and manage an acquired candidate. The expert's extended relationship with Carborundum, and with the market, greatly enhanced his value as advisor during negotiations and as integrator after the acquisition. The Council recognized that permanent employment could motivate the expert to report optimistically about a market. On the other hand, the expert would be responsible for integration and would jeopardize his future employment if integration were unsuccessful or performance expectations were unrealized.

Identifying Prospects. Carborundum's management utilized two different methods of identifying acquisition prospects. The first and least fruitful was intermediaries. They usually identified candidates which were either inappropriate for Carborundum because of poor fit with existing growth vectors, or unacceptable to Carborundum because their financial or managerial performance was inadequate. Mr. Patt and Mr. Eisenhardt, on the one hand, acknowledged that Carborundum had not always adequately communicated its acquisition criteria to intermediaries. On the other hand, they observed that some intermediaries appeared to totally disregard Carborundum's criteria. Although Carborundum continued to screen most of the candidates presented by intermediaries, management felt that this activity diverted its attention away from the important task of strategy formulation.

The second and more fruitful method by which Carborundum identified acquisition prospects was possible only after management had selected markets for entry and could identify most of the competitors in those markets as acquisition prospects. Scanners often identified many of the competitors in a market while gathering information about it. The Council identified others from published sources and trade associations. Also, when employed for the scanning process, experts could generally identify as prospects most of the competitors in the selected market. The Council generally felt that both identifying all the competitors in a selected market and initially screening all those identified were important to the acquisition scanning process because they prevented Carborundum from overlooking highly desirable prospects. Furthermore, since Carborundum approached many prospects who refused to be acquired, identifying all the competitors in a market increased the likelihood of locating and acquiring a candidate within that market and clarified Carborundum's understanding of the market structure.

Carborundum's management felt that it would be more effective and no less efficient than intermediaries in identifying and approaching prospects within a designated market. Since it was the major service for which brokers and finders received compensation, they generally located only companies which wanted to be acquired, and then acted as agents for those companies. Furthermore, the impersonal, albeit professional approach of an intermediary to a prospect which had not previously considered being acquired was often rebuffed for motives ranging from disinterest to fear of the unknown or to distrust of the intermediary.

Carborundum's management felt that by contrast some of these same companies might be receptive to an approach by its own executives. Several of the companies Carborundum acquired had not previously considered acquisition, but fit better than those with known interests in being acquired. Thus, Carborundum felt that relying on intermediaries to suggest acquisition candidates rather than identifying prospects itself would usually cause it to overlook otherwise promising acquisition opportunities. One exception to these normal patterns was the prospect identification of Tem-Pres Research. To identify companies engaged in research in the fields related to high temperature materials, hard materials, solid state materials, and plastics, Carborundum advertised in the trade press.[10] The rationale for such a move was the difficulty of identifying many of the small groups involved in such research and the extreme unlikelihood that more than a few would be willing to be acquired.

The Policy and Planning Council reviewed and analyzed this information to develop an initial estimate of the strengths and weaknesses of each prospect relative to its environment and its fit with Carborundum. To aid this analysis the Council involved the market expert and the managers who were responsible for the fit vectors. The expert often knew the managements of the prospects and could provide useful information about their competence, depth, and compatibility with

Carborundum's management. Based on this information and analysis, the Council ranked the prospects. Often the Council requested additional and more specific information about the more desirable prospects. The expert often gathered this additional information directly from the prospects.

After receiving, reviewing, and analyzing this additional information, the Council decided which prospects Carborundum should approach for negotiation. Usually either Mr. Patt or Mr. Sturges confidentially approached the president of the prospect to explain Carborundum's interest in a possible merger, describing Carborundum as a corporation, and stressing the fit relationship Carborundum felt should motivate further exploration of a merger possibility. This initial meeting was not the opening of negotiations; rather, it was an extension of the information gathering process directed toward areas which could not be obtained from information sources external to the prospect. If this initial discussion were favorable Mr. Patt usually arranged for himself and one or more other managers who would be involved in the integration of the acquisition to be conducted on a plant tour of the candidate's facilities and to meet the management on an informal basis.

Mr. Patt felt that Carborundum's reputation was critically important when approaching a prospect. Since Carborundum did not attempt take-overs and had an image of integrity and product quality, even disinterested prospects willingly greeted the Carborundum management in an informal and friendly manner and listened to its proposals based on fit. Similarly, Carborundum had a reputation of fair dealing with its suppliers, competitors, and customers so that prospects provided Carborundum with information without fear of future competitive reprisals. Furthermore, Carborundum did not generally seek information of a proprietary nature, even when it had the personal relationships with the management necessary to extract it. Carborundum was willing to sign preliminary agreements or secrecy agreements with the prospect's management during these information gathering discussions. Mr. Patt generally felt that the major decision facing a candidate was "should we be acquired?" not "should we allow Carborundum to acquire us?"

The number and type of executives involved in the information gathering task with a candidate varied with the types of problems which Carborundum executives felt were important. To one company Carborundum sent a small team of accountants to review financial procedures, and Mr. Patt and the corporate treasurer visited the candidate simultaneously. In another instance, Carborundum arranged for some of its technical experts to investigate the research and development capabilities of a candidate. During his initial plant tour, Mr. Patt felt he and his associates could learn much about the efficiency of the production operations, age of the assets, and the morale of the employees. They were also able to detect early the possible incompatibility of the candidate's management with Carborundum management.

Summary. Carborundum's formal domestic diversifying acquisition scanning process began when a member of the Policy Group obtained information which suggested a market which Carborundum might enter through acquisition. Members of the group gathered information about the market from sources both inside and outside the firm with increasing formality and detail as Carborundum's entry into the market became more favorable.

The two major factors which influenced the group's enthusiasm for a market were the fit of the market with Carborundum's other activities and the market's potential growth and profitability. During the process of gaining and analyzing market information, the group usually identified many of the competitors within the market and could easily identify the remainder either through public sources or trade association lists. Based on cursory information obtained from the acquisitions consultant, Carborundum screened all the competitors as prospects, disqualified some and ranked the remainder according to the degree of interest the group exhibited for each.

The major criteria for ranking prospects included the particular fit of the prospect with Carborundum, the potential financial impact of that fit, and the geographic proximity of the prospect to Carborundum's headquarters. The ranking of prospects provided a sequence for approaching the prospects to learn the interest of each in being acquired and if interest were indicated, to gather more detailed information about the operations and strategy of the candidate. After discussion, plant visits, and mutual exchanges of information, the negotiation process began, the group was then committed to acquiring the candidate if an acceptable price could be negotiated.

Factors Influencing the Acquisition Process

Several factors influenced the acquisition scanning process at Carborundum. These factors included Carborundum's strategy, Mr. Wendel's leadership and organization, and the general environment. Several of these factors were mentioned earlier, but their comparative impact is discussed below. The history of the domestic diversifying acquisition program at the Carborundum Company highlights the factors that influenced and constrained the program and the acquisition scanning process. The entire seventeen-year period beginning in 1955 is considered a single program because of the continuity of principles and people that guided acquisition activity during that period. However, the program did have several distinct periods. The first three acquisitions of the program were well planned and executed responses to perceived marketing needs for Carborundum's abrasives business. The second phase (1964-1967) was a response to the realization that future growth in the domestic abrasives industry was limited and that Carborundum's substantial cash flow could support a significant expansion and diversification program. These acquisitions were intended to broaden Carborundum's market base through the technological expertise and manufacturing methodology growth vectors just as the first three had broadened the technological base through the marketing experience growth vector. The third phase was a period of inactivity resulting from several factors: reduced cash flow from the abrasives business, expected performance of several internal development projects, and unanticipated managerial problems with the Commercial Filters acquisition. By 1972, Carborundum's management realized that its performance expectations for its internal development projects were too high and it would once again need acquisitions to achieve the corporate growth objectives.

Strategy.   The acquisition process employed throughout the program was responsive to the needs of the corporate strategy which emphasized technologically concentric diversifications. The nature of the fit, the vector of growth, and the information required about potential markets for entry were all well defined by the strategy. Some of this information was readily available from the divisional managers. One information requirement was a list of the major participants in these markets.   Once again, the divisional managers could supply this. Acquisition size would facilitate coordination with a division.   The geographic proximity of an acquisition to the corporate headquarters would also facilitate coordination. Furthermore, the product reputation of an acquisition was crucial to enhance or maintain a division's own product quality reputation.

Carborundum's disciplined adherence to the concepts of fit and vectored growth prevented managers from gathering large quantities of information about markets for entry or prospects for acquisitions which could not meet these criteria. Proposals for markets to enter through acquisition were acceptable to Mr. Wendel only if they were consistent with the corporate strategy or they represented a proposal to change the strategy.   Adherence to the concept of vectored growth did not discourage reviews or revisions of the corporate strategy, but did discourage acquisitions to capitalize on opportunities unrelated to Carborundum.   Without this relationship, the information gathering process used at Carborundum would not be effective, since management would not have access to appropriate sources of information.

Adherence to the fit criterion was also important. Early evaluation of fit provided some indication of the potential benefit Carborundum might obtain from entering a particular market through acquisition alternatives. In addition, it provided a rationale for acquisition proposals to facilitate early negotiations. Furthermore, it encouraged management to identify the particular activities of an acquired company which were crucial to achieving synergistic benefits and to identify the particular managers at Carborundum who would be responsible for achieving that integration. Identifying these managers involved them in the information gathering and encouraged them to state early in the process the extent of their support for the proposed acquisition. Thus, managers who would later have integration responsibility usually either became advocator of an acquisition proposal early in the information gathering process, or the acquisition proposal was rejected. In either case, information gathering resources were not expended before advocacy was well established.

Mr. Wendel. Mr. Wendel's extensive and frank discussion of many acquisition issues with many corporate and divisional managers encouraged support for the program and cooperation among the participants. Managers were encouraged to contribute their information and points of view about market or prospect alternatives as soon and completely as possible to the common base of information available for the Policy and Planning Council. By establishing a supportive atmosphere for an open exchange of information, Mr. Wendel informally monitored the positions and priorities of various managers, thus determining when consideration of a market or prospect should receive higher or lower priority and when gathering information about a market or prospect should be accelerated or retarded.

Furthermore, Mr. Wendel encouraged managers to reassess their positions and priorities with respect to acquisition alternatives in light of new information which became available. Managers felt free to contribute to Mr. Wendel any information about markets for entry or prospects for acquisition which they had available to them. Mr. Wendel could thereby quickly gather information which was available within the organization about an acquisition alternative before determining if information should be obtained from external sources. This process was considerably less expensive and more efficient than going to external sources for information that was already available internally. It also accentuated the areas of incomplete or inconsistent information and facilitated further information gathering by indicating what particular information should be sought.

Mr. Wendel maintained relatively frequent communication with the corporate and divisional managers who gathered information from external sources about markets or prospects.   By doing so, Mr. Wendel could determine when requesting additional information might overburden these managers and either reduce their enthusiasm for the acquisition program, or adversely affect either the quality of their information gathering effort, or the performance of their primary responsibilities.   Also, Mr. Wendel could determine when obtaining information from external sources might be more appropriate than continuing to gather information internally.

Organization.   Immediately after he became president, Mr. Wendel changed Carborundum's organization in several ways.   First, he created three group vice president positions.   Part of their responsibility included helping Mr. Wendel determine directions for Carborundum's future growth and markets for entry to achieve that growth.   More important, part of their new responsibility was the coordination of activities under their jurisdiction, including the integration of acquired companies into the Carborundum organization.   Their role in Carborundum's acquisition program was well defined.

Similarly, Mr. Wendel broadened the responsibilities of the staff vice presidents to include not only concern with current Carborundum markets and activities, but also interest in future directions in which the company should develop.   He could request information from the various staff vice presidents at the corporate level.   The small, but highly competent market research staff under the marketing vice president could efficiently gather information, such as the size, expected growth, concentration, and major competitors of most industrial markets which might fit with Carborundum's operations.   Similarly, the corporate finance department could quickly obtain financial data on publicly owned companies within a market to estimate some effects of market entry through acquisition on earnings, future corporate growth, and financial risk.   In addition to the corporate staff, managers of divisions with which a proposed acquisition would be coordinated often could easily gather information from external sources.

The organization also included a director of corporate development to maintain contact with intermediaries and with the acquisition consultant, to conduct more formal industry or market studies on particular markets or groups of markets which appeared desirable to the policy group, and to coordinate the more detailed investigation of acquisition prospects after negotiations with those prospects had begun.   During the 1967-1972 period, Mr. Sturges had this responsibility in addition to his responsibility as vice president of research and development.   Combining these two responsibilities was appropriate for three reasons.   First, the major thrust of acquisitions became the technological expertise vector, and as such became an alternative to research and development. Second, part of the function of research and development at Carborundum was the "nurturing" of pilot programs for new products, which involved skills quite similar to the integration of new acquisitions. Third, Mr. Sturges apparently had more available time for acquisitions activity than the other members of the policy group which also had direct responsibility for operating divisions.

This combination did have some adverse effects, since after 1967, no acquisitions were consummated. In addition to the reduced cash flow to support an acquisition program during this period, corporate management also developed an optimistic forecast for the impact of new products from the research and development department. With responsibility for both acquisitions and internal development, Mr. Sturges may have favored the latter since with his background and experience in research and development he had more confidence in his ability to fulfill his responsibilities in this area. From Mr. Wendel's point of view, assigning Mr. Sturges to the dual role and reducing his own involvement in the acquisition program was a manifestation of his own desire to temporarily reduce Carborundum's acquisition activity.

Environment. Carborundum's management believed it had defined criteria for acquisition prospects sufficiently well that it ought to be able to communicate those criteria to intermediaries and learn quickly when companies fitting those criteria were available. If intermediaries cooperated as expected, Carborundum might have been able to locate and acquire acquisition candidates much more efficiently than by screening through all the competitors in a particular market. In addition, with cooperation from intermediaries, Carborundum would not need information about all the acceptable competitors in a market before contacting them.

Information availability also influenced the acquisition scanning process at Carborundum. Since most of the prospects Carborundum sought to acquire were small, privately-owned companies, no information about them could be obtained from published sources. Through market research, Carborundum could obtain information about product performance, customer service, pricing policies, distribution strength, etc., but could not obtain information about the finances, production equipment, current technological staff, managerial depth, etc. For information which provided some indication of these factors about a prospect, Carborundum used the acquisition consultant. However, this information was often tenuous and Carborundum's management felt that while useful for screening prospects within an industry, this information was not sufficiently accurate or detailed to justify major commitments for the company. Therefore, gathering information on finance, production, and management became the major objective of early negotiations with prospects who were willing to begin negotiations.

Summary. Carborundum's acquisition program and process was influenced by many factors including the company environment, strategy, organization, Mr. Wendel's background and experience with acquisitions and his personal involvement in the program and process. Each of these had different kinds of effects upon the process, so that determining which had the greatest or least impact would be difficult; however, Mr. Wendel was a central figure influencing many of the factors (e.g., strategy, and organization) which then influenced the process. In that sense, he dominates the acquisition process. Managers in the organization and many independent observers of the company feel that Mr. Wendel was responsible for the success of the program, just as he was responsible for the success of the company. The evidence presented in this part of this chapter tends to strongly support this dominant and effective position of Mr. Wendel.

Acquisition Scanning Processes Compared

The concluding part of this chapter compares and contrasts the domestic diversifying acquisition scanning processes at Norton and Carborundum. The similarities and differences between them are examined in terms of the factors which influenced these processes. The firms were considerably different in several respects. Many of these differences related to differences in the strategies and organizations of the two firms.

Scanning Processes Compared

Norton and Carborundum gathered different types and amounts of information about acquisition alternatives, as reflected by their acquisition criteria.[11] Norton focused on information related to achieving organizational integration and synergy. Carborundum apparently gathered somewhat more information because its criteria were more difficult to apply to acquisition prospects. Nevertheless, Carborundum gathered some financial information and Norton expected to gather some information about integration and synergy for Type I acquisitions. For other types of acquisitions, financial criteria of growth, return on investment, and dilution of earnings clearly dominated the scanning process.

Partially because of the types and amounts of information they required, Norton and Carborundum gathered information from different sources. Market information was more available to Carborundum since

Norton focused on more unrelated market acquisitions which were unfamiliar to most of its executives. Carborundum's executives not only had access to more sources of information, but also were motivated to gather and communicate it. For Type II and Type III acquisitions, Norton gathered information from more impartial sources to facilitate acceptance of proposals.

Prospect information was often more available to Norton because it relied on intermediaries to identify prospects or it searched for publicly owned Type II acquisitions. For Type I acquisitions, Norton would gather some prospect information from divisional managers, as did Carborundum. However, Carborundum's focus on integration and synergy led it to identify more competitors in a related market or industry and to employ sources which could provide more detailed information about them. Since Norton maintained a wider market scope, locating and hiring similar sources was less practical.

Neither firm formally processed much information. Rather, they both used sources which had previously processed significant amounts of information. Norton used simple pro forma financial analysis and Carborundum did some market surveys. Norton generally felt that external experts were more reliable, accurate, and impartial than internally generated studies. At Carborundum, the focus on integration and synergy required more processing, but it limited the applicability of formal information processing approaches. Much of this informal processing occurred during the deliberations of the Planning Council. Norton had no similar organizational vehicle.

In both firms, responsibility for acquisition scanning resided in an executive who reported to the president. However, Carborundum apparently involved many more managers in the information gathering process than did Norton. Most of Carborundum's major participants were or had been abrasives managers, whereas only Mr. Johnson had any experience related to Norton's abrasives business. Mr. Griffin of Norton was the only executive in either firm with prior acquisiton experience in other firms. The mutual experience of Carborundum's participants facilitated its search for and evaluation of related markets for entry. The experience which Mr. Griffin brought to Norton also had a significant impact on its scanning process.

The sequence of scanning activies varied considerably between the two firms. Carborundum identified markets and gathered information about them before gathering information about individual prospects. Norton gathered little market information until it was assured that candidates would be available within that market. This explained why little information had been gathered about markets for entry through Type I or Type II acquisitions.

Influences Compared

Describing and comparing the acquisition scanning processes of Norton and Carborundum in terms of the characteristics outlined in Chapter II highlighted some significant differences between them. These differences were not attributable primarily or directly to environmental factors. Both firms encountered the same broad environmental trends and conditions prevalent during the period under study. Both were subject to the same cyclical financing problems of the abrasives industry. Both competed with similar and constant shares of the same abrasives markets. Furthermore, at the beginning of the period under study, these firms had similar financial resources available to them. As implied by their financial performance, they utilized those resources somewhat differently.[12]

However, as previous sections of this chapter emphasized, Carborundum adhered to a strategy of technologically related market entry whereas Norton's program really focused on small unrelated market entry. Because of this difference, Carborundum needed to gather considerably more information about the prospects and markets it identified to accurately estimate potential synergy benefits and the ease with which those benefits could be realized. Although Norton's management realized the need for integration to achieve synergy benefits from the clusters of Type III markets it planned to enter, this need was not formally reflected in its scanning process.

Related to this difference in strategic thrust was a difference in organizations. Carborundum's organization facilitated communication among managers in different markets and between operating managers and the corporate research and development staff. At Norton, the abrasives business was organizationally isolated from the other businesses. Also, these other businesses had little relation to one another. Because they were not related, they needed very little coordination; however, the organization discouraged or prevented the involvement of many managers in the acquisition scanning process.

Some differences were also attributable to the difference in the leadership styles of the chief executive officers and the support of the board of directors for the diversifying acquisition program. Mr. Wendel became involved in as many phases of as many businesses at Carborundum as his time would permit. He fostered a spirit of cooperation among managers and had gained the support of the board for the program through his early acquisition successes. At Norton, Mr. Cushman provided considerable autonomy to Mr. Melville and the diversifying acquisition staff. Furthermore, division managers had been granted considerable autonomy for several years. They felt no incentive to participate in the acquisition scanning process. Norton's board of directors was cautious about entry into new markets because of severe problems with acquisitions in the past. Their full support would come only after the new program completed several successful acquisitions. Thus, while the scanning effort received inadequate resources, it was required to document its acquisition proposals much more completely than was required at Carborundum.

Finally, the backgrounds and experiences of the participants within the two firms had considerable impact on the scanning process. Mr. Griffin was the only participant in either firm with a broad multi-firm experience in all phases of acquisition activity from strategic planning to negotiation. Based on this experience, Mr. Griffin relied heavily on intermediaries to identify candidates and would only gather information about markets after he was convinced that companies could be acquired. This assurance was important, but unnecessary at Carborundum, whose interest was in small fragmented markets with many competitors. The likelihood of locating candidates within these markets was high, just as it was for the safety products industry which Norton entered.

Differences in organization, leadership style, and participants were all apparently correlated with differences in diversification strategy. They tend to corroborate the hypothesis proposed in Chapter II that firms with different diversification strategies would adopt different scanning processes. However, this conclusion must remain tentative until the examination of the remaining four firms in the study is completed in Chapters IV and V.

NOTES

[1] See Exhibit III-1 for description of these diversifying acquisitions.

[2] See Exhibits III-2 and III-3 for summary of Norton's product-market scope.

[3] Messrs. Melville, Griffin, and Johnson were all interviewed as part of this research.

[4] See Exhibit III-4 for a list of related product lines for diversification.

[5] One example of a Type III acquisition was Lakeville Plastics. Norton sought to establish a national network of high precision molded plastic parts design, manufacture, and distribution for a wide variety of industries. Markets within the molded plastics industry were highly fragmented with $1 million as the average annual revenue per competitor. Having acquired Lakeville, Norton's criteria for further related prospects included that they each expand the geographical limits of Norton's markets, that each provide some new kinds of products or new technical capability, and that their physical plant be adaptable to manufacture of products produced by Lakeville. In addition, Norton especially sought a molder with a good cost control system which could be applied to other acquisitions. A second example of a Type III acquisition was Newton Glove. Norton sought to acquire a group of small companies, each competing in a different market or market segment within the safety products industry. This industry was highly fragmented and Norton felt a group of related acquisitions could permit the use of a common channel of distribution. Therefore, in seeking candidates in the safety products industry, Norton was primarily interested in the product reputation, manufacturing capability, and continuity of management as criteria for acquisitions. These criteria were important since Norton had no common technology base among safety products acquisitions as it did among precision plastics acquisitions. The competitive edge sought in safety products was breadth of product line, whereas in precision plastics, it was geographic distribution of proprietary technology.

[6] See Exhibit III-5 for a description of the major diversifying acquisitions.

[7] See Exhibits III-6 and III-7 for a summary of Carborundum's product-market scope and systems capabilities.

[8] Messers. Wendel, Patt, and Eisenhardt were interviewed as part of this research.

[9] For example, Tem-Pres and Copeland are examples of this type of information gathering.

[10] See Exhibit III-8 for an example of an advertisement for an acquisition.

[11] See Exhibit III-9 for a scanning comparison of the acquisition scanning process of Norton and Carborundum. The exhibit utilizes the process characteristics described in Chapter II. Comparing the acquisition scanning processes of Norton and Carborundum is difficult. Carborundum had only one program, whereas Norton had three programs. Moreover, managers who were involved in Norton's first two acquisition programs were not available for this research.

[12] See Exhibit III-10 for a financial comparison of Norton and Carborundum.

EXHIBIT III-1

Major Diversifying Acquisitions of Norton

1963   National Research (Manufactures high vaccum equipment; produces tantalum, superconductors and superinsulation; distributes tungsten and molybdenum products; and conducts exploratory and contract research):   Stock, Pooling, 374,733 shares.

1964   Clipper Manufacturing, including Everady Bricksaw, Pavement Specialists, and Air Placement Equipment (Masonry and concrete saws and blades, core drills and bits, joint sealing and insert equipment, curing machines, power trowels, concrete gunning equipment and pumps, concrete conveyors and placers, plastering equipment):   Cash, Purchase, $8.5 million.

1966   U.S. Stoneware (Tower packings and tower internals, chemical ceramics, ball mills and mixing equipment, metal and plastic fabrication, air and water pollution control units, plastic tubing, extruded plastic sheet and film and profiles, molded plastic and rubber products, radomes, and electrical ceramics):   Cash, Purchase, $10 million.

1966   Chamberlin Engineering, a division of U.S. Stoneware (Development of fluidized bed powders and other developments in the area of plastics and synthetics):   Stock, Pooling, 135,000 shares.

1969   Koebel Diamond Tool Co. (Single and multi-point diamond dressing tools used to keep grinding wheels sharp, and formed dressing rolls, which cut shapes into grinding wheels):   Stock, Pooling, 83,250 shares.

1970   Sandon, Inc. (Polyvinyl chloride foam materials in pressure-sensitive tape form with excellent growth prospects for the construction industry and other markets):   Cash, Purchase.

1972   Lakeville Precision Molding (High precision plastic products, such as gears and bearings for industrial use):   Cash, Purchase.

1973   Newton Glove (Industrial and safety gloves):   Cash, Purchase.

EXHIBIT III-2

Product-Market Segments of Norton

Products / Markets	Abrasive Mat'ls	Grinding Wheels	Diamond Tools	Coated Abrasives	Tape	Ceramics	Chemical Process	Plastics	Metals
Mining	X	X				X	X		
Construction	X	X		X	X	X		X	
Ordinance	X	X	X	X		X		X	
Food		X		X	X	X	X	X	
Textile		X		X	X	X	X		
Lumber & Wood		X		X	X				
Furniture	X	X		X	X			X	
Paper & Printing	X	X		X	X	X	X	X	
Chemicals		X		X		X	X	X	X
Petroleum		X		X		X	X	X	X
Rubber & Plastics	X	X		X	X	X	X	X	
Leather		X		X		X	X		
Stone, Clay, Glass	X	X	X	X		X	X	X	
Primary Metals	X	X		X	X	X	X	X	X
Fabricated Metals	X	X	X	X	X	X	X	X	X
Machinery	X	X	X	X	X	X	X	X	X
Transportation	X	X	X	X	X	X		X	
Instruments	X	X	X	X	X	X		X	X
Other Manufacturing	X	X	X	X	X	X	X	X	X
Wholesale & Retail	X	X	X	X	X			X	
Government	X	X	X	X	X	X	X	X	X

EXHIBIT III-3

Product-Divisions of Norton

Abrasive Materials

Abrasive grain, flours, aluminas, tubing, media, non-skip flooring abrasives, electrical and metallurgical materials.

Grinding Wheels

Grinding wheels and segments, diamond wheels and hones, cut-off and mounted wheels, reinforced wheels, metalworking fluids, truing and dressing tools, pulpstones, abrasive sticks and bricks.

Diamond Tools

Diamond dressing tools, rotary diamond dressing devices and diamond drills.

Coated Abrasives

Coated abrasives, cleaning and finishing products, sharpening stones, accessories.

Tape

Pressure-sensitive tapes, tape dispensers and accessories, and sealants and mounts.

Industrial Ceramics

Refractories and ceramic components.

Chemical Process Products

Tower packings and internals; fractionating trays; grinding, mixing, and blending equipment, including ball and jar mills; mill jars, grinding media; fume scrubbers and towers; drum handling equipment; alumina ceramics; chemical stoneware; porcelain equipment; tank linings; catalyst carriers; vat supports; molecular sieves and adsorbents.

Plastics and Synthetics

Plastic tubing, hose and gasketing, custom compounded and extruded thermoplastic profiles and sheeting, aircraft radomes, laboratory grinding and mixing equipment, laboratory sinks, and laboratory fume scrubbers.

Metals

Tantalum, tantalum alloys, tungsten, molybdenum, and fabricated parts.

Construction Products

Masonry saws; concrete saws, diamond and abrasive blades; core drills and diamond core bits; insta-trowels; ceiling grinders; grinding disks, saucers, and cup wheels; and joing routers and router bits.

EXHIBIT III-4

Norton's Related Product Lines for Diversification

Chemical Process Products. Norton currently manufactures tower packings and internals, catalyst carriers and supports, catalysts and absorbents for chemical and petrochemical industries. It is interested in acquiring businesses which manufacture these or other products (preferably consumable rather than capital equipment) which are sold to the chemical industry.

Specialty Plastic Products. Norton currently manufactures TYGON tubing and other specialty plastic products for the industrial, bio-medical, and R & D markets. It is interested in acquiring businesses which manufacutre the following types of specialty plastic products:

1. Reinforced pressure tubing or hose.
2. Industrial plastic products such as gears, bushings, bearings, and pulleys.
3. R & D laboratory products.
4. Plastic and rubber components for bio-medical use or for bio-medical instruments and equipment.

Sealants. Norton currently manufactures PVC foam sealants in tape form for weatherstripping and accoustical use in transportation equipment, mobile homes, the construction industry, and other markets. It is interested in acquiring businesses which manufacture other types of sealants or specialty calking products.

Industrial Ceramics. Norton currently manufactures a broad line of ceramic products which are used in a wide variety of industries in operations where resistance to high temperature (over 2,000^{0}F) is required. It is interested in acquiring businesses which make similar industrial ceramic products.

Chemical Specialties. Norton currently manufactures grinding fluids and has excellent distribution through industrial supply distributors. It is interested in acquiring companies which make chemical specialties such as cutting oils and fluids, buffing and cleaning compounds, metal treating and cleaning fluids, specialty adhesives, etc.

Waste Water Treatment. Nc.ton currently manufactures ceramic porous pipes, domes, and other media for waste water treatment. It is interested in expanding this product line through acquisition.

Air Pollution. Norton currently manufactures fume scrubbers for air pollution control. It is interested in broadening its fume scrubber line and in acquiring companies making disposable items for air pollution, such as filters or filter bags. It is not interested in acquiring companies which make major capital equipment for air pollution control.

EXHIBIT III-5

Major Diversifying Acquisitions of Carborundum

1954   Stupakoff Ceramic and Manufacturing Company (Pennsylvania):   Ceramic components used in electrical and electronic industries; tubular electrical insulators and dielectrics, low loss and precision formed insulators, capacitors and resistors, printed circuits, metal-to-glass seals, metal-to-ceramic seals, and Kovar metal for sealing to glass.

1954   American Tripoli Corporation (Missouri):   Sole producer of tripoli, an unusal form of silica which was an essential ingredient of buffing compounds.

1954   Borolite Corporation: New company formed for the development, manufacture, and sale of various high temperature metal borides which were expected to have promising uses in industry and national defense.

1955   Curtis Machine Corporation (New York):   Engaged in the manufacture of high quality sanding, polishing, and grinding machines which used large quantities of abrasives.   Most of the Curtis product line used coated abrasives (e.g., sandpaper), and was sold to the woodworking industry.

1962   Tysaman Machine Company, Inc. (Tennessee):   The largest producer of stone working machinery in the United States, specializing in the production of a full line of equipment for the cutting and finishing of stone, marble, and granite. It had also begun to design and construct equipment for use in the metalworking industry.

1963   Pangborn Corporation (Maryland and Pennsylvania):   A world leader in blast cleaning and descaling machines, dust and fume control equipment, steel abrasives, and vibratory finishing equipment.   Its Rotoblast descaling machines were wisely used in the steel and steel processing industries to clean sheet, plate, billits, bars, wire and rods, and to provide corrosion protection for ships, building, bridges, and tanks.   An airless, mechanical system using loose abrasives and controlled centrifugal force, Rotoblast was widely used for shot peening and for deflashing a wide range of metal, rubber, and plastic parts, and for cleaning castings and forgings.

1964   Basic Carbon Corporation (New York), Falls Industries Incorporated (Ohio): Both manufactured and sold carbon and graphite products, particularly to the chemical, metallurgical, electrical, missile, and rocket industries.   Basic Carbon also added a new class of non-metallic fabrics and fibers to those of Carborundum which had established a strong position in high-temperature and corrosion-resistant applications.

1966   Tem-Pres Research and Development (Pennsylvania):   Materials research for high-temperature and high-pressure conditions.   Its staff ranked among the leading investigators in their fields and were closely related with Pennsylvania State College.   Tem-Pres had established commercial markets, primarily scientific laboratories, for a number of sophisticated control and measuring devices, and worked on contract research for defense and aerospace agencies and contractors.

1966   Lockport Felt Company (New York): Third largest manufacturer of paper machine felts in the United States. These felts were endless woven belts of woolen and synthetic fabrics used on paper machines in the drying process.

1966   W. T. Copeland & Sons, Ltd. (England): Manufacturer of Spode English bone china and other fine dinnerware. Its bone china, stoneware, and earthenware were distributed internationally with a reputation for high quality and elegant design. For generations, special designs were supplied to distinguished persons and royalty and were collector's items.

1966   Metal Pumping Services: Manufactured and sold pumps for moving molten aluminum with potential for other metals.

1967   Commercial Filters Corporation: Manufactured a wide variety of types of equipment and filtering media for gases and liquids for use in air and water filtration, industrial waste control, aerospace, chemical and food processing, and petroleum.

EXHIBIT III-6

Product-Market Segments for Carborundum

	Chemical	Foundry	Aerospace	Steel	Paper	Electrical	NonFerrous	Autos	Wood Prod.	Stone	Consumer	Machinery	Nuclear	Others
High Temperature Processing	X	X	X	X		X				X		X		
Ceramics Technology	X	X	X	X	X	X	X			X	X		X	X
Inorganic Fiber Production	X		X			X	X			X				
Textile Design & Fabrication	X		X	X										
Composites Technology	X	X	X	X	X			X	X	X	X	X		X
Systems Design & Assembly	X	X	X	X				X	X	X		X		X
Coating Techniques	X		X	X				X	X	X	X	X		X
Electronic Technology	X		X			X		X		X				X
Metallurgy		X		X		X				X	X			
Filtration	X	X		X	X		X	X	X					X
Stock Removal		X	X	X	X	X	X	X	X	X	X	X		X

Percent of Carborundum Sales

	Chemical	Foundry	Aerospace	Steel	Paper	Electrical	NonFerrous	Autos	Wood Prod.	Stone	Consumer	Machinery	Nuclear	Others
1 - 5%	X		X		X		X		X		X		X	
5 - 10%		X				X		X		X				
10 - 15%				X								X		
Over 15%														X

EXHIBIT III-7

Carborundum's Related Product Lines for Diversification

Division	Abrasives Systems	Pollution Control Systems	Process Equipment Systems
Bonded Abrasives	Grinding Wheels & Machines & Ceramic Cutting Tools	Diffusion Tubes & Filter Bed Supports	Ceramic Filter Media & Pulp Stones
Coated Abrasives	Coated Abrasives & Machines	Treated Filter Fabrics	Impregnating Resins
Electro Minerals	Abrasive Grain & Motion Finishing Machines, Media, & Compounds	Primary Refractory Materials	Primary Refractory Materials, Catalyst Carrier Bed Support, & Sink-Float Media
Process Equipment			Corrosion Resistant Molten Metal Plumbing Systs.
Lockport		Fabric Filtration Media	Paper Machine Felts
Graphite Products	Electrodes for Electrical Discharge Machining & Electrical Arc Cutting	High Temperature Filtration Media	Electrodes, Anodes, & Graphite Molds
Refractories & Electronics	Wear-Resistant Parts & Blasting Nozzles	Wear & Heat Resistant Linings for Dust Collectors & Incinerators & Inorganic Fiber Filters	Refractories, High Temperature Insulation, Catalyst Carriers, Wear & Corrosion Resistant Linings & Heating Elements
Harbison-Carborundum	Wear Resistant Parts		Fused Cast Refractories for Linings & Structural Members & Fused Magnesite Chrome Grains
Tripoli	Buffing & Polishing Powders	Coagulants	
Commercial Filters	Filter Systems for Grinding Machines	Liquid Waste & Bi-Product Recovery Systs.	In-process Filtration Systs. & Filtration Systs.
Pangborn	Blast & Peening Machines & Dust Collectors	Fume & Dust Control Systems & Replacement Fiber Filter Media	Separators & Collectors for Air-Suspended Products, Bi-Products, & Waste
New Products Branch of R&D	Crush Rolls	Inorganic Hot Gas Filtration Fibers for Research	Thermowells & Electro-Thermal Sensors

EXHIBIT III-8

Advertisement for an R & D Acquisition by Carborundum

Wanted

Independent R & D

Laboratory Affiliation

Ideally the facility we are seeking is presently staffed by 35 to 100 (or more) highly qualified professionals who have a genuine desire to do really creative work in fields related to high temperature materials, hard materials, solid state electronic materials, and plastics. In addition, a demonstrated proficiency in some other areas of scientific inquiry would also be welcomed. The organization should have a range of competence that includes fundamental research, product deveopment, and process engineering.

The Carborundum Company expects to make available the financial support and managerial assistance necessary to enable the laboratory to engage in forward-looking research and development that might otherwise be beyond its means. This can permit both an extension of present capacity for outside research contracts, as well as company funded in-house programs devoted to basic research and fundamental investigations.

The present research and development personnel may expect to enjoy attractive opportunities for professional growth as a result of their association with a company that has ample financial resources and a tradition of recognizing and appreciating the importance of basic and applied research.

For the principals, financial affiliation with Carborundum can provide the means of satisfying personal goals without sacrificing the continuation of existing management.

For Carborundum this proposed association is another move designed to insure our continuing and accelerating growth as a leading creator and manufacturer of high performance materials.

If your facilities and interests are compatible with the above description, please write or phone Mr. Niles C. Bartholomew, Vice President, Corporation Planning. Your disclosure will be held in complete confidence.

EXHIBIT III-9

Abrasives Firms Compared

NORTON	CARBORUNDUM

Types of Information or Acquisition Criteria

Industrial consumable products only
Nonconcentrated markets only
Noncapital intensive markets only
Growth greater than abrasives
R.O.I greater than Norton's
Dilution less than 5¢ per share

I Overcome divisional weaknesses
Acquire only for cash

II Countercyclical to abrasives
Good management to remain
Assets between $30m & $120m
Significant market position

III Growth greater than 10% annually
Fragmented markets
Sales between $1m & $20m

Nonregulated industries only
Bookvalue less than $10m only
Markets in developmental stage
High quality image products only
Technologically based concentricity
Headquarters near Niagara preferred
R.O.I. greater than Carborundum's
Build on existing strengths

Sources of Market Information

I Corporate committees
Nonabrasives division managers
Industry trade associations
Publications

II Publications and consultants

III Nonabrasives group management
Intermediaries and consultants
Market research & publications
Trade associations

Corporate executives determined vectors of
growth, usually to extend technical
capability to new customers
Corporate officers began with personal
knowledge based on relationship with
the market
Market research occasionally
Former Industry Executives

Sources of Prospect Information

I Intermediaries

II Intermediaries & publications
Consultant reports

III Intermediaries
Market research
Consultant reports
Prospects themselves

Identified as part of gathering information
about markets
Acquisition consultant
Industry experts
Division managers
Prospects themselves

EXHIBIT III-9 (cont.)

Types of Information Processing

I   No formal processing

II Computerized search techniques

III No formal processing (done by
consultants)

No formal processing techniques
Discounted cash flow techniques introduced
in 1972

Participants in the Process

Executive vice president — former marketing
executive for an industrial products
company, no acquisition experience
Director of business planning — former
Norton division manager in industrial
ceramics
Director of corporate development —
former acquisition consultant who also
held similar positions with other firms

Senior vice president — former executive
with abrasives division and in international division where acquisitions were
important
Director of research and development —
primary experience in product and
market development
Manager of acquisition analysis — former
financial analyst and finance teacher
with little corporate experience

Sequence of Scanning Activities

I   Industries identified (no further action
until candidates found)

II S&P computer data screened to identify
potential prospects
Some candidates presented by
intermediaries
Published information gathered
Prospects contacted

III Market identified
Availability of candidates determined
Published information gathered
Markets approved for entry
Prospects identified and contacted

Markets identified
Information about markets gathered
Individual prospects identified
Some information about prospects gathered
Prospects contacted
Additional information gathered about
candidates

EXHIBIT III-10

Financial Comparison of Norton Company and Carborundum Company

Year	Net Sales		Net Profit		Earnings/Share		Return on Invst.	
	Norton	Carborundum	Norton	Carborundum	Norton	Carborundum	Norton	Carborundum
1960	$177m	$142m	$12.3m	$ 7.6m	$2.26	$2.15	8.0%	7.8%
1961	179	141	11.6	6.3	2.05	1.77	7.6	6.4
1962	213	150	14.8	7.0	2.62	1.95	9.2	6.7
1963	216	162	14.1	6.4	2.49	1.76	8.6	6.1
1964	251	185	18.2	11.2	3.25	3.10	10.4	6.6
1965	273	202	18.4	13.4	3.30	3.69	9.9	10.7
1966	311	231	18.8	15.3	3.32	4.27	9.6	10.4
1967	305	238	12.1	11.8	2.14	3.23	6.5	7.6
1968	324	255	15.2	14.0	2.72	3.83	8.3	9.1
1969	353	290	16.1	14.9	2.92	4.03	8.2	8.9
1970	359	302	11.3	14.5	2.09	3.97	6.2	8.4
1971	347	311	11.4	13.5	2.12	3.68	6.6	8.3
1972	374	340	14.5	16.3	2.70	4.42	7.4	9.0

CHAPTER IV

DOMESTIC DIVERSIFYING ACQUISITIONS
IN THE TOBACCO INDUSTRY

This is the second of three data chapters. It describes and analyzes the domestic diversifying acquisition process in two companies within the tobacco industry. This chapter begins by describing some of the major issues which confronted the managements of the companies in the industry as they planned and executed their domestic diversifying acquisitions. This section points out a major difference between the issues facing executives in this industry and those facing executives in the abrasives industry. For about twenty years, the tobacco industry faced a relatively high risk of obliteration from governmental and/or social pressures. The cause of these pressures was increasing and more widely publicized evidence linking tobacco smoking to various debilitating, chronic, or fatal diseases, particularly cancer. The second and third parts of this chapter describe how Philip Morris and American Brands (formerly American Tobacco Co.) attempted to diversify through acquisition. The final part of the chapter compares and contrasts the scanning processes of these two companies, with particular emphasis on the causes of major similarities and differences.

The Tobacco Industry

The tobacco industry was considerably larger and more visible than the abrasives industry. During the 1950-1970 period, the United States tobacco industry continued its moderate growth and profitability despite increasing medical, political, and social pressures against the use of tobacco products. This note describes the major markets in the industry, and analyzes the major environmental trends and conditions which had an impact on the tobacco markets during the 1950-1970 period.

Structure of the Industry

Both abrasives and tobacco products are consumable, or frequently repurchased, but unlike abrasives, tobacco products are a retail consumer good. Since 1970 cigarettes represented 90% of all tobacco industry sales. The remainder was comprised primarily of cigars, pipe tobacco, chewing tobacco, and snuff. The cigarette market was further segmented by filtration, menthol content, tar and nicotine content, length, and taste. The two filtered cigarette brands sold prior to 1950 were a negligible portion of all cigarette sales. However, by 1970 the portion of filtered brands increased to over 78% of all cigarette sales. This was perhaps the most significant and pervasive trend within the industry during the period under study. The segmentation by filter was sufficiently strong to characterize filter cigarettes as a separate market from nonfilter cigarettes, since few consumers would alternate from one to the other. The preference for menthol cigarettes grew from a negligible portion to about 20% of total sales during the period under study. Cigarette brands which contained larger amounts of tar and nicotine (compared to others) were discriminated against by some consumers who feared that these substances induced or caused cancer. This distinction was further reinforced by the tax structures which evolved in some cities and states during the period under study favoring low tar and nicotine brands. Length was not as strong a determinant for preference as other dimensions. A final segmentation variable was taste. Each cigarette brand was a unique blend of several of the over 60 different kinds of tobacco leaves.

The tobacco industry was concentrated. Six firms (American Brands, Brown & Williamson, Liggett & Meyers, P. Lorillard division of Loew's Theaters, Philip Morris, and R. J. Reynolds) manufactured over 99% of all cigarettes sold in the United States. Eight firms manufactured about 83% of all cigars, and eight firms manufactured about 81% of all smoking and chewing tobacco.

Prior to World War II, each cigarette manufacturer sold one major brand of cigarettes. After the war, proliferation of brands increased until those same six firms produced over 110 different brands in 1972. However, the seven largest selling brands were over 20 years old. The 20 largest brands accounted for 90% of all cigarette sales and the 40 largest accounted for 98.5%.

Barriers to Entry

There were high barriers to entry into the tobacco industry. The high failure rate of new brands and large advertising investment discouraged new competitors. Strong brand loyalty was encouraged by product differentiation and the brand images created by advertising. Established brands allocated from 3% to 10% of dollar sales to advertising, whereas a new brand might spend up to 65% on advertising and distribute many free samples to acquaint smokers with its taste properties to encourage brand switching. Advertising generally encouraged brand loyalty by developing a public image of the characteristics of the brand and of the consumers who purchased it.

Distribution channels present a second barrier to entry. The six major cigarette companies distributed their brands through about 4,500 wholesalers and over 1.5 million retail outlets (excluding vending machines) to about 40% of the adult population.   Many potential competitors failed to understand how to manage or service these channels.   In addition, the major competitors would discourage the wholesalers from distributing brands of new competitors.

Manufacturing capability and purchasing skills also would be difficult to develop as a new competitor. Although the industry had no significant economies of manufacturing scale, as evidenced by the over 500 plants spread throughout 30 states in the United States, the art of properly blending tobaccos and the high-speed machinery designed by the cigarette manufacturers was not readily available to others.   The manufacturing process began with the purchase of green leaf at tobacco auctions since none of the major firms grew their own tobacco crops. Purchasing at public auction required considerable skill, since tobacco represented over half the manufacturing costs and over 20% of the wholesale price.   After purchase, green leaves were stored, aged, and cured for over two years and then destemmed, cut, and blended. This required substantial investments in raw materials inventory.   Thus, in both manufacturing and purchasing, the major competitors had created barriers to market entry in addition to the strong marketing barriers.

Trends and Problems

During the 1950-1970 period, tobacco products in general and cigarettes in particular were in the mature phase of the product life cycle. Between 1925 and 1950, the compound annual growth rate of unit sales of cigarettes was about 7%, whereas between 1950 and 1970 the growth rate was about 2%. Also during the earlier period, the compound annual growth rate of per capita consumption of cigarettes was almost 4%; during the latter period it remained almost stagnant, growing slightly through 1966 and then declining through 1970. The dollars sales growth of the industry remained almost constant throughout the entire 1925-1970 period because wholesale prices during the early period increased at less than 1% per year while during the latter period they grew at about 4%. Throughout the earlier period, net profit margins (on gross sales) decreased from almost 30% to 8% with about 12 percentage points of this decrease caused by increases in federal excise taxes from $3.00 per thousand cigarettes to $3.50 per thousand between 1940 and 1942. During the latter period the margins further slipped to about 5%, the result of a further increase of the federal excise tax to $4.00 per thousand and increased new product development and advertising expenditures. Nevertheless, return on equity averaged about 15% for the major competitors throughout both the earlier and later periods.

Slowing growth in unit sales was attributed to two major environmental trends: (1) Saturation of the slow growth tobacco market by cigarette consumption and (2) increasing medical evidence relating smoking to serious health problems. The pound per capita consumption of tobacco products in total grew at an annual compounded rate of 1.25% between 1925 and 1949 compared with the 4.0% compounded growth of cigarette consumption per capita. Cigarette sales then increased from 32% of all tobacco sold in the United States to 78% during the earlier period and increased to 90% during the latter period.

Although not a recent issue, the legal and social attitude toward smoking and health intensified after World War II. The major cause of this trend was mounting statistical evidence which associated cigarette smoking with numerous chronic, debilitating, and fatal diseases. In response to the mounting statistical evidence, the major cigarette companies adopted advertising themes and copy to counter it. Several brands depicted doctors endorsing cigarettes as health remedies until the Federal Trade Commission stopped most of this type of advertising with court suits. Nevertheless, medical evidence widely published during 1953 and 1954 led to the first two years of consecutive decline in cigarette sales since the 1929-32 depression period. Sales turned upward again in 1955, despite continued adverse publicity.

Responses to the 1953-1954 downturn occurred at both the industry and the firm level. At the industry level, the Tobacco Industry Research Committee (TIRC) was formed as an independent organization to sponsor a program of research into the questions of tobacco use and health. Operationally, the TIRC formed an advisory board of scientists disinterested in the cigarette industry to sponsor and fund the research of other scientists who published the results of their own work independently of the TIRC. During the 1954-1963 period, the TIRC spent over $7 million on 425 research projects conducted by nearly 155 scientists in 95 hospitals, from which over 280 articles were published. This research was financed by the various major cigarette manufacturers in proportion to their market shares. TIRC also published its own interpretation of the studies reaffirming the industry claim that there was insufficient experimental and clinical evidence to demonstrate that cancer or other diseases were *caused by* cigarette smoking. In 1958, this work was reinforced by the formation of a new trade association, the Tobacco Institute, to provide a unified spokesman for the industry. It also acted as a lobbyist for the industry.

At the firm level, each cigarette manufacturer introduced new brands of filter cigarettes. The function of the cigarette filter was to trap condensates, including nicotine and tars, from the smoke. The cigarette firms attempted to reassure smokers that the adverse publicity was unfounded but that the filter provided a more pleasurable smoke by reducing tar and nicotine content while eliminating loose tobacco ends. The sales increases of these new brands at the expense of existing major brands altered market shares and caused brand proliferation.

A second and related move of individual competitors was the introduction of menthol cigarettes to reduce the apparent irritation of smoking by creating a "cooler" tasting smoke.   During the 1954-1960 period, tobacco advertising presented consumers with multiple conflicting claims for lowest tar and nicotine content brands.   Also during this period, published research and political pressure against smoking increased.   In 1956, the U.S. Public Health Service reviewed and appraised sixteen separate studies conducted in five countries over an eighteen-year period.   It concluded there was a causal relationship between excessive cigarette smoking and lung cancer.   In March 1957, it issued a report recommending the initiation of public health measures designed to reduce the per capita consumption of cigarettes.   In June 1957, the British Medical Research Council completed a similar review and reached similar conclusions.

By 1960, the U.S. government remained too fragmented in thought and ambivalent in action to deal with the health issue.   While the tobacco industry finally had a unified spokesman through the Tobacco Institute, various legislative committees, executive agencies, and judicial decisions avoided direct confrontation of the potential problem. A major reason for their reluctance was the economic importance of the tobacco industry to the nation and the political power which it possessed. By 1962, tobacco leaf was the fourth largest United States agricultural cash crop and the third largest agricultural export commodity.   Tobacco manufacturers employed over 100,000 people.   Also, the industry's media advertising expenditures exceeded $250 million annually.   Finally, excise and sales taxes from tobacco products provided over $3 billion in revenues to federal, state and local governments.

Amidst the medical, political, and social debate, only two of the six major cigarette manufacturers began to diversify.   Through acquisition, Philip Morris entered some flexible packaging markets in 1957, personal products markets in 1960 and 1963, and the chewing gum market in 1963. R. J. Reynolds began to sell aluminum foil as a packaging material and in 1963 entered fruit drink markets through acquisition.   The other four competitors reaffirmed their faith in the continued growth and profitability of the tobacco industry and claimed that diversification was a popular fad affecting all industries, somewhat detrimentally.

However, the major cigarette manufacturers were more concerned about a special advisory committee which was established in 1962 under the U.S. Surgeon General to review existing evidence on the relationship of smoking and health.   The advisory committee was particularly important because it represented the most outstanding and impartial group of scientists gathered to date for this purpose and its conclusions were expected to determine the future course of FTC action, legislation, and public health programs. The 387-page report of the committee, published in early 1964 concluded that "Cigarette smoking is a health hazard of sufficient importance in the United States to warrant appropriate remedial action."

The immediate and subsequent verbal response of the tobacco industry through both the Tobacco Institute and its members was disbelief, righteous indignation, and continued claim that the scientific evidence was not adequate. Cigarette sales dropped sharply, although within four months they returned to former levels. The political implications were more far reaching and long lasting. The Federal Trade Commission began hearings concerning the form and substance of remedial action suggested by the Surgeon General's report. The Congress began considering several legislative acts which would impact the cigarette industry. The Departments of Agriculture and Health, Education and Welfare began considering the impact of the report on their own activities.

Outside government, the various advertising agencies which serviced the tobacco industry began re-evaluating their position with respect to cigarette advertising services, and the National Association of Broadcasters attempted to develop a code of ethics for televised cigarette advertisements. Various private associations and foundations concerned with health issues began considering their role in remedial programs. The Tobacco Institute also began mapping strategy for the expected responses of these various groups, particularly the Federal Trade Commission. The direction of its response was outlined in an editorial published in *Tobacco* magazine (January 17, 1964):

> The reality now - however unpleasant - is that the problems confronting the industry have moved from the smaller area of scientific debate to the larger stage of economic impact. The tobacco industry is as vital to the economic health of the nation as it was before January 11, 1964, when the advisory committee's report was made public.
>
> Clearly, the task ahead for us tobacco men is two-fold. We must cooperate to the limit of the industry's powerful resources in making the product's requisite changes. We must be eternally vigilant to ward off restriction and retaliation born, not of sincere concern for the nation's health, but of spite and animus on the part of those who never could tolerate the indulgence of fellow citizens in such pleasures as smoking.

The strategy for the industry was then clearly one of survival. The public statement to the contrary, the industry leaders began to seriously question the future of the industry. Furthermore, four of the major competitors diversified, one was acquired by a conglomerate, and one was a subsidiary of a large international firm. Within the United States none of the major tobacco companies remained totally committed to the domestic tobacco industry. It was within this milieu that the diversification programs of two firms in the tobacco industry are analyzed in the following parts of this chapter.

The Philip Morris Company

In 1972, Philip Morris was a multiproduct, multimarket, multinational corporation with $214 million in profits and $2.1 billion in sales of which about 18% was from nontobacco products. Since 1960, the compound annual sales growth rate of Philip Morris was about 12.7% and the earnings per share growth rate was about 14.0%. During this period, the firm acquired about 21 companies, 12 of which were based in the United States and 7 of these were acquired to enter new markets.[1] During the same period, the firm divested 3 acquisitions which constituted the surgical supply division, and obtained partial ownership of several overseas companies related to the tobacco business. Philip Morris also established arrangements with several overseas companies through which the firm's products were sold in over 160 countries throughout the world. Although Philip Morris strengthened its research and development capabilities substantially during this period, its focus was on existing products and not on developing products with which the firm could enter new markets.

Program History and Participants

All of the firm's diversification occurred after 1957, prior to which the sole business of the firm was tobacco. Philip Morris increased its share of the domestic cigarette market from 9.2% in 1950 to 18.2% in 1971. Three factors explain this remarkable growth relative to its competitors: (1) Philip Morris concentrated on filter cigarette brands earlier and more completely than other major manufacturers, (2) Philip Morris had a more creative and innovative marketing organization than its competitors, and (3) the Marlboro "flip-top-box" was a packaging innovation which enhanced its product differentiation and brand loyalty. Also, while Philip Morris attempted to diversify, it did not reduce its emphasis on tobacco products.

Philip Morris was organized into five relatively autonomous divisions (Philip Morris USA, Philip Morris International, Industrial Products, Miller Brewery, and Mission Viejo) reporting to the corporate President, Mr. George Weissman. Four staff vice presidents (finance, general counsel, personnel, and planning), together with Mr. Weissman, reported to the Chairman of the Board of Directors, Mr. Joseph F. Cullman, III.

Mr. F. Harrison Poole, Director of Corporate Planning, reported to the planning vice president. He had major responsibility for reviewing long range plans for the divisions and for identifying and analyzing diversification opportunities. He joined the company in 1955 as part of its initial diversification planning activity and reported to Mr. Parker O. McComas, Mr. Cullman's predecessor. Eight corporate planners worked under his direction, all of whom had earned M.B.A. degrees. One staff planner was Mr. Douglas H. Nelson, who joined Philip Morris in 1968 after earning an M.B.A. degree from Dartmouth University, where he majored in marketing. Another staff planner was Mr. Robert M. Delaney,[2] who earned an M.B.A. degree from the University of Pennsylvania and operated his own businesses for about one year before joining Philip Morris in 1971. His business experience was primarily importing and exporting consumer goods. Both planners expressed high regard for Mr. Poole and his superiors and praise for Philip Morris as a company for which to work. The staff work was about equally divided between diversification analysis and internal planning, with all staff members allocated to both types of activity.

Following the tobacco industry sales decline in 1953, Mr. Parker O. McComas reviewed Philip Morris operations and concluded that it had adequate capital to enter new markets. Management claimed that initial diversification was motivated by Philip Morris' low market share position in the industry rather than by adverse publicity attacking the total industry. To evaluate diversification opportunities impartially, Mr. McComas hired two executives who had no previous experience in the tobacco industry. One of these executives was Mr. Poole, who helped Mr. McComas prepare the first diversifying acquisition proposal submitted to the board of directors. It was rejected. In subsequent meetings, Mr. McComas convinced the board members of the appropriateness of entering new markets, despite their confidence and experience in the tobacco business.

Philip Morris' first diversifying acquisition, Milprint[3] was a flexible packaging converter. The board approved this acquisition for two major reasons. First, flexible packaging was a raw material for Philip Morris and therefore the acquisition had more the appearance of backward integration than diversification. Second, Philip Morris had recently introduced the "flip-top-box" package for its Marlboro brand of cigarettes and attributed its rapid market acceptance partially to that package, indicating to the board the importance of packing to the future success of the firm. However, the acquisition was diversification and not integration. Milprint subsequently produced less than 20% of Philip Morris' packaging requirements and sold only a small portion of its output to Philip Morris. As part of the acquisition, Philip Morris also assumed ownership of a specialty paper mill, Nicolet Paper Company, which was a subsidiary of Milprint. Mr. McComas viewed the Milprint acquisition as the first of a series of acquisitions which would make Philip Morris a major competitor in the packaging industry. Therefore, the next acquisition he proposed was Polymer Industries which manufactured adhesives used not only to secure packaging materials, but also used throughout the cigarette manufacturing process. Again, Polymer had the appearance of backward integration, but fulfillment of the integration was never attempted.

In late 1957, after the Milprint acquisition, Mr. McComas died suddenly and unexpectedly. Former executive vice president, Mr. Cullman was elected the chief executive officer. He did not want to move forward with the diversification program immediately. Although the Polymer acquisition was completed, several other commitments were more easily held in abeyance. For example, a folding box business, a joint venture on a paper mill, and a small floor wax and cleaning products company were all under consideration, and Mr. Cullman requested that they be avoided if possible.

Mr. Cullman rationalized the Philip Morris diversification program and examined its corporate strengths and weaknesses. He concluded that the corporation's major skill was the mass marketing of consumer products, and substantially reoriented the direction of the diversification program. The first acquisition under this new program was American Safety Razor, a company well known to Mr. Cullman, who had been a member of its board of directors for several years. Mr. Cullman expressed his belief that American Safety Razor would benefit from the resources of Philip Morris, particularly the greater efficiency of Philip Morris' extensive media franchises and the advice of merchandising and other marketing experts at Philip Morris. However, the major benefit for American Safety Razor was the financial support for a major product line development and upgrading. Later, Burma-Vita was acquired to complement and complete the shaving products line and DeWitt Lukens and Hospital Supply and Development were acquired to extend the surgical blade business of American Safety Razor. These last acquisitions were later divested together with the surgical blade business of American Safety Razor.

After Mr. Cullman became president in 1958, Philip Morris maintained an acquisition program through which it searched for two types of diversifying acquisitions. Type I acquisitions were to enter markets closely related to existing Philip Morris businesses, for example, Burma-Vita, Koch Convertograph, and Armstrong. These acquisitions would be combined with the existing divisions to which they closely related; some remaining as separate profit centers and others integrating fully with the operations of the division.   Type II acquisitions were to enter markets or businesses unrelated to other activities of Philip Morris, for example, American Safety Razor, Clark Gum, Miller Brewing, and Mission Viejo.   These acquisitions would be constituted as separate operating divisions, reporting to the president.   Also, acquisitions were conducted by the international division of Philip Morris and were not a responsibility of the planning group under Mr. Poole.

Acquisition Criteria

Most of Philip Morris' acquisition criteria applied to both Type I and Type II acquisitions.   The primary criteria applied to markets for entry through acquisition, although some which applied to individual prospects were also important.   One major criterion was that a market for entry should have an international growth and profitability potential no less than Philip Morris had achieved historically, or that an acquisition prospect have that potential through superior competition within an otherwise unacceptable market for entry.   Neither the time required to realize that potential or the horizon over which it should be sustained were well defined.   Considering its own rapid growth, Philip Morris felt that acquiring firms with a slower growth rate and profitability would not be an appropriate utilization of its resources, particularly since the company required large investments in tobacco leaf inventories to support future growth.   Furthermore, during most of the 1950-1970 period, Philip Morris' price/earnings ratio had remained low, despite its strong earnings per share growth.   Therefore, growth companies could not be acquired for stock without significant dilution.

Because Philip Morris was so large, acquisitions which would have any impact on sales growth or earnings per share would also require substantial initial cash investments.   Unless future growth and profitability at least equaled what Philip Morris' other activities were expected to be, acquisitions would have decreasing impact on diversification over time rather than contribute to it.   This balance was important to offset eventual deceleration of the tobacco business.   If deceleration occurred over the short term, acquired companies would be needed to continue the growth record of the firm.   If it occurred only in the longer term, then only acquired companies which at least equaled Phillip Morris' performance would improve the balance substantially.   In either case, when the growth of its tobacco business decelerated, Philip Morris would realize a considerable cash flow from leaf inventory adjustments available to support diversification.

The international potential aspect of the criterion reflected the firm's intention to utilize its worldwide tobacco business base to develop overseas markets for the products of acquired domestic companies. International expansion of domestic acquisitions would require substantial cash flows. Thus, the expected futurity of the tobacco business strongly influenced Philip Morris' ability to realize the international potential of an acquisition. Availability of funds to support international expansion in 1972 was limited by the firm's plans to construct the world's largest and most modern cigarette manufacturing facility in Richmond, Virginia.

A second acquisition criterion was that acquisitions manufacture low-technology, quality-image, mass-marketed consumer products for which advertising and promotion were important determinants of success. This criterion applied primarily to Type II acquisitions. American Safety Razor was the first company acquired after this criterion was established. Since cigarettes were sold in almost every retail outlet where razor blades were sold, Philip Morris began wholesaling through its 600 nationwide salesmen. Later Burma-Vita products and Clark Gum were sold through the same sales organization. However, this approach did not succeed. Philip Morris salesmen could secure placement and distribution, but then would be out-sold because each product received inadequate sales attention relative to its competitors.

Nevertheless, Philip Morris management did demonstrate that it could improve the sales and distribution of mass-marketed consumer products, because it had the skill to manage these activities. Similarly, the management's advertising skills and leverage with the media were important resources for acquired companies. These supportive contributions of Philip Morris to its acquisitions reflected Mr. Cullman's desire to both contribute and control acquired companies. He wanted to be assured that if something went wrong with an acquisition, someone in the Philip Morris organization could diagnose the problem. Furthermore, he did not want Philip Morris to become a "conglomerate." In this sense, Philip Morris also avoided high technology businesses, for which research and development skills were a stronger determinant of success than marketing skills. Although Mission Viejo was a real estate business which did not exactly meet the acquisition criteria, it was conceived as an investment with a good long-term growth prospect rather than as an acquisition.

Philip Morris sought products which did not "fleece the public" or garner a distasteful image, but rather, products which contributed substantively to the quality of life. Although Philip Morris' initial entry into the cigarette market was based on a quality or premium image, the rationale for the criterion was stronger than tradition. With the tobacco industry subject to public criticism on consumer health grounds, anything that would detract from the "ethical" image the tobacco companies were trying to project could have devastating impact on the industry in general. Furthermore, products which consumers perceived as necessary to the quality of life would have more predictable demand.

Another criterion was that markets for entry be nonseasonal, noncyclical, unconcentrated, and uncontrolled. Not only did the Philip Morris management have little experience with seasonal business, but also it felt that these businesses were more difficult to predict and they complicated Philip Morris' cash flow problems. Although some other firms sought financial strength through counterbalancing cyclical or seasonal businesses, Philip Morris felt that to maintain that balance while attempting major growth and diversification was unnecessary, undesirable, and possibly unmanageable.

Concentrated markets posed similar managerial and financial problems which corporate management sought to avoid, in addition to which such markets were often mature with slow growth. Philip Morris had observed the problems facing a Philip Morris competitor, Gillette. These companies dominated their respective industries, but to grow rapidly Gillette was forced to diversify. Although a small competitor might grow rapidly within a mature market, by gaining market share, Philip Morris felt it could not afford the substantial and sustained losses required to build that market share. After Philip Morris acquired American Safety Razor, it introduced the stainless steel razor blade considerably ahead of Gillette and gained market share during the interim period. However, it was unable to maintain its position after Gillette introduced a comparable product. By comparison, Philip Morris expected high growth from acquisitions which could gain market share in relatively unconcentrated markets.

Market share competition was more feasible in uncontrolled industries. As evidenced in the cigarette market, governmental action had often changed the balance among competitors as it grappled with the public health issue. Philip Morris felt that the antitrust limitations imposed on the brewing industry were a predictable and continuing force reasonably well understood by competitors. Control was also a concern among diversified competitors. For example, one tobacco company had significant control over transatlantic shipping which could adversely affect Philip Morris' overseas shipping capabilities. In general, this criterion implied that management wanted relatively predictable but not overly constraining market environments in which to compete.

A final criterion which applied to all acquisitions, but primarily to Type II acquisitions, was that a prospective company have good management willing to remain after the acquisition. After returning from a visit to a prospective acquisition, Mr. Cullman reportedly said that he did not try to evaluate the operation of the company, just its management. Mr. Cullman was concerned not only with the quality of management but also with the compatibility of personalities with those of the Philip Morris corporate management. Since the planning staff members were generally young and with little top management line experience, they could not assume divisional management responsibility.

Although size was not an explicitly stated acquisition criterion, the management criterion implied that a prospect must be large enough to have depth of management as well as quality of management. Furthermore, Mr. Cullman wanted only a limited number of operations reporting to Mr. Weissman, because if the number became too large, the amount of corporate attention available for each could not provide adequate planning and control. In addition, if Philip Morris were to increase its non-tobacco sales significantly without adding many new businesses, each business would need to be quite large. For example, Miller Brewing had sales exceeding $200 million in the year it was acquired, an amount about equal to the growth in the tobacco business for the same year. Mission Viejo, acquired for about $60 million, might be viewed as a lower size limit and only acceptable because of its great growth potential extending many years into the future.

Thus, the major acquisition criteria which Philip Morris applied to markets for entry or companies for acquisition were future financial potential, consumer product markets, freely competitive markets, and well managed prospects. Financial potential, both sales growth and profitability, was essential to achieve greater diversification. Consumer product markets provided Philip Morris' corporate management with the maximum opportunity to utilize corporate skills for mass-marketed, strongly advertised products. Freely competitive markets, without high concentration or strong regulation, would best permit effective impact of the corporate marketing skills. Acquiring only well-managed companies would reduce the likelihood of operating problems which corporate management could not effectively diagnose and solve with its limited manpower.

The Acquisition Scanning Process

Philip Morris searched for acquisition alternatives in several ways. First, division management, corporate management, and the planning staff identified markets which the firm might enter through acquisition. When the planning staff and the corporate management agreed that Philip Morris should enter an identified market, the planning staff actively searched for acquisition prospects which competed in that market. Second, members of the firm, particularly members of the board of directors, identified acquisition candidates about which the planning staff gathered information. Third, intermediaries who were aware that Philip Morris was searching for acquisitions identified candidates.

The planning staff gathered some information about all acquisition alternatives. If the planning staff had already determined that the firm should enter the market in which the candidate competed, then the staff usually had some information already about the candidate and would quickly approach the candidate's management to gather additional information. If an identified candidate competed in a market about which the planning staff had not gathered information, a member of the staff gathered information from published sources about the market to determine if more information should be gathered. For many markets, a staff member would gather information over a two-year period before Philip Morris became committed to entry. However, only a small fraction of the 1500 candidates identified annually by intermediaries either competed in those markets or triggered information gathering about those markets.

Markets for entry. Markets for entry through acquisition were identified in numerous ways. For Type I acquisitions, the business units within Philip Morris to which market entry related usually identified markets for entry and gathered information about them. The corporate planning staff reviewed the information gathered and added any information they had previously gathered about the market. If the planning staff concurred with the business unit's market entry decision, then search for appropriate acquisition prospects was initiated or prospects already identified by the business unit were approached to gain additional information about them. When intermediaries identified acquisition candidates which the corporate planning staff thought might benefit the operations of a business unit, the staff asked the business unit management if further action should be initiated. However, the business unit managers were not forced or coerced to accept acquisition candidates which they did not feel would improve their performances. For example, management of Miller Brewing had refused to accept responsibility for a potential acquisition to enter another alcoholic beverage market, and as a result the acquisition was not consummated.

For Type II acquisitions, markets for entry were identified in many different ways. Occasionally, they were suggested by members of the board of directors or by top executives. One particular market was inadvertently suggested by an executive who was considering a substantial personal investment in a company competing in the particular market. He inquired if the planning staff had any information about that market which would assist his own decision. Many markets were identified when intermediaries proposed particular acquisition candidates. Regardless of the potential of a particular candidate identified, Philip Morris usually gathered some information about its market. One small company came directly to Philip Morris seeking financial support rather than acquisition and promoted a major study of its market. One market was identified by a previous acquisition candidate. The candidate owned over 20% of a company. Philip Morris gathered some initial information about the company as part of its evaluation of the candidate. Although the company was an inappropriate prospect, Philip Morris later gathered much information about its market for entry.

Members of the planning staff also identified potential markets for entry. They read extensively in general business publications and tried to develop a wide variety of professional associates. In addition to this informal identification of markets, the staff deliberately exposed itself to sources of new ideas. For example, during the early years of the acquisition program, Mr. Poole and members of his staff would visit the Philip Morris research center periodically to discuss general trends and interesting new discoveries in technology which might forebode emerging new markets. Although these "brainstorming" sessions did not lead to any specific market entries, they did stimulate the general thinking of the planning staff as well as identify several markets for further study. More recently, Philip Morris subscribed to the Hudson Institute study and the Long Range Planning Service of the Stanford Research Institute. These has the same general impact as had the earlier brainstorming sessions.

After Philip Morris identified markets for entry through acquisition as worthy of study, information was gathered from many sources. Usually Mr. Poole assigned the information gathering task related to a specific market for entry to one of his planning staff members. The staff conducted many brief studies of new markets each year. The purpose of a brief study was to determine if a thorough study would likely be a worthwhile investment of planning time. This judgment considered the information about the market and its environment and the amount of support indicated by other Philip Morris executives.

About five thorough studies emerged each year. Once a planner received responsibility for the research task Mr. Poole monitored his progress closely though frequent communication. A thorough study usually involved a concentrated information gathering period of between three and six man-months during which a planner became an expert on that market and a protracted period during which the planner followed new developments and deepened his understanding while working on other projects. Within the planning department over four man-years of effort were allocated to acquisition scanning each year. Although no dominant pattern for search emerged, probably because of the widely different markets under study and particular research methodologies of the various planners, generally a wide variety of sources contributed information. Philip Morris financed the requisite travel to contact those sources when necessary.   Several examples of information gathering about markets for entry are presented below to support this observation.[4]

Product A.   Mr. Delaney gathered information about the major markets for Product A. Philip Morris had gathered information about these markets in 1958 and 1963 but found them unacceptable for entry. Before Mr. Delaney began his study of the market, a few companies in the market had approached Philip Morris for financing, but corporate management remained uninterested.   One director was somewhat familiar with the market through other directorships as well as a personal interest in some products peripheral to the market.   Mr. Poole approached him in 1972 seeking information.   The director replied that he thought Philip Morris should consider entering the market by acquiring a substantial position.   Mr. Poole and the director discussed the futurity of the market with a member of the Hudson Institute staff.   Based on their enthusiasm Mr. Poole concluded that more detailed study was warranted.

Mr. Delaney completed a brief industry analysis.   His ten-page report utilized business publications[5] and several friends introduced by his own stockbroker as sources of information.   His report concluded that this unconcentrated market was expected to grow rapidly from its embryonic base.   However, it was capital intensive with no short range returns expected.   Also, it had not achieved earlier growth predictions. These conclusions generally confirmed what Mr. Poole had learned.   Two months after Mr. Delaney submitted his brief report, the board of directors requested an intensive thorough study of the market for possible corporate investment through acquisition.

During the ensuing three months, Mr. Delaney prepared a 300-page report on the market.[6]   The report described the market in terms of growth potential causes and inhibitors, cost structure, revenue determinants, operating requirements, equipment suppliers, and competitor profiles.   As part of his thorough analysis of a market opportunity, Mr. Delaney also identified the major competitors in the market.   For each, he gathered some information to indicate typical and atypical problems of competing from many information sources, particularly proprietary reports, personal associates, and market experts. Mr. Delaney had read almost every report written on the market, but he felt his network of acquaintances was his most valuable research asset because they could often provide information not available in written form.   Also they could readily respond to questions.   Although Mr. Delaney began the study with almost no information, he was increasingly becoming a source of information to others interested in the market.

Mr. Delaney felt that the cost of writing planning staff reports rather than retaining external consultants to write them was worth the benefit because outside consultants would not adopt the Philip Morris point of view. They would write about a market opportunity irrespective of the particular concerns and information needs of the firm. He felt that a clinical point of view and detailed information were required for both, but that a planning staff member could better respond to the needs of corporate management. This seemed particularly important since Mr. Delaney might maintain currency in the market for several years before Philip Morris formally entered it. After entering it, he could knowledgeably review plans for competing in that market.

Product B. Mr. Nelson gathered information about the market for Product B. Interest in the market began in a more general way when the vice president of planning decided that he would like Philip Morris to take a minority position in a company which competed in an emerging market. He anticipated that a minority position would provide high potential return with minimal risk and dilution of management attention from Philip Morris' other businesses. In discussing this with other corporate officers he learned that the treasurer had recently purchased stock in a small company designing Product B. He suggested that members of the planning staff meet with the financial backers of the company. The backers claimed that the company had a revolutionary new technological concept which satisfied a well established market need and had potential sales exceeding $1 billion. They further claimed that no large companies were then currently developing a product for this market and that this company had technological leadership.

Market information was not available since the market was yet nonexistent and the company had developed its information based on limited work with a potential customer. Philip Morris did not manufacture products requiring the technologies upon which Product B. was based. Recognizing the limitation of available information, Philip Morris management decided to proceed with a more detailed and comprehensive study. Messrs. Nelson and Poole then met with the financial promoter and the two principal founders of the company to gather more information. Although they were unable to evaluate the technical aspects of the product, they left the meeting with a feeling that the information they received did support the basic concept. A report based on this information was also favorably received by top management.

In order for Philip Morris to better evaluate the technology of the product, several of its scientists and engineers reviewed information on the product. They agreed that the product design was based on a unique combination of known technologies. They also described some of the manufacturing costs and feasibility and the inhibitors to larger scale testing. Mr. Nelson concluded that the company needed credibility, money, and management, which it hoped to obtain from association with Philip Morris or a company like it. Then with a favorable report from the research and development department, Mr. Nelson continued to gather information by helping the company develop a five-year plan and a strategy, including financial projections, available market information, and a ten-year scenario of the industry. This plan was submitted to both the company management and the Philip Morris management.

Top management did not feel it could act upon the report. No one understood why the company could not obtain necessary financing from the potential customers if the product concept was so technologically sound and the need for the product so strong. Mr. Nelson approached a major management consulting firm which had an expert in the technological and market problems related to the product. Based on a brief exchange of information with Mr. Nelson, that consultant concluded that the company had a strong financial promoter who was most likely overstating the progress of the company, although not overstating the potential of the market it sought to develop. The consultant was useful in the information gathering process in three ways: First, he could help Mr. Nelson determine what questions he should seek to ask about an area with which he was relatively unfamiliar. Second, he could help Mr. Nelson evaluate the answers he received to those questions. Third, he could later conduct some market research on the industry without involving the Philip Morris name directly. As he awaited a response from the consultant, Mr. Nelson speculated that the company would require managerial expertise to protect any investment Philip Morris might make.

Product C. Mr. Nelson also described his information gathering process about the market for Product C. He felt this study was more typical than his study of the Product B market because he was able to look at the entire industry with which the product was associated. He described his approach to the study as taking a rather macro approach beginning with simple things like the market's potential, customers, distribution, and major production problems. Finding these things all favorable, he attempted to identify the industry leaders and determine if any of them would be suitable acquisition candidates. He also noted that this approach was easier to use for emerged markets than emerging markets about which little information was available.

While gathering information about the housing industry as part of his evaluation of Mission Viejo, Mr. Nelson noticed a particular market which appeared to meet Philip Morris' criteria more clearly than the others. It was easier to understand, had better returns, and although it plateaued occasionally, its demand was not cyclical. The information he gathered contradicted some of the conclusions reached in a Stanford

Research Institute report regarding major limitations for the future growth of the market. Because of its relationship to the housing industry in general, information related to this market was abundantly available from published sources and the National Association of Home Builders. In addition, Mr. Nelson attended building conferences and conventions where he gathered further information from many market experts.

All of this information indicated continued growth potential. Therefore, Mr. Nelson gathered financial information about four of the industry leaders to determine if the market was really profitable. He learned that earnings growth had exceeded sales growth, suggesting the possibility of economies of scale within the industry. Mr. Nelson then attempted to construct a predictive model of housing starts which would indicate some of the key economic variables which affect demand for the industry in general and the market he was studying in particular. As he discovered that money availability had a major effect on demand for housing, he approached a staff economist with a major financial consultant who had access to a model of money markets and also had an interest in the housing market. Mr. Nelson established a good rapport with him and later met him at several conferences. He provided Mr. Nelson with responses to his ideas and analyses, lending either support or constructive criticism. Although Mr. Nelson learned much it would probably be several months or years before any definite decision was reached.

Prospects for Acquisition. After markets for entry were selected, identifying acquisition prospects generally followed one of three patterns. As with Product B, sometimes the candidate came to Philip Morris either directly or through an intermediary prior to the market study. Sometimes prospects were identified as part of the market study as with Product A. Also, in some cases, Philip Morris waited for candidates to be presented which competed in the markets selected for entry. Mr. Poole indicated that his staff had several reports approved by the board of directors to enter selected markets for which Philip Morris was still waiting for acquisition candidates to reveal themselves. The information files about these markets and their competitors were periodically updated to keep them current.

Miller Brewing Company was one of these latter acquisitions. Philip Morris had studied the brewing industry for about five years before the acquisition. After one staff planner was hired from Carling Brewing Company, the original studies were updated and the market still appeared attractive to Mr. Poole. The analyst's persuasive task was more difficult than his analytical task. He kept talking to the chairman, the president, and the executive vice presidents, but they were not interested in the beer business. One day over lunch he asked the chairman why not and received a long list of objections all of which he later refuted or admitted would be satisfied only by one of the three nationally distributed premium beers. None of them were available. While the planner was revising his report on the beer market, Mr. Poole learned from an intermediary that Canadian Breweries was a candidate and the president of Philip Morris International convinced the chairman to bid for the company. The bid was announced but opposed by the Canadian government. However, when Philip Morris retracted its offer, W. R. Grace, Inc. offered to sell Philip Morris its 53% ownership of the Miller Brewing Company for the amount that Philip Morris had bid for Canadian Breweries, $130 million. Philip Morris accepted the offer and later acquired the remainder of the company.

When Philip Morris had not previously studied the market of an acquisition candidate, the planning staff first gathered historical financial information from the candidate or the intermediary which presented it to assess past performance and managerial competence. This information was gathered about Mission Viejo before a major study of the housing market was undertaken. In addition, Philip Morris gathered information about the housing market for almost three years before investing in Mission Viejo. It did not fully acquire the company for another three years, while it attempted to gather more information about the market and the company by assigning two Philip Morris executives to work with the company. When historical information about the candidate was not available, as in the case of the market for Product B, Philip Morris gathered information about its market, similar to the way Mr. Nelson evaluated the market and the candidate simultaneously.

Mr. Poole described several cases in which Philip Morris directors had access to information which was useful for evaluating a candidate. A director of a competitor of one candidate which manufactured consumer Product D, was also a Philip Morris director. When asked about the possible acquisition, this director explained his opposition. He concluded by telling Mr. Poole that he could not attend any board meeting at which the acquisition was discussed, because of his conflict of interest. However, he would strongly oppose it if he could attend. Later, the candidate was acquired by another firm, and the results predicted by the director became reality.

In a similar case, a small company which manufactured Product E claimed it would eventually sign a major purchasing contract with a firm with which Philip Morris shared a director. This director confirmed the firm would let a contract such as the one the candidate described. Philip Morris later acquired this candidate. The information gathered from the director had little direct influence on the decision. However, Mr. Poole noted that the information had motivated gathering further information which did lead Philip Morris to acquire the candidate.

Philip Morris had gathered information about one market for several years. Mr. Poole maintained contact with a consultant specializing in that market who could provide him with information about candidates which he might identify. Occasionally the consultant also identified candidates. No candidate had been acquired because none had been large enough to operate as an independent division of Philip Morris, although some market competitors were of sufficient size.

One important type of information which Philip Morris could not gather from sources external to an acquisition prospect was the quality of the management. Its past performance relative to competitors and statements from its customers could have provided some indication of the quality of management. However, Mr. Poole and other Philip Morris executives felt that this evaluation required personal contact with the incumbent management. For Type II acquisitions, contact was usually with the chairman or president, in addition to the planning staff. Also, since many Type I acquisitions were somewhat small and privately owned, contact with the management occurred early since it was a major source of information about the company itself.

Summary. The major focus in gathering information was on many different sources of information obtained primarily about the markets of prospects before individual prospects were seriously considered. Markets and prospects were identified from many sources, particularly intermediaries who presented candidates and simultaneously suggested markets for entry. When evaluating a market for entry, the corporate planning staff analyst began with easily available information, utilizing published sources to gain perspective about the market and to determine if more detailed information gathering would be fruitful. Throughout the information gathering process, Mr. Poole maintained contact with top managers in Philip Morris to determine the consensus of his superiors. Generally, detailed studies of possible markets required several man-months of intensive work during which the analyst attempted to become an expert about the market. Often this was followed by a period of months or years during which information was continually gathered to update files and to further validate the findings of the analyst. Developing expertise about a market within the planning staff was useful to Mr. Poole not only before an acquisition, but also later to evaluate the plans of an acquired division. As with markets, information about acquisition prospects was also obtained from many different sources by directors and managers as well as by planning personnel.

Factors Influencing the Process

Several factors had a major influence on the acquisition scanning process at Philip Morris. These factors included the environment, the board of directors, the strategy and resources of the firm, and the organization of the firm. Of these the strategy and the board of directors appeared the most important, although the strategy was clearly a resolution of environmental conditions and trends with the firm's available resources.

Environment. Despite the threats to the future of the tobacco business, Philip Morris continued to grow through market share gains with its filter cigarettes. One major impact of this growth was that Philip Morris did not need acquisitions for their immediate impact on corporate performance. However, diversifying acquisitions which would not grow at least as fast as the tobacco business would detract from short term performance and more importantly would increase Philip Morris' exposure to industry-wide risks in the longer term. Therefore, the criterion for long term and short term growth was much more important than immediate contributions to earnings.

The effect of this criterion on the remainder of the scanning process was clearly visible. Philip Morris' management needed information about the long term futurity of the markets it entered and the companies it acquired. The quality of long term forecasts available from outside experts was often inadequate for the major investments which would be made. Hiring planners to develop expertise in particular markets of interest improved top management's access to more sources of more detailed information than publications or intermediaries could provide.

Board of Directors. A second major influence on the scanning process was the board of directors and the top management of Philip Morris. Mr. Cullman had led Philip Morris to very successful performance. Because of this success, he could have convinced the board to adopt almost any course of action he wanted. However, he chose to work with the board on important decisions, seeking its advice, counsel, and participation. Diversifying acquisition decisions were particularly important in this context. Nevertheless, he did control what issues came before the board. Acquisition proposals were not brought before the board until Mr. Cullman had satisfactory answers to all the questions which he asked or expected other members of the board to ask. Planners were expected to submit detailed reports about markets for entry to the chairman and to be prepared to answer any questions which he might pose to them. This provided powerful motivation for the planners to be sure that they had relatively complete and accurate information as the basis for their reports.

In addition, Mr. Cullman expected the planning staff under Mr. Poole to stimulate him with suggestions for markets which might be appropriate for entry. Part of the way he judged the effectiveness of the planning department was in terms of the number and quality of these suggestions. Mr. Poole maintained a wide variety of external contacts, including consultants to provide him with new suggestions, and he encouraged his planners to suggest things which interested them for further investigation. The adequacy with which Mr. Poole's staff met these needs could be measured in terms of the many years he remained with Philip Morris working for Mr. Cullman.

Strategy and Resources. The strategy of Philip Morris had three resource allocation priorities. The tobacco business had first claim to resources, other existing Philip Morris businesses had second claim, and the diversifying acquisition had the final and lowest claim. During several of the years under study, Philip Morris did not have adequate cash for diversifying acquisitions or had forecast that it would not have adequate cash to support them in the future. However, the planning staff continued to search for and evaluate markets for entry during these periods. The major reason was that Philip Morris wanted to maintain an inventory of markets acceptable for entry at some time in the future. The strategy was based on the premise that when the firm's cigarette business decelerated or declined, it would provide a strong cash flow which management would need to invest immediately.

Responding to this strategy, the planning department continually monitored the environment for information related to the markets which it identified as appropriate for entry. Encouraging planners to develop expertise within these markets helped insure a continuing supply of information regarding the latest developments related to or influencing those markets. Furthermore, Mr. Poole worked closely with the planners to be sure he too developed access to sources of their information in the event they left the firm. It was also this future thrust of the strategy that focused the scanners' attention more on market information than on information about individual competitors within those markets.

Organization. The most important influence of the organization structure was the combined planning and acquisition staff under Mr. Poole. Although thoroughness of research was encouraged by Mr. Cullman to insure good acquisition decisions, it was also encouraged by Mr. Poole for a second reason. If an acquisition were consummated, one task of his department would be to review the plans formulated by the new acquisition's management and to help that management establish a formal planning system, in some cases. Developing the expertise to evaluate adequately the subsequent plans during the acquisition information gathering process would help insure the proper execution of the planning department task. Mr. Poole further argued that in future years, when tobacco products became a less dominant part of the company, the resource allocation priorities would need to change. Part of designing and managing a new set of priorities, he felt, would involve better knowledge about the various divisions' long range futures. Gathering relatively detailed information about markets for entry would also assist in solving this problem.

Also, as part of the organization process, the planning department was staffed by well trained but inexperienced graduates from good business schools such as Harvard, Wharton, and Dartmouth. These planners usually had few prior conceptions of a particular industry based on their experience, but they did have relatively powerful analytical techniques and often extensive research experience. They were appropriate for the type of job they were hired to do. Mr. Poole felt that the jobs of planner and of acquisition analyst required many of the same skills and his planners agreed.

American Brands, Inc.

In 1972, American Brands, Inc. was a multiproduct, multimarket corporation with $123 million in profits and $3.0 billion in sales, of which about 30% was from non-tobacco products. Since 1960, the compound annual sales growth rate of American Brands was about 7.8% (since 1965 it was about 13.6%), and the earnings per share growth rate was about 5.75%. During this period, the firm acquired 14 companies, 11 of which were based in the United States and 11 of which were acquired to enter new markets. All of the firm's significant diversification resulted from acquisitions completed after 1967.[7]

Program History and Participants

During the 1960-1972 period, American Brands increased the number of cigarette brands it sold in the United States, improved its research capabilities in both tobacco and non-tobacco products, and significantly increased the long term debt portion of its capital structure. However, during this same period, its share of the domestic cigarette market dropped from 26% to 18%, primarily because the firm did not move into the filter cigarette market as quickly, aggressively, or successfully as some of its competitors. In addition, the firm's participation in overseas tobacco markets was limited by licensing arrangements with the British-American Tobacco Company until it acquired the British based Gallaher Limited in 1968. In addition to entry into the overseas tobacco markets, Gallaher was a base for diversifying acquisitions in the United Kingdom.

The diversification program at American Brands was formulated and implemented by Mr. Robert Walker. He was chief executive officer of the firm from April 1963 until his death in January 1973, ending 35 years of service to the firm. Most of his managerial experience involved marketing in the tobacco industry. He began studies of diversification alternatives and acquisition methodologies soon after becoming president by retaining a consulting company. Mr. Walker faced diversification with corporate strengths and weaknesses.

One major resource was the availability of cash flow and unused debt capacity to support acquisitions. The cash flow was provided by stabilizing tobacco leaf inventory needs caused by declining market-share. His predecessor had used some of the cash flow to reduce American Brands' long term debt. Mr. Walker could also use this benefit from previous years to finance diversifying acquisitions. Cash was important since American Brands did not have an attractive price/earnings ratio. This severely limited the range of companies which American Brands could acquire for stock without diluting its earnings per share.

In addition to financial resources, Mr. Walker also inherited limited managerial resources. The top executive group had all of its managerial experience in the tobacco business. This group was not prepared to manage other businesses or to manage a diversified firm. These executives also composed the board of directors. They were committed to the tobacco industry and would not allocate resources for diversification that were needed to rebuild American Brands' primary business. To help change the board's attitude toward diversification, Mr. Walker nominated his firm's first outside directors to the board. The first three outside directors were Mr. George Woodward, president of the management consulting firm of Welling and Woodard, Inc.; Mr. Alvin Jennings, former executive partner of the accounting firm of Lybrand, Ross Bros. & Montgomery; and Mr. Boone Gross, retired President of the Gillette Company, a firm which also diversified through acquisition. They all had prior experience with diversifying acquisition programs.

The acquisition scanning activity was coordinated through the treasurer's office, with Mr. Charles Mehos responsible for financial analysis. Mr. Mehos joined American Brands in 1950 in the treasurer's department and became assistant treasurer in 1962, treasurer and a director in 1967, and vice president of finance in 1969. Also involved in the acquisition scanning activity was Mr. Robert Heimann, who succeeded Mr. Walker as president. Mr. Heimann had joined American Brands in 1953 after serving as a security analyst and managing editor of *Forbes* magazine and after earning a doctorate in sociology. With this wide background, Mr. Heimann brought to the acquisition program information about many markets and access to sources of additional information. By 1972, Mr. Richard Walter also was involved in the acquisition scanning process in addition to his responsibilities as pension fund analyst.

Acquisition Criteria

American Brands retained most of the criteria which Mr. Walker established in 1965. The first criterion was that markets for entry have stable product demands with predictable determinants of growth. The second criterion was that acquired companies immediately and significantly improve American Brands' sales and profits without diluting earnings per share. The third criterion was that the managements of acquired companies be both capable and willing to remain with American Brands after acquisition. Most of the acquired companies were themselves the result of previous acquisitions. Although this was not a criterion, it did provide American Brands with new personnel experienced in acquisitions. For example, Sunshine had grown through numerous acquisitions of local cracker companies and potato chip manufacturers. Duffy-Mott had grown and diversified through several small acquisitions into canned vegetables and sea food products. Also, Acme Visible Records and Swingline were both the results of several major mergers.

The criterion that markets for entry have stable and predictable demand related to the firm's experience in the tobacco industry. Management had felt that tobacco demand was stable and predictable prior to the adverse publicity concerning the relationship between smoking and health. If the demand for tobacco products declined predictably and stably, new markets entered would counteract this decline so that the firm as a whole could continue its growth in the future. American Brands' management best understood how to compete in markets with these demand characteristics and were not as well prepared to cope with seasonal or cyclical demands. The predictability of demand was particularly important since if the causes of growth were better understood, growth could be forecast further into the future with less risk. Foods and beverages were such markets because man's need to eat and drink could be forecast for significant periods into the future. Acquisitions both proposed and consummated through 1969 purported to enter these types of markets.

For example, the first proposed acquisition in 1965 was a merger with Consolidated Foods, Inc. Additional early announcements included Royal Crown Cola and Buckingham, Inc., the importer of Cutty Sark Scotch Whisky. Many of these markets also had an habitual-use nature to them which created a stability of demand relative to disposable personal incomes. These markets had financial characteristics similar to those of tobacco. Also, they often used agricultural crops as did tobacco.

American Brands sought to enter only consumer-products markets early in the program. Although manufacturing was an important part of the firm's developed skills, consumer marketing was the real key to success in the tobacco industry. Management planned to use its understanding of consumer psychology and market share competition to improve the companies it acquired. American Brands did not consider integrating the operations of the acquired companies with the tobacco operations, or utilizing common channels of distribution. Rather, through management transfers and communications, acquired companies could benefit from American Brands' experience in the tobacco business. American Brands could not make similar contributions to companies in industrial product markets. The firm's skills did not relate as well to the complex and often political purchasing decisions involved in many industrial products.

American Brands' marketing experience was particularly valuable for repeat-purchase, habitual-use products such as tobacco, liquor, or snack foods. The marketing programs to support these types of consumer products markets were very familiar to tobacco managers. In addition, purchases of these habitual-use products were not sensitive to economic conditions or to style changes or fads. For many of these consumer products, merchandising, advertising, and extensive distribution would have an important influence on both primary demand and brand market shares. American Brands had competed in cigarette markets with these characteristics with great success for many years. Beverages, particularly alcoholic beverages, had many of the same consumer characteristics as cigarettes. Food products in general did not have these characteristics, but particular food markets did, for example, potato chips, laxative fruit juices, and to some extent carbonated beverages. Within these markets, particular manufacturers could develop brand loyalties through advertising which reinforced or created the illusion of minute product differences or through convenient distribution which satisfied other needs of the consumer for frequently purchased products. All of these were characteristics of marketing programs which related to a consumer psychology that the marketing managers at American Brands understood well.

The eventual diversification to commercial and industrial markets in 1970 was based on the management expectation that its skills had broadened and were more universally applicable than they had been in 1964. Furthermore, the board of directors accepted the importance of diversification for the future performance of the firm. Also, through its informal scanning, management became aware of some strong growth markets beyond consumer goods which could improve American Brands' investor image. In these markets also, marketing was the primary factor which determined product success and market share.

As a second criterion, American Brands only wanted to acquire companies which would have a significant impact on its earnings and sales in both the immediate future and longer time horizons. American Brands' cigarette market share had been declining within a market which would eventually exhibit slow growth or decline. Therefore, acquired companies necessarily represented a base of growth products for several years in the future. At the same time American Brands' cigarette sales were declining, acquisitions which did not contribute immediately to improved performance would represent ineffective uses of corporate resources quickly noticed by the investing public.

At the beginning of the program Mr. Walker assured the board of directors that diversification would not be detrimental to the tobacco business. However, acquisitions which did not produce significant and immediate performance improvement would reduce the board of directors' interest in diversification. Thus, small acquisitions were generally eschewed. Also, large acquisitions which would require major infusions of new capital for revitalization without commensurate immediate returns would be inappropriate. Simultaneous with his diversification program, Mr. Walker expected to help American Brands regain its leadership position in the tobacco industry—an expectation which would require substantial cash investments to achieve. Therefore, utilizing the debt capacity and cash flow afforded by the declining tobacco business required unusually good investment opportunities. Major acquisitions which would immediately increase earnings per share but would not grow for several years to come would also represent poorer investment alternatives than would the tobacco industry.

As a third criterion, American Brands only acquired companies with good management willing to remain and manage their business. Past financial performance was used as a good measure of management competence. Companies of this nature usually had major market shares of growth markets and well established brands supported by effective advertising programs and wide distribution. Often, companies which could achieve significant positions had strong managements. Although many of the companies which American Brands actually acquired were managed by their founders or second generation executives, most were publicly owned. These owners had sold equity to obtain cash necessary to support rapid expansion. They had a personal interest in their companies above and beyond their financial investments. Often they wanted to remain after the acquisition to insure the continued success of their business. In addition many had grown to sufficient size to develop successor management and establish adequate management control systems.

The need for good management, although an initial criterion, was reinforced by early experiences with Jim Beam and Sunshine. Beam was a well managed company with unusually creative and alert marketing management to complement its quality products. Mr. Walker and his subordinates allocated very little of their time and energy to the Beam operation. However, Sunshine had several operating problems which remained for many of the next seven years. Several managers were hired from the outside or transferred from the tobacco business to improve the operations. Much of Sunshine's previous growth had been through acquisition of inadequately managed and financed potato chip manufacturers. American Brands management believed it could redirect the cracker business to emphasize snack foods through these acquisitions, but found its facilities inadequate. In retrospect, the plans of American Brands for Sunshine appeared appropriate from a marketing point of view, but the Sunshine management was not able to implement the plan smoothly.

After this initial experience, good management became more important to American Brands. When acquired in 1970, Swingline was a publicly owned firm still controlled by the original founder. It had an active chief executive who wanted to reduce his participation. American Brands acquired Swingline only after it was satisfied that the executive had adequately developed a successor management.

Each of these criteria was necessary, based on the previous experience of American Brands' management. It had witnessed the importance of growth markets through its own slow response to the filter cigarette development. It had witnessed the power of consumer marketing in the brand introductions of its competitors as well as in its own past success. Its major strength was consumer marketing. Its major problem was to attain short term performance. Immediate performance required good management in growing markets.

Acquisition Scanning Process

American Brands' acquisition criteria did not limit its market scope sufficiently to permit the identification of desirable markets on a systematic basis. Furthermore, in its pursuit of immediate results, it generally identified only companies willing to be acquired. Seeking primarily large publicly owned companies simplified its scanning process considerably. A major problem of the acquisition scanning process was gaining acceptance for the diversification program.

Market and Prospect Identification. American Brands did not attempt to identify markets for entry before it identified candidates for acquisition, although it did identify areas of particular interest. Before the proposed merger with Consolidated Foods was first announced, Mr. Walker collaborated with a consultant to identify particular segments of the economy which would be appropriate for entry through acquisition by his firm. This consultant's firm specialized in general management practice and long range planning. Its partners had general information about many industries based on both exposure to clients in many fields and on general reading and wide interests.

In addition to these consultants, Mr. Walker formed several management committees of tobacco executives to review the suggestions of the consultants. While these committees studied the consultant's reports, they developed familiarity with and support for the diversifying acquisition program. This was important since many of these executives were also members of the board of directors. The committee deliberations familiarized them with the need for rapid diversification and reduced their apprehension about entry into new markets. A major role of the consultant was to provide direction to the committees so that companies and markets identified would appear appropriate for American Brands.

The food and beverage industries were identified by the consultant as particularly appropriate. Not only did these industries meet the acquisition criteria, but also they were somewhat familiar to many of the corporate executives. These industries involved repeat purchases, impulse selections, extensive distribution, intensive advertising, and strong merchandising, all of which resembled the marketing skills and customer characteristics familiar to those executives. The consultant also noted similarities in distribution channels and agricultural raw materials. Finally, the technologies required to produce most foods and beverages were not complex, so that management would not discover unusual problems in trying to learn about manufacturing processes or product design requirements which required sophisticated technological backgrounds that the management did not possess. These arguments provided by the consultant were acceptable to the management and formed a platform for the consideration of particular candidates for acquisition.

Candidates were identified primarily through intermediaries to whom American Brands expressed an interest in acquisitions. For example, an investment banker identified Consolidated Foods as a potential merger partner, for he was aware that American Brands was interested in acquisitions. After the firm made its initial acquisition announcements, many bankers, brokers, and finders quickly learned that American Brands sought acquisitions and began to present candidates.

Both Sunshine and Buckingham were identified by brokers not only to American Brands but also to other firms in the study. Other firms as well as American Brands felt that Buckingham's owners wanted an excessive price for their company based on either its earnings or its tangible assets.

Generally, investment bankers had identified more useful and appropriate acquisition candidates than had brokers and finders, because they usually limited the market areas of the candidates they identified to consumer products. Acme Visible Records was presented by an investment banker who felt that American Brands could and should enter office equipment markets and demonstrated that part of Acme's market included channels of distribution which were generally familiar to American Brands management.

Because of the early advice of its consultants and outside directors, American Brands did not usually identify prospects of interest and approach them directly. With the small portion of companies willing to be acquired, sequentially approaching prospects without prior knowledge of their interest in being acquired was a slow process. This was an important consideration because American Brands wanted immediate results from its acquisition program.

Information Gathering. After identifying a candidate for acquisition, American Brands began simultaneously gathering information about both the candidate and the markets in which it competed. The initial source of information was the intermediary which identified the candidate. This intermediary could provide financial statements, product literature, and management profiles. American Brands' financial department could analyze the financial information it obtained to determine historical growth, profitability, capitalization, etc. From the product literature, management could determine what the company's management felt were its real strengths in product design as well as something about channels of distribution and perceived customer needs. From the management profiles, American Brands could initially determine if the management were capable of continuing after the acquisition (age) as well as what the backgrounds and experiences of the managers were and how compatible they might be with their own. For many of the identified prospects which were publicly owned, American Brands could also obtain financial analysts' reports and annual reports which indicated some of the company's future plans and projections as well as past performance.

After the markets of the candidate were identified, management could begin gathering information about those markets from published sources, particularly trade publications. Reviewing the information in these publications over time revealed some underlying trends in those markets. For example, the emergence of frozen foods as a convenience product, as well as a method of preservation, became apparent as these publications noted the rising sales and competition in complete frozen dinners. Similarly, management observed the size of the snack food markets as people had more leisure time, and utilized it increasingly for home entertainment purposes. Further investigation suggested that although some of the snack foods markets were primarily fads, potato chips would continue to be a stable and growth snack food. In addition to gathering information from published sources, American Brands' management had the capability to interpret gathered information relative to what it already knew about the markets in which it already competed - tobacco. This ability of management to interpret the market information it gathered was particularly evident in snack foods. Because of its consumer marketing orientation, American Brands also envisioned the potential for market share growth in the fragmented potato chip market. The potential was in combining competitors from local markets to effectively utilize consumer advertising.

This skill was also evident when it entered the office equipment markets through the acquisitions of Swingline and Acme Visible Records. Management had considerably less experience in or exposure to these markets. However, it retained a management consultant to gather information about those markets emphasizing the future growth and profitability which might be expected based on broader trends and conditions in the environment. As a consumer of office equipment, the management also had some internal information from an examination of its own needs. Much of this information was gathered in 1967 when American Brands moved its corporate headquarters within New York City and considered its own office equipment and information handling needs. Some of these same needs were also considered as management evaluated the changing information processing needs required by its own increasing diversification.

However, information gathered for these purposes was primarily background information which motivated sufficient interest in the Swingline and Acme acquisitions to engage a consultant to provide more systematically collected and analyzed data. It also served to provide management with some background for assimilating the information provided by the consultant. Generally, American Brands did not itself gather large amounts of information about markets for entry. Rather, it usually gathered some preliminary information from published sources and then retained the consultant for more detailed investigations and analyses.

For particular acquisition candidates identified by intermediaries, American Brands obtained and analyzed information available from the intermediaries and from published sources relatively quickly. If the candidate appeared to fulfill the screening criteria, the intermediary was asked to arrange a meeting between the managements of the two companies to gather additional information.   During these discussions management gathered significant and useful information about a candidate.   For example, information from an intermediary and from published sources indicated that Sunshine's major business was centered in three products, Krispy Saltine crackers, HiHo round crackers, and Hydrox Cookies. However, they indicated little about its attempted entry into the snack foods and potato chip markets through a long series of acquisitions. The intermediary also indicated that Sunshine's profitability had been declining for about four years but did not indicate the reasons for these declines - high potato prices and new plant start up costs. American Brands underestimated the difficulties of consolidating Sunshine's snack foods business and overestimated the ease of creating new products.

Thus, when American Brands began discussion with Duffy-Mott two years later, it was much more concerned with management quality and the competitive situation than in developing whole new strategic approaches to their markets.   From an intermediary American Brands learned that Duffy-Mott's sales had been stagnant since about 1961 following a period of relatively rapid growth, but did not learn about the new product development and acquisition activities which had been underway during this period to provide future growth. Similarly, based on published information, management learned of Duffy-Mott's national distribution but not about the low levels of penetration in several geographic areas which indicated opportunities for the company to increase its market share in the future. Also, American Brands probed the depth of Duffy-Mott's management and learned that although the chairman of the board planned to relinquish many of his responsibilities, the president had been treasurer for almost twenty years and could ably assume direction of the company after the acquisition.

Only during discussions with the management of Swingline did American Brands learn that although the chairman had founded the company and wanted to retire, the company had developed an adequate depth of management to insure continuity of performance and product development.   In general, discussions with the owners and incumbent management were essential as part of the initial information gathering process, and postponing those discussions to gather more information from other sources was generally not as fruitful or meaningful.   Upon occasions, American Brands' marketing department had been asked to conduct market research surveys about various candidates, their products, and their reputations. These had not been major studies and had not contributed substantially to any of its acquisition decisions.

Information Processing. American Brands did not formally process much of the information which it gathered about markets or candidates. In the finance department, Mr. Mehos and his staff analyzed the financial statements provided by the intermediary to determine past performance and cash flow as well as to locate possible future financial problems such as aging capital assets or declining profit margins. This information became part of the agenda of useful topics discussed with the candidates during their early meetings. Information about the markets in which a candidate participated was generally gathered from sources which had already processed raw data to provide forecasts and/or scenarios of possible future market conditions and the rationales for each. American Brands did not generally gather information from primary sources and attempt to develop its own forecasts or its own scenarios of future market conditions. Through initial plant tours and discussions with the incumbent managements of candidates, American Brands' management again gathered information about them from sources which had already processed and distilled factual information into opinion, recommendation, and expectation.

In this respect, the major information processing which managers at American Brands performed consisted primarily of evaluating the consistency between the information provided by a candidate's management and that obtained from published sources and financial analysts' reports. It also analyzed the consistency between information about the market provided by a candidate's management and that provided by published data or consultants. In addition, management was concerned about the quality of the logic upon which the candidate's future expectations were based – a logic which American Brands' managers could evaluate in light of its own experience in consumer products markets.

Factors Influencing the Process

Several factors influenced the acquisition scanning process at American Brands. The factors included the background and experience of the firm's managers, the environment of the tobacco industry, the type and availability of its resources, and its organization. Perhaps the most important influence was the skillful planning and leadership of Mr. Walker.

Mr. Walker. Less than one year before the Surgeon General's report was released, Mr. Walker became president of American Brands. By that time American Brands had lost market share in tobacco which it could not easily or quickly regain. Mr. Walker assumed leadership with better realization of tobacco market conditions and stronger motivations to diversify than had his predecessor. Furthermore, he had the necessary resources to diversify quickly through acquisitions. He also had several limitations, most noticeable resistance from the board of directors. His leadership, skill, and vision enabled him to diffuse this resistance by rebuilding the tobacco business while involving the management in acquisition scanning.

He supported the rebuilding of the tobacco business through new aggressive marketing programs and new brand introductions. During his first year in office he introduced more new brands than were introduced during the ten years of his predecessor's administration. Most of these were filter cigarette brands supported by large advertising budgets and by a creative fee arrangement with the firm's advertising agencies. This helped strengthen American Brands' tobacco business, but more importantly developed for Mr. Walker the support of his management, which also comprised his board of directors. When he could convince the board of his concern and support of the tobacco business on this scale and showed it where additional funds were still available to support a diversification program, his chances of gaining its approval were enhanced.

Mr. Walker involved many managers in the early scanning process by assigning them to committees for the purpose of identifying areas for diversification. However, most of the scanning was the work of a consultant who presented information to the committees for their review. Mr. Walker used the committee to gauge the sentiment of the inside board members and to help the consultant develop more acceptable diversification proposals. This plus the addition of influential, knowledgeable, and supportive outside directors engendered support for the acquisition program. Information gathered by the consultants and outside directors[5] provided credible proposals for the board to approve. Thus, Mr. Walker designed a scanning process appropriate for the resistance he expected from the firm's other managers. His continuing leadership similarly guided the future development of the scanning process.

Environment. The major environmental factor affecting the scanning process was the increasing risk facing the tobacco industry and the strengthening competition facing American Brands within that industry. Because Mr. Walker's predecessor had not led his firm with an adequate response to these trends, by 1963 they demanded an urgent and potent response. To have immediate impact, acquisitions were necessarily large. Because they were large, they were usually publicly owned and much information was readily available about them. Bankers tended to identify larger candidates and were therefore more fruitful intermediaries than finders and brokers. Also, the urgency of the situation required the use of knowledgeable external scanners, like consultants, and the bankers, to gather and process information. Finally, the urgency directed American Brands toward identifying candidates rather than searching for ideal prospects for acquisition.

Resources.   The acquisition scanning process was further influenced by the resources available to the firm. Financially, American Brands could support an acquisition program focused on large acquisitions, although the number of these was limited. Functionally, the firm could not integrate other businesses with tobacco. Other tobacco firms, such as Philip Morris, had tried and failed. American Brand's strongest functional skill was in consumer marketing; however, this skill could not be spared from the tobacco business in 1964. Other functional resources were similarly limited. American Brands' manufacturing capacity and skills were not transferrable to the markets. Its raw materials had no other uses. And its research and development capabilities were inadequate for developing products not closely related to tobacco products, limiting the internal development alternative for diversification. Therefore, American Brands did not seek related acquisitions for their synergistic benefits.

However, the most influential resource was management. American Brands did not have the requisite experience to manage non-tobacco business. Therefore, it was imperative to acquire companies with good management which could be retained. Similarly, American Brands had no experience in managing a diversified firm. The consultants and the outside directors could provide some guidance but could contribute little actual skill in this regard. However, the presidents of several acquired companies had this skill. Adding them to the board of directors not only increased the board's support for the program, but more importantly, enabled the board to function as a forum for exploring the problems and alternatives of managing diversity. As the board broadened its own collective background, it widened the scope of acceptable acquisition alternatives. Thus, by 1970 the board was willing to support diversification beyond consumer products.

Organization.   Organizationally, the firm had no long range planning staff or other staff units capable of information gathering and analysis. Developing such staff groups would require time which was not available and would risk alienating the other managers in the organization, who might feel that newly hired staff managers would reduce their importance and influence in the firm. Although Mr. Walker organized several discussion groups among the current managers to focus on various aspects of diversification and recognized the political importance of doing so, he also recognized the improbability that they could develop appropriate courses of immediate and long term action without assistance. Mr. Walker was therefore forced to utilize external experts to identify markets and candidates and to gather information about them and present proposals to the board. The credibility of these sources of information also eliminated many of the uncertainties which might otherwise have engulfed and interrupted the decision process.

Nevertheless, as the program developed and more intermediaries identified candidates, Mr. Walker needed someone in the organization to perform the initial screening and to gather whatever information was readily available about the candidates and their markets. Since financial considerations were of primary importance and since most intermediaries were financially oriented, it seemed natural to involve the treasurer's office in this responsibility and activity rather than establish a separate organizational entity. Related to this, as American Brands added subsidiaries, stronger financial controls were required to insure their continuing performance. Therefore, in addition to the discussions and planning sessions of the board of directors and the establishment of two executive vice presidents, Mr. Walker also expanded the role of the treasurer's office in financial planning and control of the acquired divisions. Acquisition scanners would then also have some commitment to the future performance of the candidates which they recommended to the board.

Acquisition Scanning Processes Compared

The concluding section of this chapter compares and contrasts the domestic diversifying acquisition processes of Philip Morris and American Brands and the factors which influenced their similarities and differences. The major process differences are attributed to the difference in perceived urgency of achieving performance through diversifying acquisitions.

Scanning Processes Compared

The scanning processes of Philip Morris and American Brands were different.[8] However, both firms focused primarily on large unrelated market acquisitions. Also, the acquisition criteria of the firms were similar in that both focused on consumer markets for which advertising, distribution, and merchandising were important competitive weapons. Also, both wanted good managers willing to remain with their firms after they were acquired. Philip Morris criteria were explicitly focused on long term expected growth. American Brands did not ignore long term performance, but emphasized the immediate effects of acquisitions on financial performance. This difference in time horizon had a substantial effect on the remaining characteristics of the scanning systems.

American Brands used intermediaries to identify markets for entry and candidates for acquisition. In contrast, Philip Morris' corporate executives, including members of the planning staff, identified and selected markets for entry. This identification process was not systematic. Its coverage was limited to the informal scanning and interests of these executives. Sources of market and prospect information also varied between the firms. American Brands used readily accessible information sources supplemented by consultant reports and other highly reliable external information processing sources. Philip Morris gathered information from many more sources. Its planning staff sought not only to improve the accuracy of its information through multiple sources but also to develop internal expertise through continuing association with these sources. Philip Morris found their approach useful since it often would follow the events in a market for several years before acquiring a competitor.

The amount and type of information processing were also quite different for the two firms. Planning staff members at Philip Morris used numerous formal analytical techniques to better understand the implications of the information they gathered. This helped them determine possible future performance of markets for entry. Predicting this performance for long future periods introduced substantial uncertainty which required more processing to evaluate. American Brands used financial analysis techniques to process information about candidates, but performed little other processing. Since American Brands identified more candidates and focused more on the short term impact of acquisitions, the amount of processing required and allocated to each candidate was less than that for Philip Morris.

The backgrounds and experience of the participants also varied considerably between the two firms. At American Brands financial executives with experience in the tobacco industry were the major participants, although their work was supplemented by external consultants. The major participants at Philip Morris were the corporate planners. They had little or no previous corporate work experience and no previous exposure to the tobacco industry. They were all graduates from reputable business schools, with widely varying academic interests. Their educations provided them with many of the information processing techniques useful for analyzing and predicting future performance.

Finally, the sequence in which acquisition scanning activities were performed varied considerably between the two firms. At Philip Morris, the planners usually focused on market information and identified prospects as part of the market information gathering process.

Also, the planners gathered information about many competitors in a market while analyzing it. American Brands only gathered information about markets after it identified candidates and gathered some information from the intermediaries which identified them. Once again, this reflected the short term focus of American Brands.

Influences Compared

Describing and comparing the acquisition scanning processes of Philip Morris and American Brands in terms of the characteristics outlined in Chapter II, highlighted some significant differences between them. These differences are partially explained by the factors which influenced them. In 1957, Philip Morris was the first major tobacco firm in the United States to begin diversifying. However, by 1972 it was the least diversified. Also, in 1957 Philip Morris had the smallest market share in the industry but grew most rapidly in sales and earnings during the next fifteen years. American Brands was the last major tobacco firm to begin diversifying, but by 1972 was one of the most diversified.

Philip Morris began to diversify as a defensive response to environmental trends and conditions. Management felt that as the smallest competitor in the industry it would be the most adversely affected by the health issue. However, as its position in the filter cigarette market strengthened and it began to gain market share, both the defensive posture and the cash flow to support it disappeared. By 1972, Philip Morris was scanning to identify markets in which it could invest cash flow when or if it became available. Its posture was decidedly aggressive.

American Brands began to diversify in 1965, the year following the issuance of the Surgeon General's report. American Brands was the last tobacco firm to enter filter markets successfully. It had been losing market share and would probably continue to do so. As unit sales leveled and declined, American Brands urgently used the cash flow it provided to support diversification. This urgent posture was the result of a perceived pressure for immediate financial improvement. The financial results of the acquisition program at American Brands are reflected in its improved financial performance.[9] Many of the differences in scanning between the two firms were associated with this major influencing factor.

To achieve results quickly, American Brands only gathered information about identified candidates from reliable sources. Not only was financial information most readily available and easiest to process, but also it most directly related to the short term corporate need. American Brands did not have a corporate planning staff and could not establish one in a short period of time which would be accepted by other tobacco managers. Finally, these managers also controlled the board of directors. The use of expert consultants as sources of information and recommendations about acquisition proposals enhanced their credibility. The contrast to Philip Morris is clear. The board generally supported Mr. Cullman's proposals, the planning staff was well established and organized, and short term financial performance was expected to be good.

Nevertheless, neither firm emphasized related market acquisitions. American Brands really could not divert its attention from short term goals and did not have adequate staff to facilitate integration. Philip Morris did try to integrate some related market acquisitions with its tobacco operations in the early 1960s and found it almost impossible because of the size differentials and market position differences. Furthermore, when Philip Morris did begin to receive the benefits from decelerating cigarette sales it too would need to effectively redeploy cash quickly. Therefore, operational integration of future acquisition at Philip Morris seemed unlikely.

Thus, the major differences in the acquisition scanning processes of Philip Morris and American Brands were apparently attributable to the posture of their diversification objectives. Philip Morris was more aggressive, whereas American Brands was more defensive. This difference enabled Philip Morris to adopt a significantly longer time horizon for acquisition analysis. This tends to corroborate the hypothesis proposed in Chapter II that firms with different types of diversification objectives would adopt different scanning processes. This conclusion must remain tentative until the examination of the remaining two firms in the study is completed in Chapter V.

NOTES

[1]See Exhibit IV-1 for a complete list of Philip Morris' domestic diversifying acquisitions.

[2]Messrs.   Poole, Delaney and Nelson were interviewed as part of this research.

[3]See Exhibit IV-1.

[4]To maintain confidentiality, these markets are not identified explicitly.

[5]He particularly cited the *Business Periodicals Index, The Wall Street Transcript,* and *The Directory of Trade Associations.*

[6]This report was later condensed to about 100 pages for presentation to Mr. Cullman and the board.

[7]See Exhibit IV-2 for a list of American Brands' domestic diversifying acquisitions.

[8]See Exhibit IV-3 for a summary comparison of the acquisition scanning processes of Philip Morris and American Brands.   The exhibit utilizes the process characteristics described in Chapter II.

[9]See Exhibit IV-4 for a financial comparison of Philip Morris and American Brands.

EXHIBIT IV-1

Philip Morris Diversifying Acquisitions

1957   Milprint, Inc. (flexible packaging, particularly printed cellophane, printed aluminum foil, and polyethylene):   Stock, Pooling, 384,612 shares.

1957   Nicolet Paper Corp. (glassine): a subsidiary of Milprint.

1958   Polymer Industries (textile chemicals and adhesives for packaging):   Cash, amount unknown.

1959   American Safety Razor Co. (razors, blades, and precision metal manufacturing): Stock, Pooling, 363,000 shares.

1963   Burma-Vita Company (men's toiletry products):   Cash, amount unknown.

1963   Clark Gum Company (chewing gum):   Cash, amount unknown.

1967   C. DeWitt Lukens Company (quality sutures): Cash, amount unknown.

1967   Hospital Supply and Development Corporation (sterile disposable hospital kits): Cash, amount unknown.

1968   Koch Convertograph, Inc. (labels for bottles and other containers, especially beer bottle labels):   Cash, amount unknown.

1969   Miller Brewing Company (beer):   Cash, $246 million.

1970   Mission Viejo, Inc. (land development):   Stock options in future.

1971   Armstrong Products Company (liquid epoxy adhesives, powder coatings for industrial finishing, and fluidized bed equipment for applying powder coatings):   Cash, amount unknown.

EXHIBIT IV-2

American Brands Diversifying Acquisitions

1966   Sunshine Biscuits, Inc. (crackers, biscuits, and snack foods):   Stock, (3,349,737 shares), Pooling, Approximately $112 million.

1966   James B. Beam Distilling Co. (distiller of Jim Beam Kentucky Straight Bourbon Whiskey and other liquor products):   Cash, Purchase, Approximately $111 million.

1968   Duffy-Most Company, Inc. (canned fruits and fruit juices and miscellaneous other food products):   Cash, Purchase, Approximately $35 million.

1970   Acme Visible Records, Inc. (design and manufacture of information storage and retrieval systems):   Cash, Purchase, $53 million.

1970   Swingline, Inc. (manufacturers of stapling equipment for consumer, commercial, and industrial markets and other office supplies):   Cash, Purchase, $201 million.

1970   Andrew Jergens Company (manufacturer of toiletries and soaps):   Cash, Purchase, $109 million.

1970   Master Lock Company (manufacturer of various types of locks):   Convertible Preferred Stock, Purchase, $75 million.

1972   Perma Products Company (manufacturer of corrugated boxes for storage of business records):   Stock, (18,767 shares), Pooling, $768,000.

1972   W. R. Case & Sons Cutlery Company (manufacturers of quality knives, shears, and scissors):   Cash, Purchase, $6.5 million.

EXHIBIT IV-3

Tobacco Firms Compared

PHILIP MORRIS   AMERICAN BRANDS

Types of Information or Acquisition Criteria

PHILIP MORRIS	AMERICAN BRANDS
Consumer products companies only	No dilution in earnings
Quality image products only	Stable product demands
Mass marketing skills dominant	Significant impact on performance
Good management to remain	Consumer marketing skills important
Long term expected growth	Basic demand products mostly
	Good management to remain

Sources of Market Information

PHILIP MORRIS	AMERICAN BRANDS
Corporate planning staff	Publications & market research
Corporate executives	External consulting firms
Many sources seen by planners	Advertising agencies

Sources of Prospect Information

PHILIP MORRIS	AMERICAN BRANDS
Publications	Intermediaries & publications
Personal associates of planners	Investment bankers
Investment bankers	Candidate managements

Types of Information Processing

PHILIP MORRIS	AMERICAN BRANDS
Various techniques depending on the knowledge and skills of planners	Financial analysis predominated Limited market research

Participants in the Process

PHILIP MORRIS	AMERICAN BRANDS
Director of corporate planning – fifteen years in Philip Morris' planning department and no experience with tobacco products	President – former experience in marketing and advertising with American Tobacco Company
Eight corporate planners – M.B.A. degrees in various functional areas and little work experience	Vice president of finance – previously financial executive
	Director of investment management – former financial executive

Sequence of Scanning Activities

PHILIP MORRIS	AMERICAN BRANDS
Detailed information gathered about industries and markets before prospects identified	Candidates identified before information gathered about them
Information gathered about prospects as part of market analysis	Information about candidate and its markets gathered simultaneously

EXHIBIT IV-4

Financial Comparison of Philip Morris and American Brands

Year	Net Sales		Net Profit		Earnings/Share		Return on Invst.	
	Philip Morris	Amer. Brands	Philip Morris	Amer. Brands	Philip Morris	Amer. Brands	Philip Morris	Amer. Brands
1960	$ 509m	$1320m	$21.0m	$65.4m	$0.91	$2.11	9.4%	9.3%
1961	529	1356	21.5	73.3	0.94	2.38	9.3	10.2
1962	551	1380	21.9	77.0	0.98	2.51	9.8	9.8
1963	585	1392	22.1	76.6	0.99	2.49	8.9	9.4
1964	641	1404	22.6	80.5	1.01	2.63	8.9	9.6
1965	705	1433	26.5	86.0	1.19	2.88	9.9	11.2
1966	772	1428	34.2	86.0	1.54	3.01	11.0	11.7
1967	905	1494	43.6	89.2	1.94	3.15	11.8	12.1
1968	1020	1898	48.9	92.9	2.14	3.32	12.6	10.4
1969	1142	2661	58.3	98.5	2.40	3.56	12.6	11.6
1970	1510	2674	77.5	108.2	2.85	3.92	13.7	11.1
1971	1852	2828	101.5	119.4	3.64	4.15	14.7	11.5
1972	2131	2999	124.5	123.3	4.37	4.37	13.8	11.7

CHAPTER V

DOMESTIC DIVERSIFYING ACQUISITIONS OF CONGLOMERATES

This chapter describes and analyzes the domestic diversifying acquisition process in two acquisitive conglomerates. The chapter begins be defining conglomerates, describing some of their major strategic and structural characteristics and identifying the dominant environmental influences which fostered their development. The chapter then describes the acquisition scanning processes of two conglomerates, International Telephone and Telegraph, Inc., and Textron, Inc. The chapter concludes by comparing and contrasting the processes of these two conglomerates, with particular emphasis on the causes of major similarities and differences.

Acquisitive Conglomerates

Conglomerates differ from the four firms previously analyzed in the treatise because they are not primarily associated with any one market or industry. Rather, they compete in many unrelated markets simultaneously. Although conglomerates created a heated public policy debate during the 1960s, this note focuses more on the growth and management of conglomerates and the environmental forces which supported or impeded their acquisition programs.

A conglomerate is a firm which grew quickly primarily through diversifying acquisitions into several unrelated markets. The largest group of related markets in which a conglomerate competes usually constitutes less than 70% of the firm's sales. In 1953 Litton Industries and Textron, Inc. became the first two conglomerates. During the 1960s, many other firms such as International Telephone and Telegraph followed their example. Highly diversified firms such as General Electric, Westinghouse, and Union Carbide are not conglomerates because they did not grow primarily through acquisition, but rather through internal development continuing over more than fifty years. Three basic hypotheses about how conglomerates manage their diverse businesses exist.

The first hypothesis is that corporate management attempts to directly supervise and evaluate the operations of each of its businesses. This hypothesis lost credibility throughout the 1960s as conglomerate corporate managements themselves claimed they did not understand the intricacies of the many diverse businesses under their control. Some continuing supporters of this hypothesis contend that the collective knowledge and skill of the corporate office, including large corporate staff groups, could solve almost any problem confronting the management of any business. However, the very large staff groups at ITT seem to have limited understanding of the vast and diverse company operations.

The second hypothesis views conglomerate corporation managements as financial investors or holding companies which enter or exit markets and expand or contract businesses to change the balance and performance of their portfolios. This hypothesis contends that corporate management only evaluates divisional performance and determines if the divisional management should be retained. The managements of some conglomerates such as LTV do view their roles primarily as financial investors or portfolio managers. Conglomerates which conform to these hypotheses tend to evaluate acquisitions as they would evaluate financial investments. Over extended periods, they tend to perform more poorly than good portfolio managers who can change their investment positions more rapidly in response to changing market conditions.

The third hypothesis might be termed the strategic process management or the resource allocation process management hypothesis. Firms which conform to this hypothesis include ITT, Textron, Litton, and Bangor Punta. The corporate managements of these firms not only evaluate the financial performance of various businesses, but also evaluate and influence the formulation and implementation of the business strategies which result in financial performance. At ITT the strategic processes of various businesses are improved through the monthly management meetings and annual divisional planning and review sessions. At Textron and Bangor Punta the strategic process of a business is influenced by the group vice president to which the business is assigned. At Litton Industries, the "opportunity planning sessions" initiated by President Roy Ash provided a forum and motivation for good strategic planning by monitoring the strategic process of the division managements. Only conglomerates which conform to this latter hypothesis are included in this study.

Financial performance is a dominant concern to conglomerate managers. Earnings per share growth is usually the predominant objective. The chief executive officers of these firms usually have small ownership positions, which represent major investments compared to their annual salaries. Therefore, in their own personal interests as stockholders, as well as managers, earnings per share growth is a major objective, apparently short term in nature. For example, they generally eschewed acquisitions which would represent substantial long term earnings growth but would cause short term dilution. Yet, the short term focus was part of a longer term financial strategy based on the observation that investors reward firms with histories of rapid earnings per share growth by awarding them high price-earnings ratios. A high ratio was a highly valued resource because it allowed a conglomerate firm to acquire companies which other investors expected to perform well in the future without diluting its short term earnings per share.

Conglomerates also have common operating characteristics. They acquire only successful, profitable companies with capable managements that would retain their executive responsibility and authority. They achieve communication between the firm and its acquired companies through an enforced planning and control process. They do not integrate the operations of larger acquired companies. Their high price-earnings ratios enable conglomerate firms to acquire successful, profitable companies. If these acquired companies continued to perform as they had in the past, the firm's earnings per share grow more rapidly with a less aggressive acquisition program. However, growth and profitability requires good managers who understand the business of the acquired company. Although prior managers had operated their companies successfully, the conglomerate firm usually had no guarantee that it could operate the firm as successfully or locate managers who could. All conglomerates are not the same. They have quite different rates of growth, different portions of growth achieved from acquisition (rather than internal growth), and different planning and control systems.

Many environmental factors influenced the development and performance of acquisitive conglomerate firms. One pervasive influence was the price/earnings ratio differential between firms during the period of economic growth and prosperity in the U.S. following World War II. This provided opportunity and incentive for acquisitions. During this same period, previously uncommon forms of capitalization were purchased by investors. These enable conglomerates to finance acquisitions more advantageously. Also, generally accepted accounting principles for financial reporting did not permit investors to distinguish between acquired and internally generated growth. This permitted conglomerates to develop growth images and improve their price/earnings ratios. Another environmental factor was the strengthening of the U.S. antitrust laws to significantly reduce horizontal and vertical acquisitions. Thus, firms who desired to grow through acquisition were forced to diversify. A final factor was the development of effective administrative approaches to managing diversity. Without these approaches, conglomerates could not maintain the growth of acquired companies.

Within these influences, ITT and Textron developed from single-product firms into conglomerates in less than ten years. Their diversifying acquisition programs and processes are the subject of the remainder of this chapter.

International Telephone and Telegraph

In 1972, International Telephone and Telegraph, Inc. was a multiproduct, multimarket, multinational corporation with $483 million in profits and $8.56 billion in sales and revenues, of which the largest portion attributable to any one industry was 22% from the manufacture and sale of telecommunications equipment.[1] Since 1960, the compound annual sales and revenues growth rate of ITT was 21.7% and the earnings per share growth rate was 11.9%. Including their post acquisition sales growth, companies acquired since 1960 represented over half of the 1972 sales volume. Since 1960, ITT had acquired over 250 companies, of which about half were overseas and about 25 were domestic diversifying acquisitions.[2]

Program History and Participants

Virtually all corporate diversification occurred after 1959, when Mr. Harold Geneen became president and chief executive officer. He was not an ITT executive prior to becoming president. In 1957, the principal business of ITT was various forms of communication and navigation systems operations, installation, and the manufacture of the components necessary to support them (e.g., wire, relays, telephones, switching gear). Also, when Mr. Geneen became president, 18% of the corporate profits were derived from activities outside the United States. Mr. Geneen quickly established two corporate objectives: (1) to increase earnings from U.S. operations sufficiently to cover dividend payments immediately through improved efficiency and effectiveness and (2) to increase earnings from U.S. operations to 50% of total corporate earnings over several years, primarily through diversification. Achievement of this latter goal (accomplished in 1966) required diversification. ITT executives felt that they could not expand domestic telephone and telegraph operations against the virtual monopoly of the American Telephone and Telegraph Company.

Since Mr. Geneen began the acquisition program at ITT in 1960, many executives participated in the program. Many of the executives involved in the program during earlier periods were no longer ITT employees in 1972. Mr. Geneen always maintained active interest and involvement in the acquisition program. He had determined the disposition of some acquisition proposals despite contrary recommendations by his subordinates. Also, he reviewed all acquisition prospects before they were proposed to the board of directors and maintained a list of industries which he desired ITT to enter through major acquisitions if the opportunities to do so arose. Mr. Felix

Rohatyn, an ITT director and a partner of Lazard Freres & Company, was also active and influential in the acquisition program. He acted as an intermediary between ITT and most of the large companies which it acquired. Other ITT executives active in the acquisition program in 1972 were Messrs. Stanley Luke, Hart Perry, Scott Bohon, Frank Prevost, Robert Smith, and James Doyle.[3] Mr. Luke, a senior vice president who reported to Mr. Perry, the executive vice president for finance, negotiated all the acquisitions for ITT. Mr. Bohon, assistant general counsel for antitrust litigations, prepared and reviewed all of the acquisition contracts, provided opinions on the antitrust aspects of acquisitions, and edited all of the acquisition proposals before they were submitted to the board of directors. Mr. Prevost was his assistant. Mr. Smith, vice president and director of corporate development and special assistant to the president for acquisitions, supervised and coordinated the work of Mr. Doyle and the directors of economic research and European acquisitions for ITT. Mr. Doyle, the manager of corporate development analysis, analyzed acquisition prospects and supervised the analytical work of three financial analysts who allocated about 75% of their time to acquisition studies.

All of the ITT acquisitions through 1964, except Aetna Finance, represented diversification into markets requiring technologies closely related to its traditional businesses. The major acquisition criteria were the future growth rate of the market and the ability of the technical staff to understand the basis for the business. The 1961-1962 acquisitions were not new technologies at all, but rather provided relationships with new kinds of customers to enable ITT to enter new markets. Most of the 1963-1964 acquisitions translated ITT systems design and construction capabilities and its electronic control technology into the air conditioning industry. To determine the appropriateness of several of these acquisitions, ITT retained a general management consulting firm. The reason for the early acquisitions was not only to improve the earnings of ITT within the United States, but also to provide the company with some experience in making acquisitions, particularly diversifying acquisitions. The major reason for retaining a management consulting firm was to observe its analytical methodology and engender the support of the board of directors. The acquisition program in effect in 1972 was essentially the same as the one which evolved in 1965.

The program sought to acquire four different types of companies. Type I acquisitions related to markets in which ITT already competed. For example, American Electric represented a new market, municipal street lighting, which was closely related to the commercial and industrial lighting business. Type II acquisitions were to enter markets unrelated to those in which ITT already competed. After 1967, all of the Type II acquisitions represented major investments, particularly: Levitt,

Sheraton, Rayonier, Pennsylvania Glass Sand, Continental Baking, Grinnell, Canteen, and Hartford Fire. In addition to those two types of acquisitions, ITT also completed a large number of horizontal acquisitions which provided it with strong positions in several markets. For example, building on the Sams acquisition in 1966, ITT acquired over 30 business, secretarial, technical, and vocational schools in various cities throughout the United States. As a final type of acquisition, Mr. Doyle's group had a counterpart under Mr. James Wolf in Europe that searched for acquisitions which could extend current European businesses or could extend current U.S. businesses to Europe. The managements or owners of several acquired companies were motivated to join the ITT organization as a method of extending their former businesses to foreign markets. Only the first two types of acquisitions are discussed in the remainder of this chapter.

Acquisition Criteria

The acquisition criteria were unwritten, but well known to all but the newest of managers at ITT. In general these criteria applied to both Type I and Type II acquisitions. The first criterion was that the industries within which an acquisition prospect operated should have had a growth rate in excess of the Gross National Product. Individual prospects should have grown at least as rapidly as their markets. Many of those industries were not well known for their growth, but markets within those industries had solid growth records. For example, the utility pole industry had relatively slow growth, but the aluminum utility pole markets within that industry had grown relatively rapidly for several years before ITT acquired Myers Industries. Also, ITT had identified a high growth segment of the relatively nongrowth fastener industry. Historical growth was viewed as an initial indicator of future potential. ITT expected operating units to grow in profitability at rates greater than the markets in which they participated. Each existing business unit was expected to return a profit which was 15% greater than the previous year, without the effect of acquisitions.

As a second criterion, ITT sought companies with strong balance sheets. These companies would have considerable unused debt capacity which ITT could use to finance their future. ITT also preferred companies which had some excess manufacturing capacity so they would not need funds for expansion immediately after the acquisition. As part of this criterion, ITT only sought prospects with positive operating cash flows. It had rejected Home Equity, Inc. as an acquisition because while a profitable company meeting the other criteria, it had a negative cash flow and inadequate leverage potential. In addition, ITT sought prospects with conservative accounting policies, so that the income statements and balance sheets of the company represented an understatement of current financial condition and future potential. This did not imply that ITT sought to create earnings through accounting manipulation after an acquisition since ITT's own accounting policies were conservative, in comparison to some other conglomerate firms.

A third criterion concerned the size and ownership of an acquisition candidate. ITT was not interested in Type I acquisition candidates with sales less than $20 million, a value which had increased since 1965. Generally, companies with less than $20 million in sales would not have successor management, professional staff services, professional financial controls, or multi-plant operations. This lack of professional management had two implications. First, ITT generally did not nurture the development of small companies in an embryonic state of development. Second, these companies were often managed and owned by an entrepreneur who would not like large complex organizational arrangements and therefore would not excel within the ITT corporate structure. For many small companies, these owner-managers were a major asset not listed on their balance sheets. If anything happened to incapacitate or demotivate these entrepreneurs, their companies would likely become less profitable. Nevertheless, privately owned companies without established market prices provided ITT with more freedom in negotiating acquisition contracts.

The size criterion applied to Type II acquisitions were considerably greater and for different reasons. The criterion of $50 million minimum sales generally applied to these acquisitions. Many such prospects were publicly owned. Since Type II acquisitions were unrelated to other ITT activities, they would necessarily report to the already lengthy monthly general management meetings. These week-long management meetings reviewed the activities of over 150 operating units. Companies which could not substantially contribute to ITT overall performance could not justify expanding these meetings. Since Type I acquisitions would become subsidiaries of existing ITT operating units, they could be much smaller. They would not increase the managerial workload of the corporate officers appreciably.

A fourth and related criterion was that ITT's planning process and financial control system would effectively apply to acquired companies. Although the cost control requirements of a company depended on the nature of its business, ITT's management felt that asset control remained similar across a wide variety of markets. This approach to asset control applied to both manufacturing and service businesses. For example, APCOA was a parking lot operator with some specialized operating cost control problems. However, costs and revenues could be forecast accurately. From ITT's perspective, the key to successful performance in this business was control of assets, rather than control of costs, by negotiating leases on favorable terms.   The other service companies which ITT acquired were asset management businesses amenable to financial control.[4] ITT's operating cost control systems were primarily applicable to manufacturing companies. Since ITT's corporate management could not fully understand the specific operating details of all of its businesses, the management necessarily relied on planning and control systems to encourage operating unit managers to make good decisions. For example, few corporate executives were familiar with the operations of the fire insurance business, yet the ITT control system encouraged the management of Hartford to improve the company's performance considerably after it was acquired. Applying this criterion to acquisition candidates was particularly difficult for some businesses.

The final criterion which ITT applied to all of its acquisition prospects was that the company had good management willing to remain after the acquisition for at least five years. The historical record indicated that ITT had succeeded relatively well on this criterion; few top management changes occurred in the companies acquired. The reason for this criterion rested with the capabilities of the ITT corporate staff and the diversity of the company. ITT had many functional experts available within the corporate staff to provide advice and direction to business unit managers. However, the staff could not build a new management organization around an existing physical asset base in a market where it had little experience. Although ITT's focus was financial, it investigated many other things, particularly the management. The reason was that when ITT acquired a company it acquired people and an organization. It could buy a collection of physical assets that duplicate those of any company in the world; however, the people who utilized these assets made the difference between success and failure.

Three factors were involved in retaining the management: The incentives ITT provided to it, the attractiveness of the ITT organization, and the health and vitality of the incumbent management. With respect to the first, ITT often paid substantial premiums to acquire companies, and never used take-over tactics to subvert incumbent managements. It also clearly indicated the organizational requirements and constraints which ITT would impose on the acquired organization so the management knew what would be required if it accepted an acquisition offer. ITT also attempted to learn what motivated the incumbent managements to sell their businesses and compared the stated reasons with the other information which it gathered about the prospective business. ITT usually asked an intermediary to explain why a company was interested in being acquired. Then it attempted to learn if the operating facts about the company were consistent with the rationale.

In addition to these well specified criteria, several other criteria guided the selection of acquisition prospects. First, and largely as a result of three antitrust suits filed against ITT by the U.S. Department of Justice, the management desired to avoid any acquisition which would likely be challenged by the antitrust division. To determine this, all prospects which fulfilled the other acquisition criteria were sent to Mr. Scott Bohon of ITT's legal department for clearance before the prospect was approached. Prospects were again reviewed more thoroughly by Mr. Bohon before acquisitions were approved by the board of directors. Second, ITT was not interested in acquiring companies which competed in regulated industries. The management's past experience with telephone operations indicated the many potential problems of such industries which ITT sought to avoid. Third, ITT generally entered through acquisition relatively low-risk businesses relative to the growth and profitability sought. Management felt that high risk businesses would not be amenable to the ITT planning systems since many future environmental conditions and trends could not be adequately forecast. Finally, ITT was particularly interested in U.S. businesses which could expand to European markets. This interest was well documented by the large portion of its businesses which ITT had expanded to the European continent.

Therefore, the financially oriented criteria applied to all acquisitions. Future growth potential (sales and profits), strong balance sheets, and size of prospect were the major financial criteria. Size actually was a surrogate for professional management and supervision while the other financial criteria were important both in themselves and as indicators of managerial capability. A second kind of criteria which also applied to all acquisitions was the probable reaction of the Antitrust Division of the Department of Justice and other governmental regulatory agencies to a proposed acquisition. A third kind of criteria, applied primarily to Type I acquisitions, concerned the contribution which a proposed acquisition could make to existing areas of ITT.

The Acquisition Scanning Process

The scanning processes for Type I and Type II acquisitions were considerably different. For both types, ITT managers monitored the stream of candidates identified by intermediaries, ITT executives, and owners of companies interested in being acquired. Company owners or their intermediaries identified over 700 candidates annually to Mr. Doyle. These sources were all aware of ITT's active and visible acquisition program. Finders and brokers identified most of these candidates but ITT acquired only two or three companies identified by these sources each year. ITT executives identified another 300 candidates annually. ITT had a large number of corporate executives with a wide variety of backgrounds and experiences. Collectively, these executives had a set of professional, social, and personal associates who were aware of acquisition opportunities and motivated to communicate them. ITT did not actively search for candidates in specified markets or approach companies which were not declared candidates.

Type I Acquisitions. Operating unit managers seldom requested the corporate staff to search for candidates, although they occasionally identified acquisition candidates. There were several reasons for this. First, the acquisition analysis group felt that generally searches for appropriate candidates at acceptable prices in specified markets were an unproductive and ineffective use of staff resources. To conduct occasional searches, Mr. Doyle retained a broker in New York City who specialized in candidate searches. Second, the ITT planning system focused on internal performance improvement and development. Operating unit managers who could plan and achieve ITT's demanding performance improvement objectives had little need for acquisitions. Third, corporate officers generally eschewed acquisitions for the purpose of solving operating unit problems. Experience had shown that acquisitions for this purpose usually compounded performance problems rather than eliminated them. Operating unit managers were often reluctant to request a search because it might infer a potential weakness in their existing operation.

When an intermediary (or an owner-manager) identified a Type I acquisition candidate, Mr. Doyle immediately requested the candidate's financial statements for the previous four or five years. He also requested information about the company, its products, its customers, and its managers and owners. Based on this information, Mr. Doyle or one of his analysts could usually determine within an hour if the primary screening criteria were fulfilled. Often to do so, analysts made assumptions which would need verification later before an acquisition was consummated. Mr. Doyle's staff members had worked in general consulting areas where they had an opportunity to look at marketing, and people, and other things. Nevertheless, they focused primarily on financial analysis. After a candidate passed the initial screening, analysts attempted to determine its cash flows and to examine changes in financial ratios over the previous several years. ITT's historical orientation was a classical approach to financial analysis. Cash flows, ratios, and trends were all compared with those of the candidate's competitors. This comparative analysis, including market share and profitability, highlighted areas about a candidate which needed further information. Analysts also gathered some quantitative and qualitative information about the candidate's market and competitors from published sources to provide some perspective and context for the financial analysis. Often the financial analysis suggested particular types of information to gather. This total analysis of a candidate required one or two weeks of an analyst's time.

If this analysis were favorable, Mr. Doyle proceeded in several directions. First, he sought a preliminary legal opinion from Mr. Bohon on the antitrust implications of the potential acquisition. Mr. Bohon felt he could render this opinion with relative assurity and without great research. A favorable response included permission for Mr. Doyle to establish a formal dialogue between the management of the candidate and ITT.

Second, Mr. Doyle and Mr. Smith and usually someone from the Office of the President determined which executive would be likely to assume profit responsibility for the candidate if it were required. Locating such a "sponsor" was important since Type I acquisitions would not report directly to the monthly general management meetings. This determination was based on how the markets of the candidate related to various other ITT activities. Often the determination was obvious. Mr. Doyle then contacted the designated sponsor to enlist his support for the proposed acquisition. Sponsors usually agreed to an initial meeting with the candidate's management. These sponsors could usually provide additional relevant and useful information about the candidates' markets and often had access to new sources of information. For example, the president of Continental Baking had already investigated the health food markets which might affect his business when Mr. Doyle asked him to review several candidates in those markets.

Third, Mr. Doyle requested Mr. Jean Keller, ITT's vice president for marketing, to conduct a brief study of the candidate's marketing skills, and sometimes Mr. Steward Flaschen, the vice president of research and development, to investigate the technical capabilities within the candidate. Mr. Doyle explained that they sent people out into the field to talk to customers. ITT had many contacts throughout ITT in most areas that it could contact to determine what kinds of introductions and receptions have been given to the company's products. From this, the marketing staff could determine a candidate's strengths and limitations very quickly. If the marketing staff did not have ready access to needed information, Mr. Keller often retained a consultant or market researcher who had expert information about the market.

Fourth, Mr. Doyle contacted the candidate's owner to arrange a meeting with its top managers and the sponsor, Mr. Doyle, his analyst, and the intermediary, if appropriate. Usually the meeting included a tour of the candidate's facilities. This initial meeting and tour was not the commencement of negotiations but rather further information gathering, particularly an opportunity for the sponsor to evaluate the potential and compatibility of the candidate's management. Also the meeting did not involve detailed investigations or audits; these activities were not undertaken until later negotiations concluded with a preliminary contract.   One focal point for this meeting was the candidate management's forecast for future activity and performance and the rationale behind it.

Based on the technical and marketing studies, the financial analysis, and the initial contact meeting, the sponsor and Mr. Doyle each prepared a forecast on the candidate's future profit and return. Regardless of which forecast was the most conservative, it was usually used for further financial analysis and for determining what price was appropriate for the acquisition. At this point, either Mr. Doyle or the sponsor could decide not to proceed with the acquisition. Sponsors were not pressured to accept individual acquisition candidates. However, if a sponsor refused several candidates which Messrs. Smith and Doyle felt should have been consummated, Mr. Geneen questioned the manager's past actions and requested that future rejections be well supported and documented. (At ITT this represented a rather strong motivation.)   If both agreed to proceed, then Mr. Doyle prepared a "Board Note," which summarized in ten or twenty pages, plus exhibits, the major rationale for acquiring the candidate. It also contained five-year annual profit and cash flow forecasts which became the basis for later evaluating the success or failure of the acquisition and the performance of the sponsor. It was like a synopsis of his first annual plan for the candidate. Because of the performance implications of these forecasts, they were of great concern to both Mr. Doyle and the sponsor, as well as to Mr. Geneen.

Occasionally these board notes indicated a dilution of ITT's earnings per share for the first one or two years after the acquisition, based on the acquiring price and terms of payment suggested in the note. ITT often paid substantial premiums for acquisitions since it could not take a tough negotiating stance and then expect its owners or managers to remain and build the company. ITT seldom acquired candidates on a contingent price or earn-out basis. Management felt a contingent price capitalized the earnings stream on the selling price and the people on the contingency, which would lead to overpayment.   In ITT's experience, after the initial period of the contingency ended, the former owner returned to negotiate another deal with the corporate management which either bought business again or lost him as a highly motivated manager. The forecasts in the board note, as in operating unit plans, never extended more than five years into the future because management did not feel it could adequately predict events further into the future than that.

The drafted board note was then reviewed by Mr. Smith who often suggested areas of further clarification or additional information which he had gathered from his vast external reading. His suggestions occasionally reflected some of the latest events and issues which concerned Mr. Geneen or members of the board of directors.   After Messrs. Doyle and Smith and the sponsor all approved the draft of the note, it was submitted to Mr. Bohon, who performed two functions. First, he reviewed the antitrust implications of the proposed acquisition more thoroughly and based on more detailed information than he had done earlier.   Second, he edited the draft to clarify or eliminate any issues which could be misinterpreted by legal investigators at a later date. In editing a board note, Mr. Bohon assumed that it would eventually become a public document scrutinized by lawyers seeking to discredit the ITT acquisition program on antitrust grounds.   This was a reasonable basis for editing since many approved board notes had been subpoenaed and published by the antitrust subcommittee of the U.S. House of Representatives Judiciary Committee as part of its investigation of conglomerate corporations in 1969.

Following Mr. Bohon's revisions, the drafted board note was submitted to Mr. Geneen.   On Tuesday evening, prior to the board of director's meetings, Mr. Geneen spent between four and five hours reviewing the accumulated board notes with Messrs. Doyle and Smith. Although Mr. Geneen did not analyze the smaller Type I acquisitions in great detail, Messrs. Doyle and Smith learned to anticipate the concerns Mr. Geneen expressed about the acquisition candidates.   First, he usually wanted to hear more about the management - e.g., What are the people like? What is the organization structure? Why are they in that market? What are their major managerial problems? - as a way of learning more about the company rather than because this information should be included in the note.   Second, he generally wanted the fit between the candidate and ITT more fully explained - e.g., Why are we buying it? What can it contribute to us? What can we contribute to it? Why should it have higher value to ITT than to others who might be interested in acquiring it? - to better understand the rationale for the acquisition and to be able to answer questions at the board meeting. Third, and perhaps most important, Mr. Geneen questioned the underlying assumptions and analysis upon which the industry and candidate forecasts were based. This was the area where Mr. Doyle had the most trouble because he did not have the time for a thorough analysis although Mr. Geneen focused on it consistently.   Fourth, he probed the financial situation, particularly the assets on the balance sheet - which were over - or under-valued and why. These fundamentals were important to Mr. Geneen since he did not want to pay too much over book value for a company. Based on this information, Mr. Geneen determined if a board note should be proposed or deferred for further analysis. The decision was important because the board seldom rejected an acquisition proposed by Mr. Geneen. Although a few acquisitions had been approved within a week, generally a month lapsed between identification and board approval.

Each year approximately 90 (almost 5%) of the two thousand Type I acquisition candidates identified by Mr. Doyle in the U.S. and Mr. Jim Wolf in Europe were submitted to and approved by the board of directors.   After the board approval, the note was sent to Messrs. Luke, Perry, and Bohon. Mr. Perry prepared the necessary financial arrangements for the acquisition.   The legal staff prepared a set of preliminary contracts outlining the terms of the agreement and specifying that final disposition was subject to ITT's audit of the company.   This audit was extremely important to ITT since much of the information gathered to prepare the board note was based on the credibility of the incumbent management.   During audit, accounting, technical, personnel, marketing, manufacturing, legal and other corporate staff experts evaluated the candidate in extensive detail.   This audit not only verified or contradicted earlier information but also provided valuable information to determine appropriate changes in the company's operations and to evaluate future annual plans submitted by the incumbent management.   Mr. Bohon noted that almost any preliminary contract could be voided on the basis of information disclosed in the audit; however, frequent cancellation would severely reduce ITT's credibility and limit its future acquisition alternatives.

Mr. Luke negotiated with the owners.   Mr. Bohon noted that often Mr. Luke would complete negotiations and obtain a signed contract on the first visit to the acquisition candidate.   Mr. Doyle noted that because ITT only analyzed companies known to be available and offered premiums for its acquisitions, few candidates refused to sign a preliminary agreement.   Of these about half were eventually acquired. Of those not ultimately acquired, about 90% were found defective (at variance with previously obtained information) and both parties normally voided the contract.   Mr. Doyle noted that between 65% and 70% of all consummated acquisitions were successful in the sense that the forecasts contained in the board note were achieved or exceeded.   The remainder were about equally divided between "marginal performances" which almost achieved forecast and "horrible mistakes."

Type II Acquisitions.   Many aspects of the acquisition scanning process for Type II acquisitions were quite different from those for Type I.   These acquisitions were very large companies through which ITT entered markets unrelated to its previous activities.   Over the years of his administration Mr. Geneen had identified several areas of the economy in which he felt ITT should compete.   By 1972, ITT had entered all but one of these areas through Type II acquisitions.   Since most of these areas had great barriers to entry, they could be entered only through major acquisitions. Mr. Geneen had selected these areas for entry based on his own reading and discussions with a wide variety of people. From these sources, Mr. Geneen had gathered information about various industries over a long period of time from which he concluded that certain industries had long term stability, growth, and profitability appropriate for ITT. To supplement and enrich this information Mr. Geneen occasionally requested information about markets or technologies which appeared unrelated to current internal issues from various corporate staff members. Also, Mr. Geneen maintained interest in organizations such as the Stanford Research Institute and the Hudson Institute, to provide some longer term information about the economy and society within which these industries would operate.

ITT did not actively search for prospects which participated in the industries selected for entry through Type II acquisitions, but rather waited for investment bankers to identify opportunities to enter these industries. Investment bankers, particularly Lazard Freres and Company, identified most of the Type II acquisition candidates. Investment bankers were interested not only in the relatively large fees associated directly with negotiating a large acquisition but also, more importantly, in the fees and commissions associated with financing these acquisitions. Often other types of intermediaries could not arrange such financing. Furthermore, almost any investment banker who had a large acquisition candidate would notify ITT of its availability since ITT was known as a major acquirer. Lazard Freres was particularly prominent at ITT for two reasons. First, it had a reputation for arranging large acquisitions so that a disproportionate number of large companies which wanted to be acquired selected Lazard Freres as their intermediary. Although companies were usually better represented by investment bankers with whom they had long-term relationships, Lazard Freres' skill in arranging large acquisitions was very beneficial. Second, Mr. Rohatyn, a Lazard Freres partner, brought many candidates to ITT as a member of its board of directors. Although to avoid a conflict of interest, Mr. Rohatyn did not participate in board discussions about the candidates he introduced, he did work closely with management to prepare the presentations submitted to the board.

Searching for these very large Type II acquisitions was an inefficient use of resources since very few large corporations were acquired each year and therefore the probability of a fruitful search in a particular industry was very low. Furthermore, if ITT actively searched within a particular industry, any company which might be interested in a merger would schedule its approach to maximize the price ITT would necessarily pay for it. For these reasons, while management felt entry into certain industries would be desirable, it neither formally analyzed those industries before candidates became available nor actively searched for those candidates.

For these candidates Mr. Doyle's group gathered information and performed financial analysis. Mr. Doyle perceived his role in the decision-making process to suggest appropriate prices and payment packages and their impact on ITT's reported financial performance. Mr. Smith became involved in the candidate evaluation process almost immediately after a candidate was identified rather than after the board note was drafted. Since Type II candidates represented industries unrelated to other ITT markets, they would report directly at the monthly general meetings. Since often a member of the candidate's management or board would become a member of ITT's board of directors, Mr. Geneen personally assumed the role of the sponsor with particular attention to the compatibility of ITT's managerial organization and personnel with those of the candidate. Also, Mr. Geneen often assumed a role of primary negotiator for these acquisitions, although this probably had less impact on the acquisition decision than on the post-acquisition integration.

Although the same general types of information were gathered for Type I and Type II acquisitions, more information was gathered about the latter. Three reasons for this were: (1) They were publicly owned companies about which much more information was readily available. (2) These larger acquisitions represented larger investments which required more serious consideration, and (3) These candidates were usually more complex to analyze since they usually had wider product lives and often participated in several markets. These larger publicly owned companies had considerably more information published about them than did candidates for Type I acquisitions, and Mr. Doyle and his staff could therefore gather much more information. Nevertheless, Mr. Doyle felt that his activities had little impact on the Type II acquisition decision and cited some acquisitions for which he believed ITT had paid excessive prices.

In summary, for all types of acquisitions the predominant criteria were financially oriented. Acquisition candidates were identified predominantly by their intermediaries or owners rather than by the acquisition staff. No information about markets for entry was formally gathered until after candidates were identified. Type I acquisition candidates tended to be small, privately owned companies while Type II candidates were large, publicly owned companies. Generally for both types financial analyses were based on information supplied by the intermediaries or owners and supplemented by data gathered by ITT's marketing staff. Information from which to evaluate a candidate's management was obtained from past performance data and meetings with

ITT executives. No acquisition candidate was recommended to the board of directors until a sponsor could be identified who was willing to accept responsibility for the post acquisition performance of the candidate. For Type 1 acquisitions, the sponsor was usually the manager of an operating unit whose business was related to the candidate's business. For Type II acquisitions, Mr. Geneen was usually the sponsor.

Factors Influencing the Acquisition Process

Several factors influenced the acquisition scanning process at ITT. These factors included Mr. Geneen, the other participants in the process, ITT's strategy and organization, and the environment of the firm in the 1960s.

Mr. Geneen. Although many factors influenced the acquisition process at ITT, the most pervasive was Mr. Geneen. Indirectly, he had formulated the initial strategy (and organization) during his early years as president. He had personally selected the major participants in the program: Messrs. Doyle, Smith, Bohon, Luke, and Rohatyn. Mr. Geneen also actively participated in the process by selecting many of the industries for entry through Type II acquisitions and enforcing the criteria for all acquisitions. His continuing concern for detailed financial analysis was a reflection of his education, background, and experience in financial reporting and control prior to joining ITT as president. His concern for solid balance sheets and accurate cash flow projections for candidates also reflected his prior experience. In describing the screening criteria, Mr. Doyle frequently referred to Mr. Geneen's concern for adherence to the criteria and his role in their formulation. These criteria, in turn, influenced the types of information which acquisition analysts gathered.

During the Tuesday evening board note preview sessions, Mr. Geneen repeatedly focused on the same issues, further reinforcing the need for certain types of information in addition to the screening criteria. For Type II acquisitions, his influence was still more direct since he personally gathered much of the information upon which he selected industries for possible entry. This was possible for Mr. Geneen to accomplish without formal information gathering programs because of the number and diversity of ideas and individuals to which he exposed himself daily and from whom he gathered a large volume of information. Furthermore, his memory for facts and ability to relate data received from different sources and times was legendary at ITT.

Other Participants. Mr. Rohatyn first became involved in 1965 when as an intermediary representing Avis, he persuaded ITT managers to acquire the company. The financial community and Mr. Geneen recognized Mr. Rohatyn for his ability to identify and arrange large corporate mergers. His election to ITT's board of directors two years later provided him a position from which to demonstrate his ability. Over the ensuing three years, he arranged most of the eight very large acquisitions which ITT consummated. His influence on the process was primarily through the identification of a different type of prospect than ITT had previously identified, which resulted from his background and contacts as a financier.

Although Mr. Doyle had some general consulting experience, his primary background and experience was in financial analysis. His staff members all had similar backgrounds and experience. Thus, the major type of information they gathered before approaching a candidate was financial. The sources of their information (for comparative purposes) were primarily publications and security analysts reports, to which they had ready access. Because of their general consulting exposure, they also sought experts in other fields (e.g., marketing and research and development) for additional information.

Strategy. Acquisition was a means for achieving diversity and earnings stability. ITT's corporate management could not systematically search for appropriate markets to enter because its market scope was too broad and undefined and because comparable information about markets was not available. Operating unit managers were not motivated to systematically search for markets to enter through acquisition which related to their existing business. The planning system imposed on these managers focused their attention on performance achievement excluding acquisitions. Their performance goal of 15% annual increases in earnings offered sufficient challenge and required full attention without acquisitions. Furthermore, Mr. Geneen discouraged defensive acquisitions and Mr. Doyle discouraged acquisition searches. Therefore, operating unit managers had strong incentives not to search for new markets to enter through acquisition.

ITT's avoidance of deceptive accounting practices, willingness to pay premium prices for acquisitions, and reluctance to divest failing operating units also affected the acquisition process. ITT required great post-acquisition growth to justify the premium prices and occasional earnings dilution for acquisitions. It would not manipulate accounting data to report growth which it did not achieve. This required more detailed financial and market analysis than would acquisitions for a holding company, which could divest poorly performing acquisitions after showing significant immediate earnings effects through accounting manipulations. In Mr. Doyle's view, historical financial analysis, comparative financial analysis, and market share analysis provided a strong indication of the quality of a candidate's management.

Retention of the management was important to insure the continuation of performance. Corporate staff could provide some expertise and the management of the sponsor's operating unit could provide some guidance. However, only the managers of the acquired company had the requisite experience and successful competition records in their market. The market analysis focused primarily on the reasons why the candidate had improved its market share and/or why the market had grown at a relatively rapid rate. Based on this information, various ITT managers could supply or gather information to estimate if the factors causing growth could also be expected to continue into the future. Although not systematically investigated, these continuity assumptions focused discussions with a candidate's management on its performance forecasts. Mr. Doyle and the sponsor of a candidate attempted to evaluate the rationale which a candidate's management forecast rather than to construct a rationale before meeting the management.

ITT's large corporate staff and diverse operating units generally had access to much information about any identified market. Mr. Doyle and the sponsor could usually rely on information from ITT managers to assess the validity of the rationale after listening to the candidate. Therefore, ITT did not retain external experts, except in unusual circumstances, to gather information. The cost of doing so would have been unnecessary in view of its internal information gathering capability. Furthermore, intensive audits of all phases of a candidate's operations after the preliminary contract was signed provided adequate opportunity to verify a candidate's resource capabilities before the acquisition was consummated.

Environment. Throughout most of his term as president of ITT, Mr. Geneen felt that investors had seriously under-valued his firm's stock. He particularly faulted the institutional investors who held about half of ITT's outstanding stock. During the 1967-1970 period, ITT's price/earnings ratio averaged about 25, compared with less than 20 throughout the remainder of the period under study. During this same four-year period, ITT consummated all of its large Type II acquisitions and over half of its total acquisitions from 1960 to 1972. The stock price increase allowed ITT to acquire larger firms on more favorable terms. However, this increased activity and the large size of some acquisitions required a shift in the acquisition process. In particular, Messrs. Geneen and Smith became more actively involved in scanning for Type II acquisitions. The audits which followed preliminary contracts with these large companies were usually the work of consultants because ITT staff could not handle the additional workload.

The impact of this accelerated activity on information gathering was also apparent. For example, three of the eight major acquisitions did not achieve the performance which was forecast in the board notes. Furthermore, Mr. Smith's predecessor apparently resigned after disagreements about some of the companies acquired during this period. The information which he gathered concerning candidates was not believed or used in reaching acquisition decisions. Therefore, the stock price influenced the volume and size of acquired companies, which in turn influenced the acquisition scanning process.

Changes in the application of antitrust laws also affected the acquisition process. Mr. Richard McLauren became Assistant Attorney General in charge of the Antitrust Division of the U.S. Department of Justice in 1969. He began challenging large conglomerate mergers because of the alleged anti-competitive effects in the markets entered by conglomerates. Because of its size, visibility, and reputation, ITT was one of the first conglomerates against which he brought suit. Although these suits were eventually settled out of court, they constrained the acquisition activity of ITT in future years. This suit, together with ITT's lower price/earnings ratio, also reduced ITT's acquisition activity, permitting more information to be gathered about each acquisition candidate. More important, the legal department of ITT adopted a more active role in analyzing acquisitions for their antitrust implications. Mr. Bohon directed this antitrust analysis which was conducted on an individual case basis, since with ITT's wide diversity, it was difficult to establish guidelines which Mr. Doyle's group could easily administer. Mr. Bohon therefore rendered preliminary opinions as soon as Mr. Doyle had gathered sufficient information to determine the markets in which the candidates competed and the financial appropriateness of entering those markets.

The availability of candidates and the role of intermediaries influenced the acquisition process at ITT also. During the later 1960s, the third major merger wave in the United States reached peak activity, and many entrepreneurs became interested and motivated to have their companies acquired by other firms for a variety of reasons. Even after the wave somewhat subsided, ITT identified over one thousand candidates per year. With this great availability of companies willing to be acquired, ITT management saw little reason to begin searching formally for competitors in specific markets to acquire. If companies within a market of interest became candidates, Mr. Doyle would usually hear about them from an intermediary or directly from the entrepreneur trying to sell his company. If no competitor in a market wanted to be acquired, then studies of desirable markets served no useful purpose.

Intermediaries collectively provided an efficient communications system for identifying candidates, and because of its reputation as a major acquirer, ITT was known by many intermediaries. Also, because many of the companies ITT acquired were family-owned, published information on their financial performance was largely unavailable except from the owners or their intermediaries. The role of intermediaries as transmitters of this financial information and profiles of products and managers of candidates significantly simplified Mr. Doyle's information gathering task. Also, Mr. Doyle focused primarily on financial information and other factual information which the intermediary could transmit with minimal distortion, and therefore could be somewhat confident in using the information he received (subject to audit verification at a later date).

Thus, the background and experiences of the managers involved in the acquisition scanning process, the strategy (and organization) of ITT, the environment of the firm during the period under study, and the role of intermediaries in the information gathering process, all affected the acquisition process at ITT.

Textron, Inc.

In 1971, Textron, Inc. was a multiproduct, multimarket corporation with $72 million in profits and $1.6 billion in sales and revenues, of which the largest portion attributable to any one industry was 23% from the Aerospace group.[5] Since 1960, compound annual sales growth rate of Textron was 13.9% (sales growth rate through 1968 was 27.67%) and the earnings per share growth rate was 9.8% (earnings per share growth through 1968 was 14.1%). Acquired companies (excluding their post acquisition sales growth) since 1960 represented about one-third of the 1971 sales volume. In most years, over two-thirds of the reported growth was derived from operations which had been part of the Textron organization the previous year. Since 1960, Textron had acquired over 40 companies, of which about 30 were domestic diversifying acquisitions.[6]

Acquisition History and Participants

Virtually all corporate diversification occurred after 1952. Prior to this Textron was a fully integrated textile manufacturer which had been built through vertical acquisitions by it president and chief executive officer, Mr. Royal Little. Responding to dim forecasts for the textile industry and his own dissatisfaction with recent past performance, Mr. Little inaugurated a diversifying acquisition program under which Textron completed over 40 acquisitions before he retired in 1960. As a goal for this program, Mr. Little selected 20% return on equity for Textron, a goal which Textron achieved in 1967. Initially, he established two acquisition criteria: companies must be profitable and their managements must remain with Textron, Although several acquisitions during this period were unsuccessful and later divested, Mr. Little developed a highly diversified firm.   His successor, Mr. Rupert Thompson, joined Textron in 1956 and continued to build and diversify the firm until 1968 when he retired and Mr. William Miller became chief executive officer. Their backgrounds were different: Mr. Little, who had been president of the textile company for many years, Mr. Thompson, who was a banker before joining Textron, and Mr. Miller, who was a lawyer by education and formerly associated with a major New York City law firm.

Throughout the years from 1953, very few managers were formally involved in the acquisition program at Textron.   Mr. Lester Cassler joined Textron in 1954 as part of the Dalmo Victor acquisition and assisted Messrs. Little and Thompson with the acquisition program until his retirement in 1966.   In 1964, Mr. Charles Chapin became assistant treasurer of Textron and helped Mr. Cassler with the acquisition program for two years, before becoming director of corporate development.   He maintained primary responsibility for Textron's acquisition program until late 1970. He was succeeded by Mr. George Murphy,[7] a former president of Textron's Speidel division with many years of experience in marketing consumer products.   Mr. Murphy was the first Textron division president to join the Textron corporate staff. His background and experience was quite different from his predecessor's financial orientation.   In addition to his acquisition activities, Mr. Murphy was also chairman of consumer product development. This job entailed the development and implementation of programs intended to stimulate the top managements of Textron's consumer product divisions toward more creative approaches to product and market development. Since 1953, the chief executives of Textron maintained active interest in the acquisition program and process.

Textron had three separate acquisition programs extending sequentially through time. The first program (1953-1959) was primarily under the direction of Mr. Little. Although the program did achieve diversity and improve performance, it did not achieve the 20% return on equity goal which Mr. Little established.   Based on historical and retrospective accounts, it was relatively informal, with few criteria and little information gathered to compare with criteria. This program is not formally a part of this research, because of the inadequate primary data available about it.

The second program (1960-1969) was considerably more selective and the criteria were better defined in terms of Textron's strategy. This was consistent with the fact that Mr. Thompson's major task during the four years preceding the beginning of this program was to rationalize

Textron's strategy and to develop an organization capable of perpetuating and managing diversity. Throughout this second period, the acquisition process remained relatively stable except that the size of acquired companies increased on the average.

The third program, which began in 1970, included a shift in emphasis toward entering consumer markets, reducing the number of acquisitions, and augmenting the acquisition process. Both the second and third programs involved two different types of acquisitions. Type I acquisitions were those which related to existing Textron divisions. These "product line" acquisitions were integrated with the existing divisions of Textron to which they related. Type II acquisitions were those which became new divisions of Textron. Combining them with other divisions would have produced no benefits to Textron. More stringent criteria applied to those new product acquisitions than to product line acquisitions. The criteria for both acquisition programs and for both types of acquisitions are described and discussed below.

Acquisition Criteria

Size, measured in annual dollar sales, was a major criterion which Textron applied to all acquisition prospects. Textron's investment capacity and U.S. antitrust laws determined the maximum size. Through 1966 and after 1969 Textron's investment capacity and price/earnings ratio was the major constraint, and during the latter part of the second and early part of the third program, antitrust laws became more significant. Although $250 million in sales was the maximum acceptable size in 1965, Textron had not acquired any company with sales greater than $100 million. Antitrust became an important constraint after the Department of Justice objected to the Fafnir acquisition in 1968. Fafnir was the only Textron acquisition so challenged.

The minimum size criterion was particularly important for Type II acquisition prospects. By 1965 the minimum size for a Type II prospect had risen from $10 million to $25 million in annual sales. In 1971, Mr. Murphy rejected all candidates for Type II acquisitions with annual sales of less than $50 million. The minimum size criterion was originally established to insure the adequate depth, development, and continuity of a prospect's management because Textron did not maintain a functional corporate staff to supplement or assist the divisional operations. Corporate officers were seldom transferred to manage divisional operations.

Since 1960, the minimum size criterion had increased for three major reasons. First, Textron attempted to maintain some size balance among its divisions and product groupings so that as divisions grew, correspondingly larger acquisitions would not upset the balance. Second, as Textron itself grew, only larger acquisitions would have a significant impact on performance. Third, Textron attempted to maintain a small corporate office and felt that divisions smaller than the minimum size criterion would require corporate executive attention disproportionate to their contributions. The size criterion also motivated several product line divestitures during the latter part of the second acquisition program. These product lines could not be combined with other divisions. The minimum size criterion was less important for Type I acquisitions since they were integrated with existing divisions. Mr. Murphy felt that Type I acquisition prospects should generally exceed $5 million in annual sales, but did not immediately reject prospects smaller than this.

A second and more pervasive criterion was that Textron foresee an acceptable rate of return on its investment in an acquisition. Generally it expected a before-tax rate of return of at least 20% and preferably greater than 25%. Although acquired companies were not required to achieve this return in the first year of ownership, Textron rejected candidates which could not achieve it within a reasonable period of time. Although a prospect's historical financial performance provided some indication of future profitability, often Textron could improve the rate of return on investment by either increasing the earnings or decreasing the capitalization of a company after it was acquired. However, Textron would only acquire companies which would immediately increase Textron's earnings per share. Since most acquisitions were purchased for cash or for repurchased treasury stock and since only profitable companies were acquired, dilution was not normally a limiting consideration. The return on investment criterion was important since one of Textron's objectives was to achieve and maintain a 20% return on its equity. The expected return on investment was difficult to determine for Type I acquisitions because it involved estimating the synergy which would result from combining the prospects' operations with a Textron division. Unless a prospect had performed reasonably well in the past, it was rejected without an investigation of synergy potential.

As a third criterion, Textron had only considered acquiring companies whose managements had demonstrated competence prior to the acquisition and whose managers intended to continue managing the company after the acquisition. The criterion was more important for Type II acquisitions, since Textron did not have a large corporate staff to supplement or improve the managerial capability of acquired companies through direct intervention into their operations. However, the group vice presidents, each of whom was responsible for the development of between five and seven divisions, usually could aid the development of a reasonably competent acquired company management. The requirement was less important for Type I acquisitions, if they related to a division which had particularly strong management and/or could be expected to derive substantial benefit from a synergism.

Past financial performance, both absolute and relative to its competitors, provided some initial indication of a prospect's management capability. In addition, Textron felt that a superior management would have developed some proprietary market position which would likely continue and hopefully improve that performance in the future. This position could be demonstrated by any of several attributes: proprietary products, a patent position, a superior sales force, a solid product reputation, an unusual manufacturing capability, or good relationships with the channels of distribution. Before approaching a prospect, Textron could often not determine if the management was willing to remain after an acquisition. However, Mr. Murphy felt that Textron provided a strong incentive for that management to remain. Textron granted considerable operating latitude to its divisions and kept them unencumbered by functional staff personnel and interferences while reducing the problems of financing and providing substantial financial rewards for good performance. Mr. Murphy described the chief executive and owner of one company acquired by Textron who desired to sell his company in order to reduce his active participation in the business. Textron acquired the company only after the owner agreed to remain active through the transition period and then to reduce his participation gradually, and only after he convinced Textron that other managers in his company were capable of successfully assuming his responsibilities. Thus, the management retention criterion was primarily a requirement that the company demonstrate an ability to continue its past performance or improve it after the acquisition.

A fourth criterion was that an acquisition prospect be a manufacturing company with quality products which did not have a high technological content.[8] Textron required quality products to insure a quality corporate image and to avoid any cross-product image deterioration. Mr. Little had stressed quality throughout his term as chief executive and convinced his successors of its worth. Although Textron did not impose many constraints in divisional operations, it did generally require that each division display the Textron trademark somewhere in its advertising. This not only increased investor awareness of Textron's diversity or scope, but also developed a corporate reputation which associated Textron's name with quality.

Textron sought to acquire only manufacturing operations[9] because of their common characteristics which facilitated the application and usefulness of the Textron financial control system and the effectiveness of the group vice presidents. Management felt the manufacturing companies were more similar to each other than they were to service companies, particularly in their use of capital and standards of performance. This became more important since group vice presidents periodically rotated their divisional assignments and need to learn about new divisions relatively quickly.

The low-technology requirement further facilitated the work of the group vice presidents. They could be more effective when they could comprehend the technological requirements and limitations imposed on the divisions for which they were responsible. They did not have a corporate staff group of technologically sophisticated people who could help them assess divisional technological issues and problems. Rotation would also be more difficult if group vice presidents were required to learn the technological intricacies of a divisions's business in order to evaluate its managerial decisions. None of Textron's group vice presidents apparently had adequate formal technological training for this purpose. Textron did have one division with relatively high technological content, Bell Aerospace, which was not the responsibility of a group vice president.

A fifth criterion applied to all acquisition prospects was that they compete in small growth markets which were not dominated by large companies. Type II acquisition prospects were the leaders in these markets, particularly during the latter part of the second program. Textron recognized the advantages of being a major competitor in a market and the problems of minor competitors in concentrated markets. Management did not want divisions to be encumbered by the problems of minor competitors. Textron could not afford to acquire the leading competitors in many markets during the early part of the second acquisition program. Therefore, it preferred to acquire companies which competed in markets not dominated by larger firms.

During the latter part of the second program, as Textron became larger and more profitable and developed an attractive price/earnings ratio, it could finance acquisitions which were major competitors in relatively small markets. Often these major competitors had achieved proprietary positions because of their excellent management and had grown more rapidly than their markets by gaining market share. Future growth could be expected only if markets continued to grow or acquired companies continued to gain market share. Continued growth was important for Textron since its strategy was to achieve size more through post-acquisition growth than through acquisition itself.

Textron felt it was important to determine that a market for entry through acquisitions serves a fundamental economic need in world markets. This need can range from consumer demands for higher living standards to machinery to reduce direct manufacturing costs. Textron searched for industries and products that fulfilled the requirements generated by changing demographic profiles; or by the needs of industry to increase production efficiencies and improve products; or by the needs of government, whether it be defense, space, or social programs.

A final criterion which related to the growth objective was an emerging interest in acquiring consumer goods manufacturers and products which could be successfully marketed in Europe. The high priority awarded to consumer product companies during the later part of the period was motivated by the excellent performance of Textron's current consumer product companies and their demonstrated stability during the recent economic downturn. Based on its experience, the strongest and most profitable franchise a manufacturer can have is a branded consumer product backed by a strong brand identification. It was not subject to the variables of industrial or government markets. Therefore, the major motivation was greater profitability through product differentiation. This shift also was evident in the corporate structure at Textron. As chairman of consumer product development, Mr. Murphy was the only corporate officer with any functional responsibilities. The interest in products which could be marketed in Europe complemented a corporate thrust toward multinationality.

In summary, Textron's major acquisition criteria were size, return on investment, retained competent management, low-technology manufacturing companies with quality products, and recently an emphasis on consumer products with distinctive brand images. With the exception of the consumer goods emphasis, European expansion interest, and the increasing size requirements, the acquisition criteria had changed very little since 1960. As another two criteria, which were more easily determinable, Textron sought to avoid any antitrust litigations which might arise from acquiring a prospect and it avoided regulated industries where profits were more limited.

Acquisition Scanning Process

Since the acquisition processes for the second and third programs at Textron were somewhat different, these programs are described sequentially below. Mr. Murphy explained a major change in the acquisition process between 1966 and 1972: "When Mr. Chapin took over in 1966, the acquisition area was still open without governmental constraints, so the pace was fast and furious. He is an excellent financial man with tremendous ability to equate all the business factors and put them together. I don't know that he personally favored any one area more than another. I think he just equated each prospect with Textron. That was back in the days when Textron might make six or seven acquisitions each year. Today, our approach is more selective. The direction is as much toward internal growth as toward acquisitions. Another new element in our strategy is foreign acquisitions."

1960-1969. During the second acquisition program, 1960-1969, Textron identified between 300 and 500 acquisition prospects per year. About two-thirds of these were candidates identified by intermediaries. Brokers identified the largest portion, followed by investment bankers and then commercial bankers. Brokers and finders were the least valuable sources of information because they appeared more interested in providing names and collecting fees than insuring that the match they suggested was sound and workable. Commercial bankers and investment bankers were most valuable since they generally considered the needs of both Textron and the candidate. They not only identified more appropriate candidates but also provided more useful information about them. About 5% of the candidates were identified by their owners or managers directly to Mr. Chapin. The remaining 25% or 30% were identified by various corporate and divisional executives. Divisional managers identified about half of these as Type I acquisition alternatives to extend the activities of their own divisions.

Some of the alternatives identified by the divisional managers were candidates known to be available and others were prospects which the managers felt would be beneficial additions to their divisions, if they were available. Mr. Chapin himself identified as many prospects as all other corporate officers and directors combined. He often identified these prospects as competitors in industries which Textron might enter if the prospects could be acquired. Those alternatives identified by other corporate officers and directors were often candidates which would be appropriate for Type II acquisitions. These candidates were identified usually through associates who were aware that Textron was interested in acquiring companies and retaining their managements. They were attempting to help either Textron or the candidates they suggested. Both Bostitch and Speidel had been identified by members of the board of directors. Usually, Textron did not systematically search through markets for companies which it might acquire, nor had most of its acquisitions been the result of such searches. Past experience indicated that these searches did not produce results as efficiently as using intermediaries.

Mr. Chapin's background as an investment analyst provided him with some exposure to a wide variety of markets and a set of acquaintances from which to gain additional and more specific information about markets after candidates in those markets were identified and initially screened. Based on his experience, personal acquaintances, and reading, Mr. Chapin became aware of a few particular industries which Textron might suitably enter through acquisition.[10] Although he maintained files on several industries of particular interest, he indicated that no substantial amounts of time were devoted to gathering information about them or discussing acquisition possibilities with the owners of the major companies which competed in them.

Approximately 80% of the identified candidates were rejected immediately after they were identified. The initial screening criteria for this rejection included that a candidate: (1) be of appropriate size, (2) be a manufacturing company, (3) immediately increase Textron's earnings per share, and (4) have historical growth greater than the gross national product. Mr. Chapin indicated that not only were these criteria important, but also that the information required for them was easy to gather when a candidate was first identified. Although management capability and continuity could not be determined directly from this information, inadequate size or poor historical financial performance was generally assumed to imply inadequate management depth or caliber.

Regardless of the candidate's initial disposition, Mr. Chapin began a file into which he inserted whatever information had been gathered. The files were not systematically maintained but they covered over 5,000 companies which Textron had reviewed since the acquisition program began. When a candidate was identified, Mr. Chapin first determined if the candidate had been previously identified by searching these files. Also, if he gathered additional information related to a previously identified candidate he would add it to the files. If a candidate had been identified previously, then he would review the reasons why the candidate had been previously rejected and determine if the impediment to acquisition remained. Mr. Chapin felt that the files were useful particularly for reviewing candidates identified a second time after several years had lapsed or for periodically re-evaluating candidates which were acceptable to Textron but not at the minimum price acceptable to their owners. A typical file would contain some of the following kinds of documents: annual reports, auditor's reports, biographies of managers, product catalogs, and any computations or analyses performed by Mr. Chapin or his associates.

For the 20% of all candidates which were not rejected by the initial screening criteria, Mr. Chapin proceeded in several directions. For Type I acquisition candidates, he presented the opportunity to the group vice president and division president who had responsibilities for markets related to those of the candidate. Generally, the divisional managers either had additional information about a prospect and the market in which it competed or had access to sources of additional information. From this information and occasionally an internal market study the divisional management could generally estimate the future growth potential of the candidate's market and some of the most important competitive requirements. Often from customers common with the candidate, the divisional marketing staff could assess the product reputation, marketing strength, production capability, and aggressiveness of the candidate. Technological assessment was generally more difficult, but less important since Textron was primarily interested in low-technology businesses.[11]

The division management also attempted to estimate the potential synergistic benefits which might result from combining the candidate's operations with its own. If the division management was interested in further pursuing the acquisition alternative, Mr. Chapin reviewed the financial implications of the acquisition more closely and either he or the division president arranged an initial meeting and plant tour for Textron's managers with the candidate's management. The purpose of this discussion was to gather more information, particularly about the feasibility and extent of synergy potential, the quality of the candidate's management, the condition of the candidate's production facilities, and the reason why the management or owners wanted to be acquired. An important area of concern was the personality compatibility of the division management and the candidate management. A Type I acquisition was not consummated unless the division management supported and desired the acquisition. The division management could withdraw its support at any point in the acquisition process. This seemed particularly necessary since the corporate management granted considerable freedom to the division managements in their own operations. Also, divisional management had the expertise to judge the appropriateness of the candidate for inclusion with the division's operations and would have the responsibility for its success.

For Type II acquisitions which fulfilled the initial screening criteria, Mr. Chapin began a more systematic financial analysis of the information he had available or could easily gather from financial services or published sources. He also informed the corporate managers of the candidate and communicated a summary of information to them. One reason for circulating information about candidates among the corporate managers was that collectively they had a broad range of knowledge and experience. Often some of these managers could supply additional information about a candidate or the markets in which it competed. Equally important, when they did not have information, they often had access to sources of information which were useful for further evaluation of a prospect. Textron occasionally retained market research firms to gather additional information about a market or candidate when managers did not have access to sources of adequate information. Most Type II acquisitions had the unanimous approval of Textron's corporate officers. Involving them in the scanning process facilitated not only the information gathering but also the coalescence toward a decision.

After gathering additional information about the candidates which it identified, Textron established communications and held discussions with representatives of about 25 candidates annually. The purpose of these discussions was the same as for Type I acquisitions. Although usually no division managers were included, often either the president or an executive vice president initially attended. For Type II acquisitions, information about the quality and continuity of incumbent management was particularly important to gather at these discussions. Usually before discussions progressed significantly, the group vice president who would be responsible for the acquired company became involved in the discussions. The legal and accounting staff became involved later in the discussions. During these discussions, Textron also carefully defined the roles and responsibilities of acquired managers so they could form accurate expectations about their future association with Textron. These discussions were an integral part of the information gathering process. About half of these discussions eventually reached the negotiation stage. Discussions were usually discontinued if Textron management determined that the candidate was deficient in some way which it could not supplement – e.g., management unwilling to remain after the acquisition or impending market problems which would prevent adequate growth. Of the negotiations which did not result in acquisition, the majority reached an impasse over the price which Textron would be willing to pay. In a few instances, the company owners decided after the start of negotiations to continue their ownership for reasons unrelated to the negotiated price.

1970-1972.   As Mr. Murphy assumed the role of director of corporate development, the acquisition program became more selective. A smaller number of acquisitions would be consummated annually, with a particular focus on consumer products companies. While Mr. Murphy continued to screen candidates identified by others, he also worked with Textron executives to identify prospects in the consumer products areas which would provide entry to desirable markets.

Mr. Murphy identified desirable prospects by selecting generally desirable product classifications, listing the important companies within these, selecting companies with specific products and reputations, gathering data on these, and then approaching those prospects which appeared most desirable. From information already in Textron's file and Mr. Murphy's own background and knowledge, he identified the major consumer goods industry segments. He reviewed these segments with Messrs. Chapin and White, among others, to eliminate those which were of relatively little interest. After eliminations, 395 firms were identified with specific products which might be of interest to Textron. For each of these firms, Mr. Murphy prepared a short information profile based on Textron's files and financial services such as Dun and Bradstreet's or

Standard and Poor's. Based on these profiles, he grouped the prospects into three priority classifications. Mr. Murphy reviewed these priorities with Mr. Miller whose major input was based on his general knowledge of business and industry and his own concept of Textron's strengths and weakness.

For those prospects who had the highest priority, Mr. Murphy gathered additional information from other published sources and financial analysts and began approaching them to determine if they would be interested in being acquired. Mr. Murphy described the process as follows: "We explain our interest and corporate philosophy so that if there is not an interest now but it develops in the future they may contact us. Sometimes a knock on a door like that will bear fruit five years later. Because of Textron's known fairness and emphasis on people and management and retaining management, some companies have been acquired because they have been threatened with a take-over by other firms but preferred to make their own choice." By the end of 1972, none of the companies which were identified and approached in this manner had been acquired.

Factors Influencing the Acquisition Process

Although no one influence dominated the design or operation of the acquisition process at Textron, its consistency with the corporate strategy was one of paramount importance.

The First Program. Other factors included the organization, participants, and environment of the firm. These are discussed below in historical sequence. The strategy during the first program was simply to achieve wide diversity through a series of companies acquired with cash conserved by utilizing Textron's large tax-loss carry-over.[12] The tax-loss was the result of unprofitable textile operations prior to 1953 and of unprofitable textile operations acquired in 1954. Consolidation of these operations and large increases of Textron's long term debt provided initial cash flow for acquiring companies, while the tax-loss carry-over retained the profits produced by those companies acquired. With its low price/earnings ratio, Textron could not afford to issue new stock to either acquire companies or obtain cash with which to acquire companies. Therefore, to achieve diversity, the acquisition program focused on small, profitable companies whose owners would accept cash, or repurchased treasury stock, as payment.

Because these acquisition prospects were small and usually privately owned, Textron did not have access to inexpensive sources of information about them. Furthermore, because of their size, and

Textron's limited cash, it could not afford detailed market research studies of all the prospects it identified. Also, because Textron planned to acquire many companies, the cost of a few mistakes would be less than the cost of gathering sufficient information to avoid them. Concerning the detail of information gathered about prospects, one executive reportedly often commented during the first acquisition program, "Maybe one of us ought to go out there and see if the plant (of a prospect) is really there." Similarly, since Textron did not limit the scope of markets it would enter and since most small companies did not want to be acquired, gathering information about prospects before Textron knew they were willing to be acquired was uneconomical. Therefore, Textron only gathered information about candidates which were identified by intermediaries.

Mr. Little also affected the information gathering process. Since he wanted to develop a diversified firm rather than administer it, he required that candidates have good management willing to remain and operate their companies after an acquisition. By his definition, good managers could be identified by the performances of their companies. Since historical financial information was available from the intermediaries who identified prospects, information to evaluate managerial capability was easy to gather. Mr. Little was a businessman who informally gathered information on a wide range of subjects through his exposure to many people over a long time period; he had not narrowed his interest to the textile industry. Based on this information he felt he could usually appraise the potential of a market in which an acquisition candidate competed and he probably rejected prospects in markets which he could not. Over a period of seven years, Mssrs. Little and Cassler developed an acquisition process which met the needs of the strategy and the skills of the managers. Some of the companies acquired during the first program were unsuccessful.

The Second Program. Somewhat arbitrarily, the end of the first acquisition program was defined to be when Mr. Little retired as Textron's chairman and chief executive officer in 1960. The transition to the second program was actually gradual because the management succession was smooth and the strategy remained relatively unchanged although more clearly defined. Mr. Cassler joined Textron in 1954 and remained involved in the acquisition program until he retired in 1966. His skill increased with his experience and his information gathering became more refined and efficient. As president from 1957, Mr. Thompson's major role in Textron's management prior to Mr. Little's retirement was to organize, to rationalize, and to some extent, consolidate the various companies which Mr. Little had acquired. As Mr. Thompson began to rationalize, he likely began to influence the acquisition program and process.[13] As a former banker, Mr. Thompson probably wanted more information about acquisition candidates and the markets in which they competed than Mr. Little had required.

Two major differences between the first and second programs, however, were important. First, as leadership changed and the corporate executive group grew in size, diversity, and competence, its members became more involved in the acquisition decision process. Their combined experiences and backgrounds increased the information available within the firm about candidates and their markets. Also, continuing his administrative involvement as he assumed the chairmanship, Mr. Thompson maintained open channels of communication with the other corporate officers. As these executives found their information requested and used, they volunteered it more freely and completely and helped to locate appropriate sources of additional information. The result was considerably more information gathered about acquisition candidates and the markets in which they competed with a proportionately smaller increase in the information gathering effort. This increased involvement also spawned the group decision by consensus among corporate executives. Thus, during most of the second program each of the corporate officers could effectively veto an acquisition alternative by submitting information which argued coherently against it.

Second, as Textron's diversity increased, companies were acquired to expand and reinforce existing divisions. Competing in more markets increased the likelihood that a candidate would be related to an existing Textron division in some way. As Textron's management structure became more clearly defined, both the problem of increasing the number of divisions extensively and the advantages of combining related divisions became more obvious. The problem of increasing the number of divisions was partially a span of control issue. It became increasingly clear that the number of independent divisions was limited by the organizational policies of minimizing the size of the corporate office and maintaining close interpersonal relationships between division managers and group vice presidents. The advantages of combining related divisions and acquiring companies related to them were primarily synergy benefits based on potential economies of scale in marketing, manufacturing, or technology. Formally recognizing Type I acquisitions encouraged a separate and different information, about these candidates and the markets in which they competed. Communicating this information and the desire for it through the group vice president was a natural development which followed from including the division managers in the information gathering process.

However, as Textron sought to integrate Type I acquisitions with the division to which they related, the division managers' role in the information gathering and decision process necessarily increased substantially. Integration was only possible if the division manager approved and supported an acquisition. Furthermore, because of their relationship to the candidate, the division managers had the most accurate and complete information and therefore corporate management upheld divisional recommendations against acquiring particular Type I candidates. In addition, the group vice presidents encouraged division managers to identify acquisition candidates which would prove beneficial to their overall performance.

Thus, the major differences between the acquisition processes of the first and second acquisition programs at Textron were related to and consistent with changes in corporate strategy and corporate management.

The acquisition process was relatively stable throughout the second acquisition program, the influence of changing corporate strategy was apparent, primarily in shifting the emphasis of the program. Mr. Chapin joined Textron in 1964 and became vice president of corporate development when Mr. Cassler retired in 1966. Messrs. Chapin and Cassler worked together for the intervening two years and both had financial backgrounds so that the change in personnel had little perceptible affect on the acquisition process. As Textron grew in size and cash flow, it increased the average size of its acquisitions, particularly Type II acquisitions, since corporate management wanted new divisions to be at least as large as existing divisions. Textron also divested several operations for the same reason.

The major development during the second program occurred in 1967, in response to an environmental change. In 1967 Textron's price/earnings ratio increased dramatically from 14 to 20, exceeding the New York Stock Exchange average. The impact was that for the first time, Textron could afford to issue stock to purchase acquisitions without significantly diluting earnings per share. Using the capability to its advantage, Textron consummated five large acquisitions,[14] which accounted for 57% of the sales increase between 1966 and 1968. Since these companies were significantly larger, much more information was gathered about them from published sources. However, the overall impact on the acquisition process of these large acquisitions was otherwise inconsequential. By 1969, Textron's price/earnings ratio returned to its former levels, again limiting the size of candidates Textron could afford to acquire. One impact of the large acquisitions was a complaint filed by the Antitrust Division of the U.S. Department of Justice against the Fafnir acquisition. Although Textron settled the complaint quickly, easily, and quietly, it promoted an increased concern for the antitrust implication of future acquisitions. It was not a primary inhibitor to future acquisitions, probably because of their small size.

A change during the second acquisition program which had little immediate influence on the acquisition process was that in early 1968 Mr. Miller became chief executive officer of Textron. Since he became president in 1960, the management continuity explained the major lack of immediate change in the acquisition process. As apparent and logical successor to Mr. Thompson, any dissatisfactions he had with the process presumably would have been reconciled much earlier than 1968. However, Mr. Miller did affect the acquisition process, and introduce the third acquisition program.

Following the major acquisitions in 1967 and 1968, Textron's overall growth and profitability stagnated. A major environmental change affecting this stagnation was the maturation of several Textron products, the severe reduction in helicopter orders for the de-escalating Viet Nam war, and a sluggish economy. In response to these and other pressures, Mr. Miller reformulated Textron's strategy to provide new opportunities for growth. The primary thrust of the new strategy was an emphasis on growth through acquisition outside the United States, principally Europe. This new thrust significantly decreased the cash available for domestic acquisitions as well as the executive interest in them. To permit the strategic change to be reflected in the acquisition process, Mr. Miller reassigned Mr. Chapin to other duties and asked Mr. Murphy to devote part of his time to acquisition activities.

The Third Program. The changes in the acquisition process were consistent with the new strategy. However, it was Mr. Murphy's background, experience, and other duties that caused the immediate change in the acquisition process. Mr. Murphy was considerably older than many Textron corporate executives, including Mr. Miller. Most of his adult career was in consumer disposable product industries, beginning in the marketing area of Montgomery Ward where he advanced to the position of marketing manager of sportswear and men's clothing. Then at Johnson & Johnson he began as manager of advertising and advanced to president of the Personal Products Division. His first major acquisition experience began in 1961 when he joined Revlon as president. He restructured the entire acquisition program and process at Revlon divesting product lines such as artificial flowers, shoe polish, and women's fashion clothing and substituting a specifically focused search for prospects in a few markets closely related to Revlon's cosmetic business, particularly fragrances and pharmaceuticals. Thus, in addition to a broad background in consumer products marketing and management, his previous acquisitions experience involved a significantly different scanning process than that previously used at Textron.   At Revlon he identified markets for entry and gathered extensive information about them before identifying prospects. Within the selected markets he gathered information about prospects without knowing if they were available and contacted them only after this information was gathered.

At Textron, Mr. Murphy introduced a similar process which he described as more selective. He selected consumer product markets for entry about which he had gathered information during his career or about which other Textron executives, particularly Mr. Chapin, had gathered information during the earlier acquisition program.   His background and experience therefore selected markets which would help implement Textron's strategy - consumer markets. Because of his broad background, Mr. Murphy had previously gathered information not only about markets, but also about many competitors in those markets, enough to categorize the desirability of acquiring them.   Much of his work was categorizing and recording information rather than gathering new information. Unlike his predecessor, Mr. Murphy approached many of the prospects he identified without knowing if they were interested in being acquired. His program had not resulted in acquisitions because of the low probability that companies wanted to be acquired.

However, the program was consistent with the corporate strategy. It required little operating cost, focused on the segment of the economy of most interest to Textron, and resulted in only a small number of very attractive acquisition alternatives while maintaining Textron's image as a company searching for acquisitions. Also, Mr. Murphy's dual role as vice president of corporate development and chairman of consumer product development conveyed to several division managers the corporate interest in their performance improvement much as Mr. Miller's earlier Profit Improvement Program conveyed to all division managers the importance to the corporate office of increasing profitability.   In addition, information gathered while searching for acquisitions might have useful implications for existing consumer products divisions.   The highly selective character of the third acquisition program also conserved cash dispersal for European acquisitions.

In summary, the Textron acquisition process evolved over time in response to major shifts in Textron's strategy or environment. The evolution was facilitated by changing the backgrounds and experiences of the participants.   The strategy itself changed more in response to environmental conditions than to change in executives, although these executives determined the direction of change.   Because most of Textron's acquisitions were small, U.S. antitrust law enforcement had little effect on the acquisition process.   The consistency between the strategy and the acquisition process was maintained throughout the period from 1953, contributing substantially to the success of Textron's several acquisition programs.

Acquisition Scanning Processes Compared

The concluding section of this chapter compares and contrasts the domestic diversifying acquisition processes of ITT and Textron[15] and the factors which influenced their similarities and differences. Both firms were actively pursuing conglomerate strategies throughout the period under study. This accounts for the great similarity between the firms.

Scanning Processes Compared

The acquisition criteria of the two firms were similar. Both strongly emphasized financial criteria and information gathering. Both also sought only companies with good managers who would remain with their businesses after acquisition. Good management was assessed initially in terms of its historical financial performance. This criterion was important for unrelated market acquisitions. Other criteria only varied slightly. For example, Textron had a more limited market scope whereas ITT was particularly interested in markets with international potential. ITT did exert more effort to determine five-year forecasts for prospects than did Textron.

ITT and Textron adopted somewhat different approaches to market and prospect identification. Both relied primarily upon intermediaries to identify candidates, although managers also identified a significant portion of candidates. At Textron, division managers were active in identifying related markets for entry and prospects which competed in those markets; whereas, at ITT, business unit managers were seldom involved in identifying either markets or prospects for unrelated markets Textron's executive group had identified a few markets for entry but usually reacted to markets identified by intermediaries. The president of ITT had identified several areas in which he would like his firm to compete but had searched for prospects in those areas by monitoring the candidates presented by intermediaries.

Sources of market and candidate information were considerably different for ITT and Textron, In both firms, information about related markets was gathered by the divisional managers. However, at Textron this information was supplemented by the group vice presidents and at ITT it was supplemented by corporate staff scanning, particularly market research studies. These same sources of information plus intermediaries were generally used for candidate information. In both firms, related market candidates were approached quickly after they were identified to gather more information.

For unrelated market acquisitions, Textron involved most of its corporate managers in the information gathering process. Each manager was expected to read widely about many areas which might be of interest. This information, plus information from published sources and some unpublished financial analyses provided the basis for decisions of whether to initiate discussions with an identified prospect. Similar sources were used by ITT except that the corporate staff could gather information from primary sources and industry experts more easily and ITT centralized the informal scanning process more than Textron had. ITT's major acquisitions were presidential decisions; whereas, Textron's were group decisions.

Both firms emphasized financial information and performed extensive financial analysis on candidate information. Also, both involved managers with similar backgrounds and experiences in the scanning process and gathered information in very similar sequences. In addition, ITT utilized corporate staff to perform market research studies or occasionally technological studies. Textron did not process information to the same extent because it did not have the staff capability to do so. For related market acquisitions, managers within the divisions of Textron presumably processed information more extensively.

Influences Compared

Many of the similarities in the scanning processes of these two firms can be traced to their corporate strategies. Because they sought wide diversity in many areas which could not be combined to yield synergy benefits, their information requirements focused on financial and managerial impacts on their firms. Both the immediate and long term financial impact of acquisitions was important to them. In the short term it provided the appearance of growth and profitability which was expected to result in higher price/earnings ratios. In the long term, it provided a measure of continuing performance. However, in the long term performance would only be achieved through effective management. Corporate management could not foresee all of the possible environmental changes which would affect its wide scope of businesses. However, competent division managements could anticipate, plan, and lead their business through changing environmental trends and conditions.

The rate of acquisition activity required by their conglomerate strategies also affected the process. Since financial information was usually the easiest to gather and process, the ability to assess management initially on the basis of its historical financial performance was both convenient and useful in the design of the scanning process. Furthermore, financial criteria could be applied systematically to a wide variety of businesses. However, conglomerate managers could not limit their market scopes sufficiently to permit systematic identification and search through markets for appropriate acquisition prospects. Rather, monitoring and reacting to the candidates identified by intermediaries improved access to information while it prevented gathering information about acquisition alternatives which could not be selected. Although Textron limited its market scope to low technology, manufacturing businesses, this did not permit systematic identification and evaluation of markets or prospects.

The environment, particularly financial investors, also influenced the acquisition scanning processes of these firms in a similar way. Unlike many other conglomerates, ITT and Textron both had low price/earnings ratios except during the 1967-1969 period.[16] These price/earnings ratios were partially an investor reaction to well established financial performance records of the firms.[17] It was during this period that both firms acquired most of their large companies because stock transactions were attractive. For ITT, it meant different participants and different roles for the participants. At Textron it meant a different pattern of information availability and sources of information and candidate identification.

Despite these strategic similarities, some significant differences in the two firms influenced their acquisition scanning processes. One difference was that ITT maintained a large corporate staff of functional experts which could gather information about identified candidates and their markets. By comparison, Textron maintained no such staff and therefore relied on information readily accessible to the managers of the firm. In this respect, ITT had the capability to gather significantly more information about acquisition alternatives. Also, ITT maintained a financial analysis group primarily to gather and process information about alternatives. This group processed both related and unrelated acquisitions. At Textron only the vice president of corporate development was active in this process and he limited his scope primarily to unrelated acquisitions. Related acquisitions were evaluated at the division level primarily. Thus, Textron had a more decentralized and coordinated acquisition scanning process than did ITT.

The similarities of diversification strategies and diversification objectives of the two firms described in this chapter tend not to contradict the two hypotheses proposed in Chapter II. These were: (1) That firms with different types of diversification objectives would tend to adopt different acquisition scanning processes and (2) That firms with different diversification strategies would tend to adopt different acquisition scanning processes. A more thorough examination of these hypotheses remains an important task to be accomplished in Chapter VI.

NOTES

[1]See Exhibit V-1 for a summary of ITT's principal products and services.

[2]See Exhibit V-2 for a list of principal domestic diversifying acquisitions.

[3]Messrs. Bohon, Prevost, Smith, and Doyle were interviewed for this research.

[4]For example: consumer credit, life insurance, auto rental, education, hotels, and fire insurance.

[5]See Exhibit V-3 for a summary of Textron's principal products.

[6]See Exhibit V-4 for a list of principal domestic diversifying acquisitions.

[7]Messrs. Chapin and Murphy were interviewed for this research as was Mr. John Henderson, Vice President and General Counsel for Textron.   Also, significant information was obtained from the Harvard Business School case series on Textron, Inc.

[8]In 1972, Textron acquired American   Research and Development Corporation for about 1.8 million shares worth about $57 million. ARD was a successful Boston-based venture capital firm under the leadership of Mr. Georges F. Doriot, ARD founder, long-time Textron director, and former Harvard Business School professor.   ARD represented a substantial departure from Textron's historical concentration in manufacturing areas. It was not included in this research. Mr. Murphy indicated that the departure was not an issue since management had been considering entry into non-manufacturing markets for some time. He further noted that the scanning process was atypical because of the close relationship between Mr. Doriot and Textron.

[9]In 1968, Textron did bid for control of United Fruit Company, primarily a banana importer. The proposed bid of $716 million would have been considerably larger than any of Textron's other acquisitions. United Fruit was not manufacturing. Presumably it would have represented a separate product group managed differently than other divisions.

[10]Mr. Chapin described for the researcher one industry in which Textron had been interested for several years, and a second about which he was currently gathering information.   For these industries, Mr. Chapin described, from memory and with no hesitation, the competitive requirements and barriers to entry, all of the major competitors, which ones he would be willing to acquire, the major strengths and weaknesses of each, the reasons why Textron had not acquired them to date, and who their principal owners and managers were. He also noted one company which Textron acquired in less than ten days after it had been identified because he had been gathering information about it for several years and therefore had a reasonable assessment of its operations and of the price Textron would be willing to pay for it.

[11]Mr. Murphy noted that when Speidel was acquired, the company not only had product patents to protect itself from potential competitors, but also proprietary automated assembly technology which he felt other competitors could not duplicate after the product patents expired.   Some technological factors such as this were

difficult to determine until after Textron initiated discussions with a candidate.

[12]Information about the strategy and acquisition program is based primarily on published information.

[13]For example, as he analyzed the problems of the steamship line, he not only recognized the operating problems inherent in the industry, but also recognized that part of Textron's problem was that it was different than its manufacturing companies.

[14]These acquisitions were: Gorham, Fafnir, Bridgeport, Talon and Polaris.

[15]See Exhibit V-5 for a summary comparison of the scanning processes of ITT and Textron. The exhibit utilizes the process characteristics described in Chapter II.

[16]See Exhibit V-6 for a comparison of ITT's and Textron's price/earnings ratios with those for a sample of other publicly owned firms.

[17]See Exhibit V-7 for a comparison of the financial performance of ITT and Textron.

EXHIBIT V-1
Principal Products and Services of ITT

Avionics · Ground and Airborne

Short range navigation
Long range navigation
Approach and landing
Air traffic control
Communications
Airborne display
Airport construction & installation

Communication Operations

Telephone
Telegram and telex
Simultaneous voice/data channels
Ship-to-shore
Alternative voice/data channels
Standard and broadband lease channels
Worldfax
Datel
Presscasts

Components · Electronic

Wire & Cable
Electron tubes
Semiconductors
Electro/optical devices
Vacuum capacitors
Relays and switches
Connectors, fittings & terminals
Filters
Antennae
Piezo electric crystals

Consumer Products

Radio & television
Phonographs & tape recorders
Refrigerators & freezers
Washers & dryers
Ranges & dish washers
Air conditioners
Small electric appliances
Housing construction
Home furnishings & supplies

Data Equipment, Systems, & Services

Systems analysis
Programming
Computational services
Data center management
Data preparation services

Education

Educational institutes
Magazines, catalogues & manuals
Books
Teaching machines

Financial & Consumer Services

Life & casualty insurance
Fire insurance
Mutual funds management
Sales management
Consumer finance
Commercial & industrial finance
Automobile & truck rental & leasing
Parking at airports & other public
    spaces
Ground transportation
Hotels & motels
Housing & community development
Real estate

Food Products

Breads, cakes, & snacks
Frozen foods & food additives

Illumination Products

Lamps
Lighting fixtures and equipment
Flash bulbs
Advertising signs

Medical Electronics

Patient monitoring

Hearing aids

Hospital equipment

Military & Space Equipment

Communications
Satellites
Navigation
Radar
Simulators
Countermeasures

Natural Resources

Forest products
Glass sand
Clay products

Office and Business Equipment

Document sorters
Document readers
Pneumatic tube distribution
Data processing equipment
Character & symbol generators
Character displays
Communication equipment

Technical & Industrial Products

Heating, ventilating, & air conditioning
Fluid handling products
Automatic controls
Automotive equipment
Fire sprinkler systems
Abrasive materials & products

Telecommunications

Public and private switching
    telephone, telegraph, & data
    exchanges
Ancillary telephone switching
    equipment
Telephone station equipment
Telegraph & data equipment
Transmission systems
Point-to-point communication
    radio links
Land line transmission
Underwater cable
Multiplex equipment
Mobile radio communication
Broadcasting

Research and Development

Material studies
Process studies
Techniques & technologies

EXHIBIT V-2

Principal Diversifying Acquisitions of ITT

1961

Jennings Radio, Inc.	Radio & television transmitters
Suprenant Mfg.	Specialized wire & cable for missiles, computers & other industrial uses

1962

National Computer Products	Diodes & other electronic components

1963

General Controls, Inc.	Automatic controls for domestic, industrial, & aerospace uses
Bell & Gossett, Inc.	Industrial & commercial pumps for heating, air conditioning & refrigeration
Nesbitt, Inc.	Heating, ventilating & air conditioning systems & equipment for schools
Cannon Electric Co.	Electrical connectors for industrial commercial, & military use

1964

Hayes Furnace Mfg. & Supply Co.	Commercial gas furnaces
Aetna Finance Co.	Small personal loans & insurance services
Gilfillan, Inc.	Airport surveillance & ground control approach radar systems
Barton Instruments, Inc.	Instruments for measuring flows of liquids & gases & detecting gas leaks

1965

Henze Valve & Instrument Co.	Repair and service for valves, meters, instruments, & similar equipment
Avis, Inc.	Automobile renting & leasing
Hamilton Management Corp.	Mutual funds & insurance
Kebby Microwave Corp.	Microwave communications equipment & components

Documat, Inc.	Microfilm equipment and devices, & other photographic equipment
Press Wireless, Inc.	Communications services for newspapers & press associations

1966

Wakefield Corp.	Institutional, commercial, & industrial lighting fixtures & abrasive products
Consolidated Electric Lamp Co.	Standard incandescent & flourescent lamps
Howard W. Sams & Co.	Technical reference services, magazines, textbooks, & technical training schools
Airport Parking Co. of America	Parking facilities at airports and other public locations

1968

Jasper-Blackburn Co.	Electrical transmission and distribution equipment and supplies
Levitt & Sons, Inc.	Planning & developing residential communities & general housing construction
Sheraton Corp. of America	Hotels, motels, & motor inns internationally
Rayonier, Inc.	Chemical cellulose, paper pulps, lumber, & silvichemicals
Pennsylvania Glass Sand Corp.	Silica & special clay products
Continental Baking Co.	Bread & bakery products, frozen foods & snack foods
Transportation Displays, Inc.	Advertising for the transportation industry, at terminals & in vehicles & timetables

1969

Yellow Cab Co. of Kansas City	Operates taxicabs & school buses
Marquis - Who's Who	Publisher & distributor of biographical reference books
Canteen Corp.	Vending machine leasing & operation & food service operations

American Building Services Co.	Janitorial & maintenance services for industrial buildings
American Electric Mfg. Corp.	Street lighting & other outdoor lighting
Pearson Candy Co.	Candy bars & other candy products
Southern Wood Preserving Co.	Creosoted & other pressure-treated forest products
Grinnel Corp.	Fire protection systems & sprinklers & pipe fittings
G. K. Hall Corp.	Library reference materials publisher

1970

Hartford Fire Insurance Co.	Fire & casualty insurance
Gwaltney, Inc.	Fresh and processed pork products

1971

H.M. Harper	Industrial fasteners & communications
O. M. Scott & Son, Co.	Seeds & lawn & garden products
Peninsula Plywood Corp.	Veneer & plywood
Holub Industries, Inc.	Packaging tools & supplies sold to the building trades
McDonell & Miller, Inc.	Boiler controls

1972

Higbe Mfg. Co.	Small diameter welded tubing
Phillips Drill, Inc.	Masonry anchoring systems & equipment
Hancock Industries, Inc.	Roll formed, machined, & stamped metal parts and fabricated assemblies for the automotive industry
Meyers Industries, Inc.	Aluminum utility poles & high voltage utility transmission poles

EXHIBIT V-3
Principal Products of Textron

Aerospace Products

Military helicopters
Commercial helicopters
Rocket engines
Missile & spacecraft propulsion
    systems
Positive expulsion rocket fuel tanks
Inertial guidance and automatic
    landing systems
Air cushion vehicles
Avionic devices
Electrohydraulic actuators
Hydraulic control systems & filters
Pressure regulators
Fluid controls
Heat exchange equipment
Autoclaves
Aerospace antennae systems
Electronic warfare systems
Magnetic detection systems
Electro-optics
Automatic test equipment
Solar cells, simulators & power arrays

Consumer Products

Zippers
Chain saws
Eye glasses & frames
Expansion watch bands
Bathroom accessories
Power lawn mowers
Power generators
Pumps
Electric golf carts
Electric vehicles
Paints & varnishes
Cookware
Mail boxes
Tubular furniture
Pens & automatic pencils
Hearing aids
Ophthalmic machinery
Jewelry chain
Men's toiletries

Industrial Products

Ball & roller bearings
Cushioning materials & polyurethane
    foam
Castings for engine blocks, cam-
    shafts, & brake drums
Electronic crystals & other frequency
    control products
Chaplets & chills for casting
Electric line products
Service fittings for utilities
Malleable iron hardware
Plastic products
Hand tools
Metal abrasives
Vibration test equipment
Environmental test systems
Balancing machines
Electronic instrumentation
Appliance & automotive trim
Automobile
Corn milling products
Gas meters & regulators
Cylinders, valves, & regulators for
    liquefied petroleum
Marine fittings
Underfloor electrical distribution
    systems
Pre-engineered metal buildings

Metal Products

Staples, staplers, & fasteners
Stapling hammers & pneumatic
    nailers
Container machinery
Cold flow metal parts
Aluminum & steel foil mills
Heavy duty rolling mills
Metallurgical furnaces
Anti-vibration metal cutters
Precision grinders
Turret lathes
Hobbing machines

EXHIBIT V-4

Principal Diversifying Acquisitions of Textron

1953

R. Burkhart Mfg. Co.	Batting, padding, & upholstery filling

1954

Dalmo Victor Co.	Airborne radar antennae & related equipment
M.B. Mfg. Co., Inc.,	Aircraft engine mounts & vibrator equipment

1955

Ryan Industries, Inc.	Precision electro-mechanical devices for defense work
Homelite Corporation	Chain saws, generators, & pumps
Coquille Plywood	Plywood (later divested)
Camcar Screw & Mfg. Co.	Metal fasteners, screw-washer assemblies, and metal parts for engines.
Kordite Corporation	Polyethylene & other plastic products

1956

Campbell, Wyatt, & Cannon Foundry Company	Alloy iron & steel castings
General Cement Mfg. Co.	Liquid cement, chemicals & parts, primarily for radio, television & electronics
Benada Aluminum Products	Aluminum home building speciality products, particularly door frames & window sashes
Hall-Mack Co.	Bathroom accessories & fixtures
Peat Mfg. Co.	Die castings
S. S. LaGuardia	Passenger tourist ship (later divested)
Federal Leather Company	Plastic coated fabrics

1957

California Technical Ind.	Electronic test equipment
Accessory Products Corp.	Valves & pneumatic controls
Cleveland Hobbing & Machine Co.	Machine tools & automation equipment
Fanner Mfg. Co.	Metal devices for foundries & hardware

1958

Waterbury Farrel Machine Co.	Diversified lines of metal working machines
Shuron Optical Co.	Optical spectacle frames, cases, lenses, and optical laboratory equipment
Precision Methods & Machines	Mill components & precision machinery

1959

Nuclear Metals, Inc.	Metallurgic research & prototype construction for atomic energy fuel elements & specialized metals
Townsend Company	Metal fasteners, rivets, ball studs & stampings
Pittsburgh Steel Foundry Corp.	Steel casting & specialized heavy machinery
Randall Company	Special parts & interior metal trim for auto industry and cast iron & aluminum cooking utensils
Amsler Morton	Design & construction of soaking pits & industrial furnaces

1960

Bell Aircraft Corporation (defense group)	Rocket engines, inertial guidance systems, helicopters, and hydraulic research & manufacturing
Weinbrenner Company	Workshoes & other specialized footwear
Dorset Marine	Fiberglass pleasure boats & boat trailers (later divested)
E-Z Go Car	Electric golf carts

1961

Tilden Company	Ethical drugs (later divested)
Modern Optics	Multi-focal lenses
Sprague Meter Co.	Gas meters & regulators & marine fittings
Spencer, Kellogg & Sons, Inc.	Chemical & oil seed products, poultry & livestock feeds
M. B. Skinner Company	Clamps & service fittings
Tubular Rivet & Stud Co.	Tubular rivets & rivet setting machines

1962

American Screw Company	Industrial fasteners
Vita-Var	Paints & varnishes

1963

Continental Optical Co.	Optical frames & lenses & safety glasses
Ames Maid	Tubular metal furniture
Zenite Metals	Trim for automotive & appliance industry
Caroline Poultry Farms	Poultry growing & processing (later divested)
Parkersburg-Aetna Corp.	Ball & roller bearings, oil field production equipment, & pre-engineered metal buildings
Walker Brothers	Underfloor line of electrical distribution equipment

1964

Jones & Lamson Machine Company	Machine tools
Speidel Corp.	Expansion watch bands
Ledeen, Inc.	Hydraulic-pneumatic control systems

1966

Cleveland Metal Abrasive Co.	Metal shot for cleaning
W. A. Shaeffer Pen Co.	Writing instruments & hearing aids
Bostitch, Inc.	Staples, staplers, & nailing & container machinery

1967

Thompson Grinder Co.

Surface grinders

Gorham Corporation

Sterling silver & stainless steel flatware, sterling & silver plated holloware, crystal stemware, and china dinnerware

Eaton Paper Corporation

Social stationery, desk & photo accessories, and personal record books (part of Gorham)

1968

Fafnir Bearing Co.

Precision ball bearings for industrial aerospace, off-the-road and farm equipment fields and replacement sales

Bridgeport Machine, Inc.

Milling machines, attachments & accessories, hydraulic and optical duplicating milling machines, numerical controls

Talon, Inc.

Metal and filament zippers, threads, tapes, and other sewing accessories & electrical contacts

Polaris Industries, Inc.

Snowmobiles and snowmobile accessories

1969

Donahue Sales Corp.

Distributor of Talon products & other products

1970

Welsch Manufacturing Co.

Safety goggles, safety headgear, & plastic lenses

1971

Auto-Soler, Inc.

Automated nailing machines for shoe repairs and for high-speed fabrication of furniture, luggage, wooden articles, & fabricated houses

EXHIBIT V-5

Conglomerate Firms Compared

ITT   TEXTRON

Types of Information or Acquisition Criteria

Growth rates exceeding GNP   Pretax R.O.I. exceeding 20%
Strong balance sheets   Immediate increase in eps
ITT control systems applicable   Good management to remain
Good management to remain   Manufacturing companies only
Avoid antitrust problems   Quality products only
Nonregulated industries   Low technology industries
International potential   Small markets only
                                           Nonconcentrated markets

I   Privately owned primarily
    Sales between $20m & $50m   I   Synergy possible
    Market relationship
                                           II Sales between $5m & $100m
II Publicly owned usually
    Sales over $50m

Sources of Market Information

I   Divisional management   I   Published sources
    Associates of managers   Divisional management
    Research of corporate staffs   Group vice presidents
                                               Associates of managers
II President and staff
    Publications & consultants   II Corporate executives
    Market research   Publications
    Technical department   Market research occasionally

Sources of Prospect Information

I   Intermediaries   I   Intermediaries
    Candidates themselves   Divisional Management
    Staff research projects   Candidates themselves

II Intermediaries   II Intermediaries
    Financial analysts   Publications
    Investment bankers   Investment bankers
    Staff research   Candidates themselves
    Candidates themselves

Types of Information Processing

Financial Analysis   Financial Analysis
Market & Technical research

EXHIBIT V-5 (cont.)

Participants in the Process

President – former accountant and financial executive

Senior vice president – former staff planner

Manager of acquisition analysis – former financial analyst and financial consultant

Vice president of corporate development – former financial analyst with major financial institution

Director of corporate development – former executive with several consumer product firms & some acquisition experience

Sequence of Scanning Activities

Candidates identified

Information about markets and candidates gathered together

Candidates identified

Information about markets and candidates gathered together

EXHIBIT V-6

Price-Earnings Ratios for ITT and Textron

Year	Moody's*	ITT	Textron
1957	13.99	7.3	5.6
1958	18.03	12.1	5.4
1959	18.91	19.4	7.4
1960	18.00	20.6	7.4
1961	20.80	21.4	12.5
1962	17.11	16.8	9.0
1963	17.55	18.1	10.3
1964	18.02	20.0	11.0
1965	17.32	16.6	13.8
1966	15.90	16.8	12.7
1967	18.40	21.6	19.9
1968	17.97	20.8	23.5
1969	18.86	18.4	12.7
1970	17.70	14.3	10.1
1971	18.16	16.5	13.7
1972	17.87	14.8	14.4

*Weighted average calculation of 125 stocks selected by Moody's Industrial Manual, 1974.

EXHIBIT V-7

Financial Comparison of ITT and Textron

Year	Net Sales		Net Profit		Earnings/Share		Return on Invst.	
	ITT	Textron	ITT	Textron	ITT	Textron	ITT	Textron
1960	$ 811m	$ 383m	$30.6m	$14.1m	$0.98	$0.73	7.6%	9.5%
1961	930	473	36.1	10.5	1.09	0.51	8.2	7.9
1962	1090	549	40.7	14.8	1.21	0.74	8.3	9.9
1963	1414	587	52.5	18.0	1.35	0.85	9.0	11.8
1964	1542	720	63.2	22.1	1.55	1.02	10.2	11.4
1965	1783	851	76.1	29.1	1.79	1.31	10.6	14.5
1966	2121	1132	89.9	43.9	2.04	1.67	11.9	13.0
1967	2761	1446	119.2	61.5	2.27	2.02	10.1	15.3
1968	4067	1704	180.1	74.0	2.58	2.10	10.3	11.9
1969	5475	1682	234.0	76.1	2.90	2.14	10.7	14.0
1970	6364	1612	353.3	66.7	3.17	1.90	11.9	11.4
1971	7346	1603	406.8	71.8	3.45	2.06	11.8	12.2
1972	8557	1678	476.6	82.1	3.80	2.32	12.0	11.7

CHAPTER VI

FINDINGS, ANALYSIS, AND CONCLUSIONS

In this chapter, the findings of the previous three chapters are summarized, analyzed, and translated into conclusions. These conclusions apply only to the six firms in the study. Their implications for other firms are discussed in Chapter VII. This chapter has two distinct, but interrelated parts.

The first part contains an evaluation of the acquisition scanning processes used by the six firms in the study. Several different approaches to evaluation are explored from which two conclusions evolve. One conclusion is that the scanning processes of four of the six firms were generally appropriate. The other conclusion is that historical evaluation was inadequate for managerial action. The latter conclusion motivates the next part of the chapter.

The second part attempts to construct a model of the acquisition scanning process. Evaluations from the first part of the chapter indicate the extent to which the model should conform to the acquisition scanning processes described in the previous three chapters. The research design facilitates the construction of the model.

Evaluating Acquisition Scanning Processes

Evaluating acquisition scanning processes is a difficult task. These processes have many dimensions which are interrelated in complex ways. Also, adequate information upon which to base evaluations is often not available. For these reasons, four approaches to direct evaluation are proposed and applied to each of the firms in the study. Individually, these approaches are inadequate for credible evaluation. Collectively, these approaches indicate the general appropriateness of an acquisition scanning process for a firm.

Evaluation Approaches

Four useful bases for evaluating acquisition scanning processes are: (1) achievement of diversification objectives, (2) measurement of financial performance, (3) managerial judgment of success, and (4) analysis of specific instances. All of these bases focus predominantly on the results achieved by a firm using a particular acquisition process. The first two are quantitatively oriented, but accurate data is difficult to obtain. The last two bases are qualitatively oriented, but inputs are highly subjective. These approaches are described and discussed below.

Diversification Achievement.   One approach to evaluating an acquisition scanning process is to measure the impact of acquired companies on the diversity of a firm.   This impact is most easily measured as the portion of sales attributable to diversifying acquisitions at the end of the period under study.   This approach is more useful when diversity can be compared to an objective established at the beginning of the period.   None of the firms in this study explicitly formulated such objectives. Without these objectives, comparisons of the achieved diversity among the firms in the study provides a reasonable basis for evaluation.

One problem with this approach is that performance is confounded by the size and growth of businesses existing at the beginning of the period and by the timing of a series of acquisitions. The same series of acquisitions will achieve less diversity for larger firms and for firms which grow more rapidly than others during the period. Similarly, the same aggregate volume of acquisitions will achieve less diversity if acquired later in the period than earlier because the firm will receive less benefit from post acquisition growth.   Thus, this approach to evaluation favors smaller, slower growth firms which acquired companies earlier in the period.   It also favors firms which achieved higher post acquisition growth from acquired companies.   This problem can be reduced by judicious analysis of the available data.

Another problem with this approach is that diversification achieved through acquisition is a tenuous measure of scanning process appropriateness.   Achieved diversity tends to indicate an appropriate scanning process only when other acquisition objectives, such as financial performance goals, are achieved.   For the firms in this study, diversity was not generally viewed as a final objective, but as a means to more important objectives.   When diversity is not achieved, the scanning process cannot be deemed inappropriate without further examination. For example, an appropriate scanning process may discover that no suitable prospects are available, whereas an inappropriate process may fail to locate suitable candidates.   This problem can also be reduced by judicious use of research data.

Financial Performance.   Another approach to evaluating an acquisition scanning process is to measure the financial performance of specific or collective acquisitions.   Measures such as sales growth, profit growth, and return on invested capital are all appropriate for this purpose.   However, some of these measures can be adequately determined only for acquired companies which continue to remain operationally independent from the acquiring firm.   Most of the firms in the study which attempted to determine performance measures were unwilling to provide detailed or aggregate financial performance data for acquired companies. Using more aggregate firm data for evaluating financial performance inevitably lessens the usefulness of the conclusions which can be drawn from it.

The same problems which limited the usefulness of the diversification achievement approach also apply to the financial performance measurement using aggregated data. Unless acquisitions represent substantial diversification, their financial impact will be difficult to determine. In addition, relating financial performance to scanning process appropriateness is difficult when acquisitions have good financial performance and is tenuous otherwise. Poor performance may result from poor integration of an appropriate decision or from a poor decision based on inadequate information.

Another problem with financial performance measures is determining appropriate criteria for judging financial performance and the time horizon appropriate for judgment. Improving growth and profitability through diversification was a major motivation for acquisitions in all of the firms in the study. However, firms used different measurement dimensions, performance levels, and time horizons. Thus, comparisons among firms on performance measures alone distort intentions. Similarly, aggregate financial data limits the reliability of conclusions drawn from financial performance measures. In addition, the financial performance cannot often be achieved from an acquisition for several years so that financial performance is not reliable for more recent acquisitions.

Financial performance approaches to evaluation are therefore difficult to use and tenuous in result. Nevertheless, they can be important indicators when combined with other evaluation approaches and tempered with nonquantitative information. The remaining two approaches to evaluation attempt to systematically incorporate qualitative information into the evaluation process.

Managerial Judgment. A third approach to evaluating acquisition scanning processes is to ask the managers in the firms the extent to which they are satisfied with the process or the acquisitions which it produces. These managers apparently can evaluate the scanning process and the acquisition decisions with reasonable accuracy. The criteria which they use include not only some of the more objective measures of performance and impact, but also an assessment of the problems which the scanning process faced. These might include the internal resource limitations which hindered the scanning process.

The subjective nature of this form of evaluation makes it somewhat suspect. Managers involved in the process may tend to see acquisitions as more successful than do others in the firm or they may be unwilling to admit some inadequacies of their own programs. However, these evaluation problems were partly countered by the fact that most of the managers in the study could appraise the acquisition programs of their competitors. Generally these external appraisals corroborated the internal appraisals.

   Specific Instances. One final approach to evaluating acquisition scanning processes consists of examining particular acquisitions or opportunities for acquisition which highlight potentially appropriate or inappropriate scanning processes. This final approach is more selectively focused than those which were concerned with the overall results obtained by a firm's acquisition program. This approach permits some more detailed analysis than the other approaches. Perhaps more important, it is a major means for examining decisions not to acquire acquisition candidates.

   This approach lacks some reliability and validity since conclusions from the specific instances cannot be transferred easily to other prospective decisions or acquisition alternatives. They were selected less because of their representativeness than because the researcher felt they provided important insights into the process. Thus, while perhaps not useful for general evaluation, this approach does highlight some of the specific strengths and weaknesses inherent in the acquisition scanning processes of the firms in the study.

Scanning Process Evaluations

   When applied judiciously, these approaches to evaluation provide some indication of the appropriateness of the scanning process employed by the firms in the study. Individually, these evaluation approaches must be applied with considerable caution. However, their strengths and weaknesses complement one another. For example, financial performance is particularly meaningful when the achieved diversity is significant. Both approaches are more meaningful when compared to the managerial expectations and judgments about acquisition decisions. Specific instances provide illustrations and examples to support, or not support, conclusions drawn from the other three approaches.

   Below, these approaches to evaluation are applied to each of the firms in the study.[1] Data in the previous three chapters provides a basis for these evaluations.

   Norton. Norton's financial performance during the 1960-1972 period was the poorest of any of the firms in the study. However, throughout the period, Norton maintained its share of the domestic abrasives markets and expanded its participation in overseas abrasives markets. This accounted for most of the firm's sales growth. A considerably lower profit growth resulted from the unprofitable companies acquired during the 1962-1966 period, when much of the sales growth occurred, and divested later. Evidently, Norton's poor performance was largely attributable to poor acquisitions.

This evaluation of Norton is substantiated through an analysis of its diversity. Although the objective of 40% of sales from nonabrasive products by 1980 was not established until about 1970, it likely reflected earlier dissatisfaction with Norton's progress. Although abrasive products represented 64% of corporate sales in 1969, they represented 75% in 1972. This substantial increase was caused primarily by divestitures.

Managers involved in Norton's acquisition program in 1972 agreed that the previous programs had been unsuccessful. In their judgment, the potential impact of early acquisitions had not been adequately analyzed. The goals which motivated these acquisitions were short term oriented. It seems likely that the scanning system which provided information for these acquisition decisions was not adequate for the needs of the firm because of this short term orientation.

This evaluation is consistent with managerial judgments concerning the second acquisition program. These managers claimed that the top management was skeptical of acquisition proposals it reviewed. In response, acquisition scanners gathered excessive amounts of inappropriate information. One Norton manager who was not a scanner in the second program noted that he could find a reason to reject almost any acquisition proposal if that were his initial intention and disposition. He felt both scanners and top management searched for and gathered information from that point of view during the second program. Related to this credibility problem, the scanning process focused on a limited number of markets for entry. Information was gathered without regard for the availability of candidates within those markets. Later management judged this to be an inappropriate approach to scanning for acquisitions.

Although no specific instances can be cited about the second acquisition program, the 1964 acquisition of Clipper Manufacturing supported the observation that acquisitions during Norton's first program were not well planned and that inadequate information was gathered. This acquisition increased Norton's sensitivity to the capital goods cycle and thereby compounded its problem of fluctuating sales, earnings, and cash flows.

Since the third acquisition program had been in existence for only a short time and since only two small companies had been acquired by 1972, financial performance and achieved diversity were not appropriate approaches for evaluating its scanning processes. Nevertheless, management felt that the problems of the earlier programs had been rectified and that the objectives of the third program were modest and well within Norton's foreseeable financial constraints.

Two specific instances, both nonoccurrences, raised some questions concerning the appropriateness of the scanning processes for the third program. The first was that during the previous two years Norton had not consummated any Type I acquisitions. Management felt that no candidates were available in markets related to Norton's existing nonabrasives divisions. However, division managers had not been motivated to search for or gather information about any candidates which might compete in related markets. In view of this organizational limitation, and the limited scanning resources available to the corporate staff, it seemed inadvisable for Norton to pursue Type I acquisitions. However, Mr. Johnson began his investigation of the plastics industry to help and encourage one division to plan for acquisitions and internal development. Without some organizational changes the likelihood of his success appeared low.

As a second specific instance, the search for Type II acquisitions had also proved fruitless during the previous two years. There were indications that it would continue to be fruitless in the future. Mr. Griffin claimed that because only a small number of companies were willing to be acquired, gathering significant amounts of information before availability was determined was an inefficient approach to acquisition scanning. This same logic would suggest that pursuing several large companies, with the hope that one might be willing to be acquired, was also inefficient. Yet, Mr. Griffin adopted this course of action. Managers in others firms in the study either had similar fruitless experiences in tracking specific companies or attested to its inefficiency. Furthermore, reflecting on its past experiences, top management would likely remain skeptical of proposals which would involve substantial investments until the acquisition staff had demonstrated some positive results. Therefore, active search for Type II acquisition prospects appeared inappropriate for Norton.

These two specific instances did not indicate that Norton's third acquisition program would not succeed. Rather, examination of the two Type III acquisitions suggested likely success. The industries in which both of these companies competed were discovered by accident, as was a third potential industry for entry. Unless this experience was unusual, Norton could expect to continue to identify an adequate number of industries for entry through Type III acquisitions. Furthermore, by the acquisition criteria, these industries were fragmented and in a developmental stage. Under these conditions, it could be predicted that either horizontal or related acquisition candidates could be identified easily. Therefore, the acquisition scanning process for Type III acquisitions appeared appropriate for Norton. Nevertheless, the probability of achieving the diversity objective could be improved by temporarily abandoning searches for Type I and Type II acquisitions and focusing limited scanning resources primarily on Type III acquisitions and Type I acquisitions which related to them.

Carborundum.   Although Carborundum's overall financial performance was considerably below that of several other firms in the study, its overall growth of 7.5% was somewhat better than Norton's and its profit growth of 6.5% was substantially better.   Like Norton, Carborundum maintained its share of the domestic abrasives markets. However, it expanded more vigorously overseas during the period than did Norton.   Much of this sales growth and profit growth occurred during the early part of the period when Carborundum completed most of its acquisitions.   Therefore, early period growth can be largely attributed to Carborundum's acquisition activity.   Since Carborundum's profitability remained stable during the later part of the period, early acquisitions appeared to be relatively successful in financial terms.

The success of the acquisition program in terms of the diversity achieved is difficult to determine.   Carborundum had not established explicit diversification objectives for its acquisition program.   Overall diversification plans include internal development and joint ventures in addition to acquisitions.   During the 1968-1972 period, Carborundum did not acquire any companies to increase its diversification.   Nevertheless, 30% of 1972 sales and about 70% of all sales ·growth was attributable to companies acquired after 1960.   This indicated a substantial impact of diversifying acquisitions on Carborundum's diversity.

Several managerial judgments provide perspective for these quantitative measures and further indicate that the diversifying acquisitions and the scanning process which generated them were generally appropriate.   Management felt that this program had been successful.   Carborundum's published statements attempted to convey the impression that the company was highly diversified as a result of sound management decisions.   Nevertheless, several managers acknowledged that Carborundum should have acquired more companies during the late 1960s.

Managers felt that reduced acquisition activity in the latter part of the period did not indicate any inappropriate scanning process. Rather, they felt this resulted from strategic priorities which were based on overly optimistic forecasts of the impact of new product development. Because of these forecasts, Carborundum had reduced its emphasis on acquisition as a means of growth and diversification.   Most managers believed that Carborundum's financial performance and diversity would have been higher if the emphasis on acquisitions had not been reduced. Implicitly they assumed that additional acquisitions would have been successful.

Some managers hinted that this problem might not have occurred if the same manager had not been responsible for both research and development and acquisition scanning. That manager had little formal experience in acquisition scanning prior to assuming the role in 1967 and Carborundum had not acquired any companies since that time. Although this might indicate an inappropriate participant in the scanning process, the broader context of the acquisition program indicates otherwise. The participant was apparently selected because of a change in corporate priorities and behaved within the context of those priorities.

Two specific instances tend to support the general appropriateness of Carborundum's acquisition scanning process, but indicate some opportunity for improvement. Carborundum's acquisition of Curtis and Tysaman suggested the importance of relating acquisitions to the overall strategy of the firm. The purpose of these acquisitions was to support Carborundum's market position in abrasives. They were capital goods manufacturers which affected Carborundum's cash flow much as Clipper affected Norton's. Carborundum eventually sold its capital goods product lines partially for that reason.

However, Carborundum considered these acquisitions successful whereas Norton considered Clipper a failure. Carborundum's acquisition objectives were achieved because the acquired companies did help the firm maintain its abrasives market position, even though they were not themselves highly profitable. Carborundum then did gather and process sufficient amounts of information to set realistic objectives for each of its acquisitions.

Yet, a second specific instance suggests that Carborundum's acquisition scanning process was overly structured or focused. Pangborn was acquired for the same reasons that Curtis and Tysaman were. Outside observers, as well as managers, commented that Pangborn was the firm's outstanding acquisition because it provided entry into several pollution control markets. Thus, the major benefit of the acquisition was not recognized prior to its consummation. Carborundum's information gathering focused primarily on its abrasive machinery operations, which were the major motive for the acquisition.

Apparently Carborundum's management profited from this fortuitous acquisition in experience, as well as in monetary terms. By 1967 Mr. Wendel was claiming that Carborundum could diversify into any market through its concept of vectored growth. The Copeland acquisition exemplified this broadened attitude vividly. Thus, these specific instances suggest that the firm's acquisition scanning process was generally appropriate.

Philip Morris. Although Philip Morris performed very well by most financial measures, its acquisition program was not the major cause. Throughout the period, tobacco industry sales had been growing moderately, but Philip Morris doubled its market share through its strategic concentration on filter cigarettes. In addition, it expanded vigorously in overseas tobacco markets. Because raw material price differentials favored filter cigarette manufacture, Philip Morris also enjoyed high profitability. Under these conditions, the firm achieved its goal of compound annual sales growth greater than 10%.

This performance could not be attributed to diversifying acquisitions because by 1972 Philip Morris was still relatively undiversified. It had a larger share of its sales in one product line than any other firm in the study. Because of the rapid growth of the tobacco business and the commensurate limited availability of funds to support diversification, any objectives related to corporate diversity had been revoked as impossible to achieve. This problem was best exemplified by the Miller Brewing acquisition. Although Miller was large enough to be among the 500 largest industrial companies in the United States when Philip Morris acquired it, Miller's total sales about equaled Philip Morris' cigarette sales increase for that same year.

Therefore, in terms of diversity achieved through acquisition, the Philip Morris acquisition scanning process could not be evaluated. Similarly, its financial performance results could not be evaluated, except to the extent that Miller apparently continued to gain market share in the brewing industry following the acquisition. The scanning process seemed adequate for the needs and capabilities of the firm. Whether it could provide for increased diversity in the future when tobacco business decelerated could not be assessed by the criteria of diversity achieved or financial performance.

All of the managers at Philip Morris indicated that its acquisition programs had been successful. Mr. Poole indicated that he would have preferred to acquire more companies, but felt that within the constrained resources available for acquisitions, the program had been very successful. He also indicated that Philip Morris was in a good position to make future acquisitions when resources became available. He felt that his staff's information gathering had not only provided the basis for acquisitions in the future, but also had provided the basis for intelligently monitoring the future planning of acquired companies.

However, two specific instances challenged the appropriateness of the acquisition scanning process at Philip Morris. In both cases, management did not fully understand the competitive requirements for successful competition or how to respond to them.

First, in acquiring Clark, Philip Morris planned to market chewing gum in the same way it marketed cigarettes. Management apparently felt that Philip Morris had important marketing skills which could be successfully applied to any frequently purchased and intensively advertised and distributed consumer product. However, by sharing Philip Morris' marketing resources, Clark could not gain and maintain its market share. Part of the problem was that the marketing organization was unwilling to direct sufficient resources from its dominant and successful cigarette products. The other part of the problem was that the chewing gum industry did not have an emerging growth market into which Clark could position itself as Philip Morris had done in cigarettes.

Second, Philip Morris's entry into, and relatively rapid exit from, several hospital supply markets in 1967 indicated that the acquisition scanning process had not identified the major requirements for success in those markets. The purpose of these acquisitions was to strengthen American Safety Razor's position in surgical blade markets. Unfortunately, the major competitors in these markets were wide-product-line producers (e.g., Johnson & Johnson) with superior distribution systems. Philip Morris' surgical supply business did not have the requisite volume to support such a system. Its acquisition scanning system did not identify this major requirement for success.

However, as a third specific instance, the acquisition of Miller in 1969 indicated that Philip Morris had improved its scanning process considerably. Unlike most breweries, Miller was an acceptable candidate because it had a strong product position in the growth market of the industry and it had the marketing resources to develop that position. Furthermore, Philip Morris understood that national distribution was a major competitive requirement for long term success in the industry. Thus, while some earlier acquisitions indicated inadequacies, the scanning process which gathered information about the brewing industry was appropriate.

Two factors about the Miller acquisition suggested a possible future scanning problem for Philip Morris. First, the planner who finally persuaded management to enter the brewing industry had managerial experience in that industry, which provided him with access to significant amounts of information. Second, much information was published about the brewing industry as it matured. Several of the markets or industries about which Philip Morris' planners were gathering information were still in developmental stages. The information available about these industries was much less complete and less certain than information about the brewing industry. Also, none of the planners had previous experience with them.

The potential problem was whether or not planners could adequately forecast the competitive requirements and developmental rates of these markets. The thoroughness with which planners gathered and processed information about markets for entry suggested that they could forecast as well as anyone.   However, accurate information about the future of developing markets was unavailable and anyone's forecast was highly uncertain.   For entry into these types of markets, Philip Morris' acquisition scanning process was apparently adequate.

American Brands.   In terms of aggregate financial results, American Brands' performance was mixed.   Its growth rate throughout the period was among the lowest in the study.   Although its return on investment was satisfactory, it was not as good as its competitor, Philip Morris.   However, these aggregate results are deceiving.   As a late entrant to the filter cigarette market, American Brands' share of the domestic tobacco markets declined during the period.   While sales growth rate for the entire period was 7.0%, growth rate since 1965 was 13.6%.   Also, all of American Brands acquisitions were completed after 1965, including one major acquisition in overseas tobacco markets.

The impact of acquisitions on this performance is more clearly represented in the diversity which American Brands achieved after 1965. Most of is 30% nontobacco sales had been acquired in the five years from 1966 to 1970.   This diversity compared favorably with the 26% achieved by Norton and the 30% by Carborundum in considerably longer time periods.   Although explicit goals had not been articulated for diversification, management apparently sought to diversify as rapidly as possible.   There were indications that American Brands did not have the financial and managerial capacity to diversify at a more rapid rate than it did without injuring its tobacco business.   Since the financial performance was improved and maintained following these acquisitions, the acquisition program was apparently successful.

In addition, American Brands generally felt that the acquisition program had been successful and that the companies which it acquired would provide strong growth and profitability in the future.   Sustained performance following the acquisitions indicated the success of its acquisition scanning process.   This was particularly true in light of the handicaps facing Mr. Walker at the time he began to search for diversifying acquisitions.   Although one early acquisition was not fully successful, the post acquisition performance of the others was more than satisfactory to the management.

In combination, three specific instances suggested that American Brands' scanning process was adequate by the end of the period under study.   Its first acquisition, Sunshine Biscuit, had never really been successful.   The reorientation of the product line over the years following the acquisition suggested the inappropriateness of Sunshine's strategy prior to the acquisition.   The replacement of the acquired management suggested the inadequacy of the incumbent management.   The competive problems which remained following these changes suggested that

American Brands' management did not really understand the competitive requirements of the business. Other firms in this study had rejected Sunshine as an acquisition opportunity because they had gathered information which revealed the competitive, strategic, and managerial problems plaguing Sunshine.

However, about the time Sunshine was acquired, American Brands rejected the Buckingham Corporation as an acquisition opportunity because its sellers wanted an excessive price for a one-brand liquor distributorship. The rejection was based on financial information, suggesting that this was the major type of information gathered about acquisition candidates.   Other firms in the study had also been approached by Buckingham's sellers and had rejected it for the same reasons. If evaluated primarily on a financial basis, Sunshine appeared to be an acceptable candidate.   This reinforced the observation that American Brands gathered primarily financial information during the early part of its acquisition program.

The third selected incidence was the acquisition of Master Lock. Its performance both before and after the acquisition was outstanding by several measures. One other firm in the study regretfully rejected Master Lock as an acquisition opportunity before it was presented to American Brands.   The rejection was based on a lack of fit with the firm's corporate strategy and the regret was that the performance prospects of the company were considered quite good.

Therefore, as part of its scanning process, American Brands learned quickly how to evaluate candidates in relatively unfamiliar industries by evaluating both financial and managerial capability. They related well to American Brands' strategy.   As part of this strategy, acquired companies continued to operate as relatively independent divisions under their former managements.   In this regard, American Brands resembled a holding company more than any other firm in the study. Competent incumbent management willing to remain with their company after an acquisition was essential to American Brands as was future financial performance.   American Brands' acquisition scanning process was appropriate because it apparently focused on the areas of greatest strategic concern.

ITT.   In terms of growth in sales and profits, ITT was clearly superior to the other firms in the study. Because of its conglomerate strategy, acquisitions were the major reason for this performance. Mr. Geneen, ITT's president, claimed that ITT could have exceeded its objective of 10% growth in earnings per share without its acquisition. This seemed somewhat plausible, particularly in the latter part of the period, since ITT issued stock for many of the companies it acquired. Some of these acquisitions had diluted the earnings per share, although certainly this was not the aggregate effect.   Thus, financial results strongly imply that ITT's acquisition scanning process, and the acquisitions which it produced, was successful.

The success with which ITT achieved diversity while maintaining substantial growth in its telecommunications business provides strong evidence in support of the appropriateness of its acquisition scanning process for achieving diversity.   During the period, ITT achieved all of its diversity, reducing its original telecommunications business to only 22% of corporate sales.   Nevertheless, ITT claimed that over half of its annual growth was internally generated.   In the latter part of the period, most of this internal growth was the result of companies acquired in the early part of the period.

Generally, ITT's management felt that the firm's acquisition program had been successful and pointed to its financial results and its diversity as evidence.   Mr. Doyle noted that between 65% and 70% of all acquisitions were successful in the sense that the forecasts contained in the board notes were achieved or exceeded and that only about 15% were total failures.   He felt this record was admirable, particularly in light of the large number of companies which ITT had acquired.   Nevertheless, some of management's frustrations with the antitrust law enforcement (which led to the forced divestitures of three major acquisitions) indicated some frustrations over the program.   Since there was a pronounced change in this enforcement in 1969, neither the acquisition program, nor the scanning process, could be faulted on this ground.   In general, management's evaluation appeared realistic and appropriate.   It was one of the few evaluations firmly based on the forecasts which management completed prior to its acquisitions.

One major acquisition at ITT highlighted a potential weakness in the scanning system.   This major acquisition was a total failure in terms of both revenues produced and post-acquisition investments required to maintain it.   The acquisition analysis group recommended that ITT not acquire this company.   Mr. Geneen acquired the company despite the recommendation.   In retrospect, the information gathered by the analysis group was accurate and its predictions correct.   Thus, Mr. Geneen's formally constituted scanning process was more appropriate, for this acquisition, than his own formal scanning system.

The potential problem was apparently a result of the decision maker, Mr. Geneen, also assuming the role of sponsor or advocate for a candidate.   In light of the acquisition staff's historical performance, acting counter to its recommendation without adequately analyzing the conflicting information seemed inappropriate.   Not only did it produce a poor decision, but also, if repeated occasionally, could destroy the morale and motivation of the acquisition scanning group.

Textron.   Although Textron's financial performance appeared admirable during the period, further analysis revealed some problems. Its return on investment was higher than that of the other firms in the study and remained over 11% in every year after 1962.   Its growth in sales was second only to ITT's.   However, all of this growth came prior to 1969 and return on investment dropped considerably after that time. Some of this change was attributed to significant reductions in helicopter sales and in overall acquisition activity.   Some of it was also attributable to the slow growth of companies acquired earlier in the period.   During the 1961-1965 period, Textron claimed that over 75% of its annual growth was internally generated; that growth rate was not sustained in the 1969-1972 period.   Nevertheless, Textron exceeded its objective of 20% pre-tax return on investment throughout seven of the last eight years of the period under study achieving 28% in 1967.   Major attempts to expand overseas toward the end of the period suggest that while achieving return, management also wanted to continue corporate growth. In this sense, Textron's acquisition scanning process may have been inadequate.   Financial data does not permit an evaluation of the acquisition program which began under Mr. Murphy in 1971.

Generally speaking, the success with which Textron achieved diversity provided evidence to support the success of its acquisition scanning process.   However, Textron had not achieved the balance desired among the various segments of the U.S. manufacturing economy. Substantial portions of its growth during the mid 1960s resulted from rapid helicopter sales increases for the Viet Nam war.   In 1967, the aerospace product group represented 44% of Textron's sales, although no important acquisitions in the aerospace group were reported after 1960. As aerospace sales declined during the following year, new diversifying acquisitions were inadequate to maintain corporate sales growth although they did restore balance somewhat.   The acquisition program under Mr. Murphy could, if resulting in sufficient consumer production acquisitions, again upset the desired balance.   In 1972, consumer products represented 33% of corporate sales and was the fastest growing product group at Textron.   However, the new acquisition program and the new acquisition scanning process could not be evaluated by the diversity criteria.

Although Textron's management generally expressed satisfaction with the acquisition program, some evidence indicated that it was conditional on the frame of reference.   The retarded sales growth during the late 1960s disturbed the management, although the return on investment remained satisfactory.   The shift toward a "more selective program" under Mr. Murphy was possibly a response to inadequate growth.   Some Textron managers implied that they did not expect the program to produce acquisitions.   However, they were unconcerned about this expectation.   A view of other corporate activity indicated a possible explanation. The president was preparing the firm organizationally for a major overseas expansion which would require significant investments. Unless an outstanding company could be acquired on favorable terms (a highly selective approach), he would have preferred to invest available funds overseas. Under this interpretation, the new acquisition program could achieve its goals without producing a stream of acquisitions. In any event, managers at Textron did not indicate dissatisfaction with the acquisition program which the firm maintained throughout the 1960s.

Two specific instances suggested some possible inadequacies in the Textron acquisition scanning process. They were both foregone acquisition opportunities. In 1968 Textron agreed to bid for the stock of United Fruit and in 1971 it agreed to bid for the stock of the Kendall Company. Either of these candidates would have been Textron's largest acquisition. Published reports indicated that as other bidders increased their offers for these companies, Textron withdrew because it had already bid what it believed to be a full and fair price. However, comments by Textron managers suggested that Textron had gathered additional information about these firms and reconsidered their desirability. The increased offers of other bidders enabled Textron to withdraw gracefully. If Textron did not gather sufficient information about these significant opportunities before submitting its bids, then Textron may not have gathered sufficient information about some of its other Type II acquisitions. In general, Textron's record did not support this proposition. Nevertheless, Textron divested several product lines during 1966 which were not achieving the expectations of corporate management. Although the specific instance cited here raises some questions about the appropriateness of Textron's acquisition scanning process, through 1971, it does not alter the previous evaluation.

Overall Evaluation

One overall evaluation of each firm in the study can be constructed by combining these four approaches: overall financial results, achievement of diversification objectives, managerial judgments, and analyses of specific instances.[2] By all measures, Norton's acquisition scanning process through 1969 was inappropriate. For the program since that time, no overall evaluations are provided since the data is inconclusive. For Carborundum, the overall evaluation reflects the earlier evaluations. The Philip Morris program was not evaluated primarily because of its nature. Acquisitions to date were generally successful, but if the real concern of Philip Morris' management was preparedness to utilize eventual cash flow, that preparedness could not be adequately evaluated. American Brands and ITT generally had appropriate acquisition scanning processes by almost any measure. Textron's acquisition scanning process through 1970 was generally appropriate despite its growth problems toward the end of the period. The program under Mr. Murphy could not be evaluated. Since it began, Textron had not acquired any companies and managerial reactions to it seemed mixed.

One conclusion which can be drawn from this evaluation is that there was no one best way to scan for domestic diversifying acquisitions. Each of the four successful firms was different in some way. Carborundum and Textron involved the largest number of people in the process, while American Brands involved the smallest number. ITT and American Brands relied primarily on staff groups, whereas Textron and Carborundum avoided them. American Brands, ITT, and Textron all identified acquisition alternatives through intermediaries, whereas Carborundum did not. Then, the data from this research does not yield a consistent composite description of the appropriate scanning process for all the successful firms in this study. Such a composite would provide a basis for evaluating the Norton, Philip Morris, and Textron acquisition scanning programs which could not be evaluated in Exhibit VI-3.

A second conclusion is that managers need some procedure for evaluating their acquisition scanning processes independently of evaluating the results which they produce. Such a procedure would aid initial process design as well as periodic review or continual monitoring of the process. Furthermore, as indicated by the experience of Norton and Textron, the acquisitions resulting from the process sometimes cannot be evaluated for several years. Philip Morris, for example, could not afford to wait for several years after its cigarette business decelerated to decide if its acquisition scanning process were appropriate. Since this research indicates that there is no one best way to design an acquisition scanning process for all firms, the remainder of this report attempts to construct a situational model which can be used to evaluate acquisition scanning processes.

Modeling the Acquisition Scanning Process

Developing a model of the acquisition scanning process for the six firms in the study requires defining a set of dependent variables, a set of independent variables, and a set of relationships between them. These relationships will be in part derived from or corroborated by the data in the previous three chapters for the four firms in the study which apparently utilized appropriate scanning processes. The resulting model should be useful for assessing the appropriateness of the acquisition scanning processes of Norton, Philip Morris, and Textron, where the performance evaluations were inadequate. Developing and applying the model is the work of the remainder of this chapter.

Dependent Variables

The dependent variables were described in Chapter II as the characteristics of a scanning process. These characteristics were: (1) the types of information gathered, (2) the sources of market information, (3) the sources of prospect information, (4) the types of information processing, (5) the backgrounds, experiences, and organizational positions of the scanners, and (6) the sequence in which scanning activities were performed. In Chapters III, IV, and V, these characteristics provided a framework for describing the scanning processes of the six firms in the study.[4]

Independent Variables

Four general types of independent variables were anticipated in Chapter II and in the research design. These were: (1) universal variables, whose values would have the same effect on the acquisition scanning processes of all the firms in the study; (2) industry variables, whose values would have the same effect on all the firms within the same industry; (3) strategy variables, whose values would have the same effect on all the firms following the same diversification strategy; and (4) firm variables, whose values would be different for each firm, or would not be patterned in the same way as the other types of variables among the firms in the study.

Variables of each type can be identified from the research data in the previous chapters.[4] Four universal variables affected the scanning processes of the firms in the study, including, the availability of information, the state of the economy, the enforcement of antitrust laws, and the financial disclosure requirements. The most important of these was the availability of information. The major industry variables were the products, customers, competitive structures, and future prospects of the industry. The strategy variable with the most significant impact was the relationship between the firm's existing businesses and those it planned to acquire. The firm variables included organizational structure, management's experiences with successful acquisitions, and the leadership style of the chief executive officer.

Relationships Among Variables

Relationships among variables can be determined in two ways. First, managers within the firms indicated some of the major factors which they felt influenced the design or operation of their acquisition scanning process. Second, the research observed some similarities and differences among the firms and industries which suggested additional factors which had substantial influence on their processes. Each of the four types of variables are discussed below in terms of their influence on the scanning process.

Universal Variables.   The relationship between universal variables and the scanning process cannot be deduced by comparing firms for which values of these variables were different. The values of these variables were the same for all of the firms in the study. Also, their values remained essentially the same throughout the period under study. Although several universal variables affected acquisition activity during this period, only the availability of information appeared to have a significant impact on acquisition scanning processes. Other universal variables which did not appear to have a major influence on the scanning process included the prosperity of the economy, the requirements for financial disclosure, and the interpretation and enforcement of antitrust laws.[5]

The lack of compatible information about specific markets for possible entry limited the ability of firms to systematically compare markets on the basis of their established criteria. Without this ability, firms could not inexpensively screen markets or portfolios of markets to optimize their performance, regardless of what criteria they adopted. The emergence of new markets represented acquisition opportunities which could not be identified easily since lists were not maintained at a disaggregated level. Information at more aggregated levels often combined growing and declining markets. The averaged data further limited the ability of firms to identify specific market opportunities.

Therefore, firms could identify markets in one of three ways. First, through informal scanning managers could identify market opportunities on a somewhat random basis. Second, managers could select an industry or group of markets which collectively had desirable properties (e.g., same technology as the firm's existing products) and monitor it for market opportunities. Third, managers could identify candidates and then systematically gather information about the markets in which they competed.

The first approach was not useful because the markets identified in this way often could not be entered at an appropriate price. The latter two approaches to identifying market opportunities were the most prevalent observed in this study. Markets for entry through related acquisitions were usually identified through monitoring broader industries. Firms usually monitored these related industries to some extent and usually had access to appropriate sources of information. This approach applied primarily to Type I acquisitions. For unrelated acquisitions, firms could often determine priorities for industries to monitor. Thus, for Type II acquisitions, firms usually did not identify markets for entry prior to identifying prospects, except to a limited extent through informal scanning. After market opportunities were identified, information about them could be gathered from many sources. For Type I acquisitions, a firm usually had access to these sources of information. For Type II acquisitions, a firm usually had access to published information and could not obtain additional information without substantial cost.

Information about privately owned companies was generally not available from published sources. Therefore, access to sources of unpublished information was important in order to evaluate most smaller acquisitions. This access was more economically available to firms which competed in markets related to those of a prospect than to firms which were unrelated. Without access to these sources of information, firms usually obtained information directly from acquisition prospects. Prospects would provide this information only if they were interested in being acquired. Thus, firms seeking to acquire privately owned companies which competed in markets not related to their existing businesses usually gathered information only about candidates. If privately owned companies competed in markets related to their existing businesses, firms could gather information about several prospects without regard for their interest in being acquired.

Information about publicly owned companies was available from published sources. Publication of this information was required by the stock exchanges and governmental agencies, particularly the Securities and Exchange Commission. However, because of their economic importance and investment potential, many general business and industry trade publications also contained information about many of these companies. This information facilitated evaluation of companies unrelated to the business of a firm. Although easy to gather, it was generally inadequate for determining the ability of a firm to achieve synergy through acquisition. Information for this determination could often be obtained only from a company to be acquired. Thus, firms seeking Type I acquisitions generally could not rely primarily on published information, whereas firms seeking Type II acquisitions could make relatively good evaluations based on published information.

Information availability then determined two general approaches to acquisition scanning, one for Type I acquisitions and one for Type II acquisitions. Firms seeking to enter markets related to their existing businesses generally identified markets for entry before gathering much information about prospects for acquisition and often sought smaller privately owned companies which would be easier to integrate with existing operations. Firms seeking to enter markets unrelated to their existing businesses generally identified acquisition candidates before selecting markets to enter and often sought larger publicly owned companies about which substantial amounts of published information was available.

Industry Variables. The relationship between industry variables and the scanning process was somewhat confounded by both the strategy variables and the firm variables. Nevertheless, the products and customers, market structure, and future prospects of an industry appeared to influence the scanning process.[6]

Differences in products and customers affected the directions in which firms chose initially to diversify. Carborundum initially entered other industrial products markets and American Brands initially entered other consumer products markets. In both cases, the firms expected that the managerial problems of competing within these types of markets would be more similar than the problems of competing among them. Similar behavior was exhibited in most of the other firms in the study at the beginning of their diversification programs. The major impact of this difference was in the types of markets rejected by the acquisition criteria and hence in the types of information gathered. The impact of this variable appeared to influence the process primarily during the early periods of the firms' programs. Later, its relationship to the scanning process appeared unimportant.

Competitive structure and future prospects appeared to have joint effects on the acquisition scanning process. The primary difference in market structure was the stability of market shares in the abrasives industry compared to the shifting shares in the tobacco industry. The primary difference in future prospects was the rate and predictability of industry growth or decline. With a continuing and stable market share in a growing but decelerating industry, Carborundum did not perceive strong pressures for immediate performance improvement through acquisition.[7] Therefore, Carborundum gathered information which focused on the ability to achieve synergistic benefits within a longer time horizon. With a declining share of an industry which could decline rapidly, American Brands perceived strong pressures for immediate performance improvement through acquisition. In response to these pressures, American Brands sought to acquire large companies with established growth trends. Furthermore, its criteria focused on financial information and avoided substantial information processing. Because its focus was more short term oriented, American Brands was unconcerned about achieving potential synergistic benefits. Finally, its scanning process identified candidates only through intermediaries to insure that scanning would be productive without long delays. Carborundum contrasted with American Brands on each of these dimensions.

Thus, industry variables appeared related to the scanning process in two ways. First, and less important, they limited the early search for markets to those with some similarity to the firm's existing businesses. Second, and more important, industry variables influenced the perceived urgency of improving short term performance through acquisition.

Strategy Variables. The relationship between strategy variables and the scanning process was more easily observed than that between industry variables and the process. Carborundum adopted a related market strategy in which every market which it entered related to other markets in which it competed. ITT and Textron followed an unrelated market strategy although they also acquired companies in related markets of existing divisions. American Brands followed an unrelated market strategy but did not search for companies in related markets.[8]

The scanning processes used by the two conglomerate firms were similar to one another and were similar to the one used by American Brands. However, all three were considerably different than the one used by Carborundum. The similarities apparently resulted from a common perceived urgency of improving short term performance through acquisition. The conglomerate firms required diversifying acquisitions to maintain their historical financial performance and thus encourage investors to increase their price/earnings ratios. In contrast, American Brands perceived urgency emanating from the tobacco industry environment rather than from its investors.

Firms generally gathered significantly more information about prospects which competed in related markets than about those which competed in unrelated markets. A major motivation for related acquisitions was the synergy benefit with could be derived from combining some parts of their formerly separate operations. To insure that synergy was attained, scanners necessarily gathered a sufficient amount of information about prospects to determine what changes would be required to combine operations. In addition, they needed to determine the impact of those changes on the competitive posture of a company in its markets or potential markets.

For unrelated acquisitions, only financial and corporate management resources of the firm were allocated between the firm and its acquired company. Operation synergy was not a motivation for these acquisitions. No changes in the operations of the acquired company would necessarily result for the acquisition to be successful. Therefore, financial and managerial information about prospects were most important. If the firm determined that the incumbent management of a prospect had the capability and motivation to meet its performance expectations through the utilization of specified resources, detailed information about how the resources were to be utilized was not required for the acquisition decision. Therefore, firms required less information about unrelated acquisition prospects than about related ones. Also, the types of information to be gathered were significantly different.

Firm Variables. The relationships of the three kinds of variables described above did not explain all of the differences in the scanning processes of the firms in the study. Nor did they fully explain why four of the firms in the study were successful while Norton's earlier programs were failures. Some of these residual differences were explained by the organizational policies of the firms in the study, the management's experience with successful acquisitions, and the leadership style of the chief executive officer, and how they influenced the acquisition scanning process.[9]

The organization of a firm had an important influence on the acquisition scanning processes for related acquisitions. Sources of information about related acquisition prospects were more accessible to the managers of business units to which their markets related. The organizational policies of firms with successful acquisition scanning processes facilitated the participation of these unit managers in the scanning and decision making. In addition to gathering information, these managers could also evaluate the significance of information. For related acquisitions, information about changes in the prospect's operation was inadequate by itself. In addition, information about the changes in the firm's operations required to accommodate the acquired company was also necessary. Business unit managers could evaluate the impact of these changes on the firm. Carborundum appeared to recognize this necessity implicitly. When seeking to enter a new market, it often located a former executive with experience in that market and hired him as a permanent employee to familiarize him with Carborundum's operations. ITT recognized this necessity more explicitly. Mr. Geneen never forced a division manager to accept particular acquisition proposals.

Organizational policy facilitated the participation of business unit managers when it induced working relationships with corporate scanners and when it motivated the effort required for scanning, negotiation, and integration. Three firms in the study established working relationships in three different ways. At Carborundum, Mr. Wendel was directly involved in the scanning process and maintained frequent, informal personal communication with appropriate division managers to insure their participation. At ITT, the stature of various corporate staff groups insured the involvement of division managers in scanning for related business acquisitions. At Textron, the close relationship between group vice presidents and division presidents facilitated the scanning process. In most firms, the increased power and remuneration of managing larger and more successful divisions often provided additional motivation for the divisional managements to become involved in the acquisition scanning process.

Organizational policy also influenced the scanning process for unrelated business acquisitions. For these acquisitions, firms needed rapid access to many types of information about many different markets and industries. They also needed to formulate judgments based on the limited information they could gather. Organizational policies which involved more managers in the scanning, encouraged those managers to develop broad networks of associates who could be sources of information, enabled those managers to develop their abilities to analyze new situations in creative ways generally, and facilitated the scanning process. However, firms without these characteristics could utilize general management consultants and financial analysts to provide adequate information. Managers with considerable acquisitions experience generally indicated that these sources were expensive and therefore useful only for a limited number of acquisition prospects or to help a firm develop its own internal acquisition scanning expertise.

Three firms in the study represented a wide range of alternative organizational arrangements to facilitate scanning for unrelated business acquisitions. With its large corporate staff, ITT could gather significantly more information about prospects and their markets than could American Brands or Textron. Staff groups with functional expertise and experience in many markets could often gather information quickly and inexpensively. The participation of most all Textron corporate executives, particularly the group vice presidents, partially compensated for the lack of functional staff to gather information. These general managers were familiar with many different market situations and collectively had often gathered significant amounts of information about market opportunities. Also, their general management experience enabled them to determine the significance of information gathered about particular acquisition candidates. To compensate for this lack of functional staff or general managers, American Brands retained consultants to help gather and use information about acquisition opportunities. No one best organizational policy facilitated the acquisition scanning process for unrelated acquisitions. To the extent that adequate resources were not provided by the policy, external resources were required.

Regardless of the organizational policies, one executive served as the acquisition scanning coordinator in each firm to combine information gathered by them inside and outside the firm. This executive worked closely with the chief executive officer. In all cases, the chief executive either proposed or endorsed acquisition proposals which the board of directors ratified. As such, they were the ultimate recipients of information which was gathered and processed by the acquisition scanners. The scanners necessarily considered the needs of both the chief executive and the board of directors. When the board habitually ratified proposals with little or no opposition, the scanners were primarily concerned with the information needs of the chief executive to make his decision. When the board did not actively support the diversifying acquisition program, the scanners were concerned with the information needs of the chief executive to both make his own decision and convince the board to make that decision.

This suggests a second and related firm variable, the amount of experience and success a firm had with diversifying acquisitions. Boards of directors were more willing to actively support diversifying acquisition programs after the firm had completed several successful acquisitions. However, until success was demonstrated, the boards needed some assurance that the proposals they received were appropriate for their firms. In providing that assurance, the sources of information and recommendation were often as important as the information itself. Directors, recognizing the potential biases of information generated from within the organization, found information from consultants, financial analysts, or other neutral sources more credible. This need for credibility was particularly apparent when firms first began diversification programs and the boards were either uncertain of the appropriateness of diversification or uncertain of the management's competence to plan for it. Most firms which had employed neutral sources of information early in their programs later abandoned this requirement after managers had demonstrated their competence. During this formative period, the organizational policies were important to facilitate development of appropriate scanning skills.

The scanning processes also varied somewhat in response to the leadership styles of the chief executive officers. This style, together with the organizational policies and experiences of the firm, helped to shape the collective work habits of the executive involved in acquisition scanning. For example, at Carborundum, Mr. Wendel maintained close working relationships with most all corporate and top divisional officers and encouraged them to do likewise. In acquisition decisions, as in other decisions, he encouraged the participation and involvement of many executives. To adequately participate, executives provided whatever information was available to them about a market or prospect. His frank discussion of many acquisition issues further encouraged these managers to contribute their points of view as well as their information. In this respect, Mr. Wendel's leadership style had a significant effect on the scanning process. It was particularly appropriate for Carborundum's related business acquisition decisions.

This same style of leadership characterized Mr. Miller and Mr. Thompson of Textron. By involving many corporate managers in acquisition decisions and responding positively to the information and analyses he received, Mr. Thomas encouraged his managers to read widely about markets beyond Textron's scope. In both Textron and Carborundum, this somewhat democratic leadership style supported relatively efficient scanning processes in the sense that available information was quickly gathered when acquisition alternatives were identified. Additional scanning effort was applied only to the more promising alternatives.

By comparison, Mr. Geneen of ITT and Mr. Walker of American Brands were much more autocratic. Mr. Geneen had personally selected many of the markets for entry through Type II acquisitions. He requested information about particular alternatives from specific internal staff groups and many individuals. Often they were not told why information was requested and often the information provided was reportedly ignored. Thus, managers were encouraged to provide information only when it was solicited and few managers were actively involved in the scanning process. Mr. Walker was also autocratic, although he may have had less choice. At the beginning of American Brands' acquisition program, managers had little information, or access to information, about nontobacco businesses. Although he formed some groups to identify acquisition alternatives and gather information about them, he relied on external sources, particularly consultants, for recommendations. In both American Brands and ITT a smaller portion of managers were involved in scanning than in Carborundum or Textron.

Summary. The research design and the research data then permitted the identification of four types of independent variables which influenced the acquisition scanning process.[10] These types of variables were universal variables, industry variables, strategy variables, and firm variables. The major universal variable was the availability of information about markets and prospects which influenced the amounts, types, and sources or information which were available to firms in the study. The major industry variable was the structure and future prospects of the industry which influenced the planning horizon within which the benefits of acquisitions should be realized. The strategy variable concerned the amounts and types of synergy sought between the firm and its acquired businesses. Both industry and strategy variables had significant impact on all of the characteristics of a scanning process. The major firm variables were the organization of the firm, which structured and motivated the participants in the acquisition scanning process, and the amount of experience and success the firm had with diversifying acquisition, which influenced the need for independent and credible sources of information.

Application of the Model

The three acquisition programs which could not be evaluated on the basis of the acquisitions which they produced can be evaluated by applying the model. These programs were (1) the Norton program after 1970, (2) the Philip Morris program after 1965, and (3) the Textron program after 1971.

Norton. After 1970, Norton searched for both related and unrelated acquisitions. Its diversification objectives did not suggest any urgency for immediate results. Its board of directors approved the acquisition objectives and the chief executive supported them. The model must be applied separately to each of the three types of acquisitions which Norton sought.

The scanning process for Type I acquisitions generally conformed to the propositions of the model for universal, industry, and strategy variables.[11] However, the process was inappropriate because it did not conform to the firm variable relationships of the model. Organizational policies did not facilitate working relationships between corporate managers and the division managers and did not motivate them to scan for acquisitions. As a result, the corporate management could not gather adequate information about markets to determine which should be entered. Furthermore, since divisional managers were not motivated to assume responsibility for acquired operations, they did not identify acquisition alternatives. Part of Mr. Johnson's role was to facilitate cooperation between corporate and divisional scanners. However, while initiating this role, he identified a market for Type II acquisitions and pursued it. Mr. Griffin's suggestion that policies should have been changed has some merit in terms of the model. If combined with more staff support or consulting help the appropriateness of the process could have been increased. Since the acquisition objectives had a long range focus, changes in organizational policies would have had an opportunity to alter the behavior and motivation of divisional managers toward acquisition scanning.

For Type II acquisitions at Norton, the scanning process was also inappropriate. Norton attempted to identify prospects through a computer price/earnings ratio to insure that an acquisition would not result in significant dilution of Norton's earnings per share. The model suggests that unrelated acquisition candidates should be identified by intermediaries because of the low probability that any of these companies would be willing to be acquired and the amount of scanning required to approach each of these companies would be excessive. Furthermore, the low price/earnings ratio of the companies identified suggested that if any candidates were identified, they would either compete in mature markets or require substantial managerial changes to improve their performances. If markets were matured, then an acquisition would increase the number of small acquisitions necessary to sustain Norton's growth rate but would not provide the resources to support it. If management changes were required, the model suggests that the prospect should not be acquired because competent incumbent management willing to remain with Norton should have been a major criterion. Furthermore, the model suggests that without previously successful acquisitions, the scanners would need to gather large amounts of information from a wide variety of independent sources to persuade the board to approve an acquisition. This would further limit resources available for higher growth potential acquisitions. Thus, the scanning process for Type II acquisitions at Norton was inappropriate. Scanners should have responded to intermediaries rather than actively searching for prospects. When candidates were identified, Norton should have focused on managerial as well as financial criteria. The financial criteria should have more explicitly recognized the impact of a large slow-growth acquisition on the corporate objectives and on the acquisition scanning program.

Type III acquisitions were different from anything which either successful or unsuccessful companies in the study had attempted. Therefore, conclusions from applying the model remain more tenuous than for other program evaluations. Nevertheless, the scanning process for Type III acquisitions conformed to several propositions of the model. The process was appropriate for the universal variable of information availability. Norton did not attempt to optimize acquisition criteria and did not gather information about markets for entry until the availability of prospects was determined. Low market concentration and intermediary identifications generally assured availability. Information gathering generally focused on the industry characteristics of related developing markets so that the aggregate market information could be used to evaluate markets. Similarly, Norton gathered information from independent and credible sources. Also, candidates were approached immediately after they were identified and became a principal source of prospect information. Since they were usually privately owned companies in markets unrelated to Norton's other businesses, they were the only economical source of sufficient information. The process was also generally appropriate in terms of industry variables since Norton did not perceive major urgency for short term performance.

However, the Type III acquisition scanning process did not conform well to the remaining propositions of the model. Norton adopted an unrelated business strategy but did not adequately emphasize the criteria that prospects have adequate management willing to remain with Norton after they were acquired. Since Norton later planned to acquire small companies in markets related to the businesses of Type III acquisitions, good managements would necessarily have adequate scanning capability to assist corporate management in identifying further Type I acquisitions. In addition the management would necessarily be capable of integrating Type I acquisitions into their businesses. Both of the companies acquired as Type III acquisitions lacked this capability. Furthermore, Norton did not generally have organizational policies which facilitated Type I acquisition scanning. Although Mr. Johnson might have adequately facilitated the scanning for Type I acquisitions by the Lakeville management, this would require most of his attention and the Lakeville management would probably not be capable of effectively coordinating and integrating a sufficient number of companies if they were acquired.

Thus, overall, the model suggests that the scanning processes used by the Norton company were inappropriate. Given the firm's organizational policies, it seemed unlikely that minor changes in the process would significantly improve it.

Philip Morris. As Norton, Philip Morris adopted a strategy of unrelated diversification and did not perceive that rapidly acquiring diversity was important for achieving short term performance. Under these conditions, the Philip Morris scanning process conformed to the propositions of the model.[12] Philip Morris gathered detailed information about possible markets for entry without regard for the availability of candidates. This was appropriate for two reasons. First, Philip Morris did not require that it enter a market as soon as it was selected, rather, management was willing to wait many years if necessary for an appropriate candidate to be identified. Therefore, even in relatively concentrated markets, the probability of identifying appropriate candidates within this time horizon was not unreasonably low. Second, Philip Morris needed detailed information in order to determine the long range futurity of the markets it would select. In the process of gathering this information, planners established a network of associates who could inexpensively supply additional information over time, providing Philip Morris with appropriate sources of information when candidates were identified. Thus, initial scanning efforts would not be necessarily wasted if no candidates could be identified immediately after a market was selected.

Textron.   The acquisition scanning process which Textron adopted in 1971 was appropriate for the firm because it was coincident with a major shift in the objectives for the acquisition program.[13]   In 1971 Textron announced a major new strategic thrust toward international expansion with particular and most immediate focus on European markets. Future corporate performance was to come from this new thrust rather than from the traditional thrust toward domestic diversifying acquisitions.   With this change in emphasis, the perceived urgency for immediate performance resulting from domestic diversifying acquisitions was reduced substantially.

Mr. Murphy did not gather significant amounts of information about prospects or markets before he determined that a candidate was available.   The probability of scanning leading to successful acquisitions was similar to the reasoning used by Philip Morris: An approach to a prospect which refused might cause an acquisition several years into the future, according to Mr. Murphy.   The prospects which generally interested Mr. Murphy were large publicly owned companies about which he could gather substantial amounts of information from published sources with little effort. In gathering information to approach them, Mr. Murphy concentrated on the quality of their managements as reflected in their market positions and in their historical financial performance. Information of this nature was appropriate for unrelated acquisitions.

Overall this process was not likely to result in substantial numbers of acquisitions. However, its highly selective nature would tend to insure that any consummated acquisitions would be unusually high quality companies.[14]   They would represent investment opportunities particularly appropriate for Textron.

Conclusion.

In this chapter the scanning processes of four of the six firms in the study were judged appropriate in terms of the successful acquisitions which they produced.   The descriptions of these processes and the circumstances under which they were used were then analyzed to derive a model of the domestic diversifying acquisition scanning process.   The independent and dependent variables of the model were anticipated in the research design outlined in Chapter II.   The relationships among these variables were deduced from the research data presented in Chapters III, IV, and V for the four firms with successful scanning processes. The scanning processes of firms which could not be evaluated on the basis of the acquisitions they produced were then evaluated by applying the model to them. The model confirmed the appropriateness of two such processes and suggested problems which were likely to prevent the success of three others. The propositions of the model suggested improvements which could be made in these three.

The model appears to support the two hypotheses suggested in Chapter II. These are: (1) Firms with defensive diversification objectives tend to adopt different acquisition scanning processes than firms with aggressive diversification objectives, and (2) Firms which follow unrelated business strategies tend to adopt different acquisition scanning processes than firms which follow related business strategies.[15]

The model is not definitive for evaluating or defining all scanning processes. However, as demonstrated with Norton, Philip Morris, and Textron, when applied with common sense, it can provide useful insights and recommendations. The remaining chapter attempts to provide some useful implications of the research and the model by developing an approach for its broader application.

NOTES

[1]Exhibits VI-1 and VI-2 contain some useful financial and diversification statistics for the six firms in the study.   More detailed financial information is contained in Exhibits III-10, IV-4, and V-7.

[2]Exhibit VI-3 summarizes the evaluations based on the four approaches and combines them into an overall composite evaluation. Each entry in the exhibit is a response to the question: Was the scanning process appropriate using this basis for evaluation? Question marks imply that evaluation was impossible. For Norton and Textron, more than one acquisition program is evaluated since the evaluation approaches strongly distinguished between programs or types of acquisitions for these firms.

[3]Exhibit VI-4 summarizes the values of these dependent variables from the study. More detailed information for each variable is contained in Exhibits III-9, IV-3, and V-5. For Norton, the variable values refer only to the acquisition program which began in 1970, because information about previous progams was inadequate to define the variables completely and accurately. For Textron, the variable values refer only to the program which existed prior to 1970, since this program was evaluated as appropriate. Values of the variables for Philip Morris and Norton are included in the exhibit but are not used to construct the model.

[4]Since the data about Norton and Philip Morris cannot be used to construct the model, the task of identifying and classifying independent variables is considerably more difficult than was anticipated by the research design. Distinguishing between variables which affect only Carborundum from those which affect all firms in the abrasives industry requires careful analysis of the data. This same problem exists for American Brands.

[5]Exhibit VI-5 describes the major values of four universal variables.   Economic prosperity appeared to insure an adequate number of companies willing to be acquired at attractive prices to motivate a significant acquisition wave. Since the economy remained more or less constantly healthy throughout the period under study, its relative impact on scanning could not be adequately evaluated. Antitrust enforcement became more rigorous toward the end of the period and firms generally responded by asking antitrust lawyers to review acquisition contracts before they were signed. Reporting requirements also had more impact on overall acquisition activity than on the acquisition scanning process.

[6]Exhibit VI-6 describes the values of these industry variables for the abrasives industry and the tobacco industry. To construct the model, only Carborundum and American Brands were used as industry related firms. Carborundum adopted a related business strategy and American Brands adopted an unrelated business strategy.   Thus, differences between Carborundum and American Brands could be attributed to either industry variables, strategy variables, or firm variables. Distinguishing among the influence of these three types of variables is possible by a more detailed examination of the research data.

[7]While responding to the same industry environment, Philip Morris adopted a significantly different scanning process than did American Brands. Although direct comparison is difficult since the Philip Morris progress could not be evaluated as

either appropriate or inappropriate, some differences were apparently attributable to competitive structure shifts. The future of the tobacco industry was highly uncertain, but in the short term, Philip Morris could anticipate a continued increase in its share of the industry, whereas American Brands could not. Also, Philip Morris executives appeared convinced that the industry was not on the precipice of a sharp decline and behaved consistently with that conviction.

[8]Philip Morris and Norton also generally followed an unrelated business strategy. Norton had been unable to identify any acquisition prospects. If it consummated Type III acquisitions, it would then search for Type I acquisitions which would relate to them. Philip Morris had also initially searched for some related acquisitions but found they would be too small to have substantial impact on the firm's growth and diversity.

[9]Exhibit VI-7 describes the major organizational policies of the six firms in the study. The policies for Norton were in effect after 1970 and applied primarily to the third acquisition program. The policies described for Textron applied to the period about 1967. These policies had changed somewhat by 1971.

[10]Exhibit VI-8 summarizes the major propositions of the model.

[11]Because no Type I acquisitions were consummated, few prospects were identified and markets selected for entry, this process is described in terms of intentions and expectations rather than operations. In designing this process, Mr. Griffin explicitly recognized the limitations of information availability and the need for somewhat detailed information about markets and prospects. Since the markets were to be related to existing businesses and since the prospects were to be small privately owned companies, division managers with access to appropriate sources of information were expected to become involved in the process. Since none of the corporate scanners had a detailed understanding of the nonabrasives businesses, the cooperation and involvement of division managers was essential to the success of the program.

[12]However, there were indications that the process might be less appropriate at some time in the future. If the tobacco business decelerated slowly, providing a small, steady cash flow for acquiring other companies, Philip Morris could maintain its long time horizon and reasonably expect appropriate candidates to be identified in selected markets for entry. If, on the other hand, the tobacco business decelerated quickly, Philip Morris could expect substantia' cash flows which would need to be used quickly to acquire other companies. Unless Philip Morris monitored many markets with many acceptable competitors, the likelihood of rapid acquisition utilizing the existing scanning process would be small. The propositions of the model suggest that as Philip Morris' objectives required more immediate results from its scanning process, the process itself would need to be altered. This alteration would not be difficult, but would not utilize much of the information gathered using the existing process.

[13]However, the process adopted in 1971 would not have been appropriate for Textron's previous acquisition objectives, which were short-term oriented in response to perceived pressures for immediate performance resulting from acquisitions. The contradictions between this process and the propositions concerning both industry and strategy variables in the model are obvious.

[14]This was somewhat paradoxical. It seemed unlikely that companies of this caliber would be willing to be acquired at price/earnings ratios which Textron could afford without substantially improving its own price/earnings ratio. However, it was unclear what would happen to Textron's investor image if the international expansion were successful.

[15]It is worthwhile to note that these hypotheses were not corroborated as intended by the original structure. This structure somewhat naively anticipated that all of the firms in the study would have successful acquisition scanning processes. Norton did not. It also anticipated that the abrasives firms and the tobacco firms would have adopted related business diversification strategies and that the conglomerate firms would have adopted unrelated business diversification strategies. Only Carborundum adopted a related business diversification strategy. Finally, it anticipated that the abrasives firms would establish aggressive diversification objectives and the tobacco firms would establish defensive diversification objectives. Philip Morris adopted aggressive diversification objectives. Nevertheless, the data collected and presented in Chapters II, IV, and V provided an adequate basis for corroborating the hypotheses and constructing the model.

EXHIBIT VI-1

FINANCIAL SUMMARY

| | | Abrasives | | Tobacco | | Conglomerate | |
		Norton	Carbor-undum	Philip Morris	Amer. Brands	ITT	Textron
Sales,	1960	$177m	$142m	$ 509m	$1320m	$ 811m	$ 383m
	1972	$374m	$340m	$2131m	$2999m	$8557m	$1678m
	CAGR	6.0%	7.5%	12.7%	7.0%	21.7%	13.1%
Profit,	1960	$ 12.3m	$ 7.6m	$ 21.0m	$ 65.4m	$ 30.6m	14.1m
	1972	$ 14.5m	$ 16.3m	$ 124.5m	$ 123.3m	$ 476.6m	$ 82.1m
	CAGR	1.4%	6.5%	16.0%	5.5%	25.6%	15.8%
eps,	1960	$ 2.26	$ 2.15	$ 0.91	$ 2.11	$ 0.98	$ 0.73
	1972	$ 2.70	$ 4.42	$ 4.37	$ 4.37	$ 3.80	$ 2.32
	CAGR	1.5%	6.2%	14.0%	6.3%	11.9%	10.2%
ROI,	1960	8.0%	7.8%	9.4%	9.3%	7.6%	9.5%
	1972	7.4%	9.0%	13.8%	11.7%	12.0%	11.7%
	AVG.	8.0%	8.1%	11.6%	10.7%	10.2%	11.8%

Notes: (1) All data refers to performance as reported, not as restated. (2) CAGR is the compound annual growth rate. (3) eps is earnings per share. (4) ROI is return on invested capital calculated as profit after taxes plus interest expense divided by long term debt plus equity. (5) AVG. is the average return on investment with each year given equal weight in the calculation.

EXHIBIT VI-2

Diversification Summary

	Sales Acq'd Since 1960*	Domestic Diver'd Sales Acq'd Since 1960**	Sales of largest single product line***	Goals of Diversifying Acquisition Program
Norton	30%	10%	75%	40% of sales from nonabrasives products by 1980 (goal established in about 1970).
Carborundum	38%	30%	63%	Goals either not well formulated or not well articulated—acquisition was expected to provide profits necessary to meet profit growth objective.
Philip Morris	38%	18%	82%	Not stated explicitly. Acquisition was expected to provide necessary sales to meet growth objective.
American Brands	68%	30%	70%	Not stated explicitly. Acquisition were to improve growth and maintain profitability.
ITT	63%	45%	22%	Form a foundation for stable future earnings growth.
Textron	60%	50%	8%	Achieve balance among various segments of the U. S. manufacturing economy.

  * Sales acquired since 1960, including post acquisition growth, stated as a percentage of 1972 corporate sales.

 ** Sales of domestic diversifying acquisitions since 1960, including post acquisition growth, stated as a percentage of 1972 sales.

*** Sales of the largest single product line of the firm in 1972 stated as a percentage of 1972 sales.

EXHIBIT VI-3

Acquisition Program Evaluations Summarized

Was Scanning Process Appropriate?	Financial Results	Diversification Achieved	Basis for Evaluation		Overall Evaluation
			Management Judgment	Specific Instance	
Norton 1962-1969	NO	NO	NO	NO	NO
Type I	?	?	YES	NO	?
II	?	?	YES	NO	?
III	?	?	YES	YES	?
Carborundum	?	YES	YES	YES	YES
Philip Morris	?	?	YES	YES*	?
American Brands	YES*	YES	YES	YES	YES
ITT	YES	YES	YES	?	YES
Textron 1960-1970	YES*	YES	YES	YES*	YES
1971-1972	?	?	?	?	?

*Indicates most probably.

EXHIBIT VI-4

Acquisition Scanning Processes Compared

Types of Information

Norton

Most emphasis on financial information and least on technological information.

Carborundum

Most emphasis on the relationships between firm and prospect.

Philip Morris

Most emphasis on market and marketing information focusing on long term future developments.

American Brands

Most emphasis on financial information with a short term orientation.

ITT

Most emphasis on financial information supplemented with market and technological information.

Textron

Most emphasis on financial information supplemented with some market information.

Sources of Market Information

Norton

Most information gathered from consultants or experts external to the firm. Multiple sourcing was important.

Carborundum

Most detailed information from former industry executives who are hired by the firm.

Philip Morris

Numerous sources of information used. Internal expertise developed through detailed study.

American Brands

Published information and consultants provided most of the information.

ITT

Published information and functional staff experts provide most information. President gathered information from many personal conversations. Divisional managers provided information about markets related to their divisions.

Textron

Published information and various Textron executives provided much of the information. Investment bankers were also consulted. Divisional managers provided information about markets related to their divisions.

EXHIBIT VI-4 (Cont.)

Sources of Prospect Information

Norton

Information on larger firms mostly from published sources. For smaller firms, intermediaries and the candidates themselves provided most information.

Carborundum

Initially provided by an acquisition consultant then supplemented by prospects themselves.

Philip Morris

Many sources used, no one seemed to dominate the process.

American Brands

Published information was supplemented by consultants and by candidates themselves.

ITT

Intermediaries, publications, and financial analysts provided information for larger candidates. Divisional management gathered information from personal acquaintances on smaller candidates.

Textron

Intermediaries, publications, and financial analysts provided information for larger candidates. Divisional management gathered information from personal acquaintances on smaller candidates.

Types of Information Processing

Norton

Little formal processing except computerized search technique for larger prospects.

Carborundum

No formal processing, discounted cash flow techniques introduced near end of study.

Philip Morris

Many techniques used by the various planners depending on their training.

American Brands

Financial analysis predominated the processing.

ITT

Financial analysis supplemented with market research techniques was the major processing.

Textron

Financial analysis was the major processing used.

EXHIBIT VI-4 (Cont.)

Participants in the Process

Norton

Organizationally isolated from the abrasives business with little abrasives experience. Acquisition experience limited to one scanner with a background in finance.

Philip Morris

Scanners with little business experience and no exposure to the tobacco industry, but powerful analytical techniques developed through formal education.

ITT

Variety of backgrounds but with primary emphasis on financial analysis.

Carborundum

Most scanners were or had been senior abrasives managers. None had extensive experience in the acquisition process before he began with Carborundum.

American Brands

Scanners with primary experience in the tobacco industry and primary backgrounds in finance.

Textron

General managers with more background in finance than other areas.

Sequence of Scanning Activities

Norton

Generally candidates identified before information gathered about either market or prospect.

Philip Morris

Detailed information gathered about industries and markets before information gathered about prospects. Often substantial lag between market selection and acquisition.

ITT

Candidates identified before information gathered about either markets or prospects.

Carborundum

Markets identified and information gathered about them before information gathered about prospects.

American Brands

Candidates identified before information gathered about either markets or prospects.

Textron

Candidates identified before information gathered about either markets or prospects.

EXHIBIT VI-5

General Environmental Conditions

(Affecting all firms)

Availability of Information

comparable information about specific markets not available

information about privately owned companies generally not available from published sources

information about publicly owned companies available from published sources, increasing with the size of the company

Economic Prosperity

generally stable economic conditions

gross national product and disposable personal income rising consistently

inflation and unemployment acceptable

industrial production somewhat cyclical but generally growing

investor confidence generally stable with increasing premiums for equity of companies with high growth histories or prospects

Antitrust Enforcement

generally limited to horizontal, vertical, or closely related acquisitions during early part of period

increasing prosecution of conglomerate mergers toward end of period

Reporting Requirements

investors could not distinguish between acquired and internally generated growth of firms during early part of period for acquisitions treated as purchases

investors could not determine premiums over book value paid for acquired companies under poolings of interest

investors could not distinguish sources of sale and earnings for diversified firms during early part of the period

EXHIBIT VI-6

Market Environmental Conditions and Trends

ABRASIVES INDUSTRY

Products and Customers

customers are solid material processors in many industries
products shape and finish solid materials by abrasion
products purchased frequently by most customers
products represent small but vital portion of production costs
technological content relatively sophisticated but not proprietary
potential new markets not foreseen

Competitive Structure

high barriers to entry and concentration in all markets
relatively stable market shares among major competitors
major competitors fully integrated

Future Prospects

future conditions relatively predictable
market growth will continue to decelerate slowly
cyclical component of demand will continue to dominate
profitability good and cash flow strong when demand is high

TOBACCO INDUSTRY

Products and Customers

customers are retail consumers serviced through extensive distribution
cigarettes are the major product, markets defined by product characteristics
products purchased from personal disposable income, representing a small portion
technological content relatively low

Competitive Structure

high barriers to entry and concentration in all markets
predictably shifting market shares among competitors based on product mix
pervasive trend toward filter cigarettes nearly complete
new brands require years to gain significant market share
consumer marketing is the major competitive skill

Future Prospects

future conditions are highly uncertain
market growth will decelerate and demand will retard, but timing uncertain
cash flow very strong as market growth slows

EXHIBIT VI-7

Organizational Policies

Norton

Isolate abrasives from nonabrasives businesses.
Avoid large functional corporate staff units.
Impose formal planning system on divisional management.
Permit considerable divisional autonomy.
Retain acquired management.
Actively recruit new managers for nonabrasives products.

Carborundum

Maintain a strong centralized research and development staff.
Maintain corporate functional staffs.
Organize worldwide on a continental basis.
Organize domestically by groups of related divisions.
Control divisions through informal personal relationships.
Promote management from within to the maximum extent possible.
Retain management of acquired companies.

Philip Morris

Organize tobacco business by geographic region (U.S. and overseas).
Organize remaining businesses in relatively independent divisions.
Impose formal planning system on divisional managements.
Use corporate planning staff to control future activities of divisions.
Retain acquired management.

American Brands

Avoid large corporate staff units.
Maintain divisional autonomy of acquired companies.
Retain management of acquired companies.
Add outside directors to the board from acquired companies.
Minimize interdivisional management transfers.

ITT

Organize structurally by continental geography.
Retain acquired managers and operating independence of acquired companies.
Centralize control of cash flow.
Maintain a large and strong corporate staff with many specializations.
Enforce a detailed planning and control system through monthly meetings.
Establish a custom for long hours and hard work.
Base rewards and punishments on achieved performance objectives.

Textron (circa 1967)

Organize structurally by groups of unrelated divisions.
Retain acquired managers and operating independence of acquired companies.
Centralize control of cash flow.
Provide no corporate staff support in functional areas.
Minimize the use of corporate policies and procedures required for divisions.
Use group vice presidents to encourage long range planning.
Avoid committees and large management meetings involving divisional officers.
Base rewards and punishments on achieved performance objectives.

EXHIBIT VI-8

Propositions of the Scanning Process Model

Universal Variables

1. When information available about markets is aggregated, outdated, and incomplete, firms cannot economically identify markets or sets of markets for entry which would optimize acquisition criteria.

2. When the probability is low that appropriate candidates competing within a market or set of markets can be identified, firms cannot economically gather information about that market through formal scanning.

3. When the probability is low that a prospect can be acquired at an acceptable price, firms can economically gather information about the prospect from published sources or associates of the firm's executives.

4. When prospects are small, privately owned companies competing in unrelated markets, firms generally do not have access to economical sources of information.

5. When the economy is prosperous, more companies are available at acceptable terms, although the percentage remains relatively small.

6. When antitrust enforcement is more aggressive, the markets which a firm can enter without challenge is reduced somewhat.

Industry Variables

1. When a firm perceives that rapidly acquiring diversity is important for achieving short term objectives, its scanning process has the following characteristics:

   a. It emphasizes financial acquisition criteria more than other types of information.

   b. It gathers less information about markets for entry and candidates for acquisition.

   c. It does not select markets for entry prior to identifying candidates for acquisition.

   d. It identifies acquisition candidates primarily through intermediaries.

   e. It gathers information about a candidate and the markets in which it competes simultaneously.

   f. It gathers information about markets for entry primarily from published sources.

   g. It gathers information about candidates primarily from published sources and from the intermediaries who identify them.

h. It limits information processing primarily to financial analysis.

i. It assigns the responsibility for acquisition scanning to executives with financial backgrounds.

2. When a firm perceives that diversifying acquisitions are an investment of resources not required for achieving short term performance objectives, it does not necessarily adhere to the pattern described above.

Strategy Variables

1. When a firm pursues a related business strategy and therefore acquires small, privately owned companies to achieve operating synergy, its scanning process has the following characteristics:

   a. It emphasizes market and operating information more than financial information.

   b. It gathers more information about markets for entry and prospects for acquisition.

   c. It selects markets for entry based on their relationship to the firm's other markets prior to identifying prospects.

   d. It identifies acquisition prospects while gathering market information and identifies acquisition candidates through intermediaries.

   e. It gathers information about markets for entry primarily from the personal and professional associates of managers responsible for operations in related businesses.

   f. It gathers information about prospects primarily from either prospects themselves or the personal and professional associates of managers responsible for operations in related businesses.

   g. It focuses information processing on those areas required for successful integration.

   h. It assigns responsibility for acquisition scanning to operating managers.

2. When a firm pursues an unrelated market strategy and acquires small, privately owned companies to achieve operating synergy with existing operating units, its scanning process is generally similar to that above, except that:

   a. It does not necessarily select markets for entry before identifying candidates for acquisition.

   b. It may identify more candidates through intermediaries while searching for unrelated acquisitions.

   c. It assigns acquisition scanning responsibility jointly to operating unit managers and corporate financial managers.

3. When a firm pursues a conglomerate strategy and acquires large companies to operate as independent units, its scanning process has the same characteristics as firms which perceive that rapidly acquiring diversity is important for achieving short term objectives, because acquisitions are important for maintaining or improving the firm's price-earnings ratio.

Firm Variables

1. When organizational policy induces working relationships between corporate managers and business unit managers and motivates business unit managers to scan, a firm is more likely to consummate successful related market acquisitions.

2. When the manager responsible for acquisition scanning is supported by numerous functional corporate staff groups, the firm can economically gather more information about prospects.

3. When the firm does not have adequate internal scanning capacity, it may rely on consultants and similar external experts to assist its scanning efforts for unrelated acquisitions.

4. When the executive responsible for acquisition scanning understands the information needs of the chief executive and reports his progress frequently to him, the acquisition scanning process is more likely to result in successful acquisitions.

5. When the board of directors actively supports the diversifying acquisition program, the scanning process can focus primarily on the needs of the chief executive.

6. When a firm has little experience or success with diversifying acquisitions, the sources from which information is gathered becomes as important as the information itself, since they establish the credibility of the information.

CHAPTER VII

IMPLICATIONS OF THE RESEARCH

The purpose of this final chapter is to extend the findings, analysis, and conclusions of the research to a larger number and variety of firms than those in the study. To accomplish this purpose, several major problems related to designing and evaluating an acquisition scanning process are identified. Resolving these problems appropriately should enable a firm to improve the efficiency and effectiveness of its acquisition scanning process and to avoid some serious and expensive mistakes. The chapter first examines the problems of designing an acquisition scanning process and then, the problems of evaluating an existing scanning process. The propositions of the model developed in Chapter VI, together with the other findings of the research, provide the underlying rationale and structure for Chapter VII.

The Problems of Designing
The Acquisition Scanning Process

The research findings indicate three major problems related to designing the process. These problems, like the characteristics of the process itself, are interrelated. Resolving them independently may lead to conflicting design prescriptions. Three major problems of design are: (1) Assessment of the firm's resource position, (2) Assessment of the firm's access to sources of information, and (3) Assessment of the firm's organizational capabilities.

Resource Position

The first problem of design is to assess the firm's present and likely future positions in the markets in which it does compete or could enter through internal diversification. This assessment should be in terms of the objectives of the firm to determine the urgency of diversification and the resources available to the firm to support it.[1]

Urgency. Urgency is great when the gap between short term expected and desired corporate performance is great. When this urgency is great, firms tend to emphasize short term performance more than long term performance. When urgency is great, the scanning process should assure the rapid identification of appropriate acquisition alternatives which can be selected on acceptable terms.[2] This can be achieved by searching for candidates rather than approaching many prospects which might not be available and by locating intermediaries, which are a prime source of candidate identification.

When urgency is great, scanning criteria usually should maintain a broad market scope and should require information that is easily available. The broad market scope is important for two reasons. First, few intermediaries limit their focus to the firm's desired market scope. Second, few companies within any specified market are likely to be interested in acquisition, so that a restrictive scope hinders the achievement of acquisition objectives. Limiting criteria to information which is easily available facilitates rapid rejection of undesirable candidates, permitting more time to scan for candidates which appear appropriate. This is particularly important since the firm will likely identify many candidates which are undesirable by using the services of intermediaries. A major risk when evaluating many candidates is that important information may not be gathered. Criteria which relate to the information often provided by intermediaries further facilitate scanning.

When urgency is not great, a firm has the opportunity to assess the long term potential of markets for entry. Although firms with greater urgency may share the same concern for long term potential, they usually cannot afford to respond as completely to this concern. Assessing this potential requires much more time and attention than assessing immediate impact because information is more uncertain and sources are less reliable and identifiable. A major risk when evaluating long term potential is adequately accounting for the uncertainty of the future. Concern with long term potential may lead to more focused and intensive information gathering concentrated on fewer market alternatives. Therefore, market scope can be more limited by the acquisition criteria and markets for entry can be selected before acquisition prospects are identified. For selected markets, the firm may not be able to identify candidates immediately, but monitoring the market over time usually will lead to identification of appropriate candidates.

When information about an identified market is less accurate, the firm may attempt to gather information from several sources. Also, the firm may find it necessary to process more information to determine the long term potential of a market since information which relates directly to acquisition criteria may not be available or only available from unreliable sources. Information processing also enables the firm to monitor the progress of these markets more easily since it will not only have access to the forecasts of future performance, but also to the assumptions and relationships upon which they are based. Finally, although forecasting methodologies may be somewhat imprecise, processing enables the firm to examine in more detail assumptions which appear to have the strongest impact on future performances. Therefore, processing guides the directions for future information gathering.

Resources. From an assessment of its future positions, a firm can determine the financial resources, particularly cash and price/earnings ratio, available to support the acquisition program and the subsequent development of acquired companies. If financial resources are limited, a firm may need to be more concerned with the future timing of acquisitions and of investments in acquired companies. One major result of limited financial resources may be that the diversification objectives, including immediate impacts on performance, may be beyond the capability of the firm to achieve. The implication of this problem for the scanning process is that the firm must reconcile its objectives, resources, and priorities before developing a scanning process.

When financial resources are limited, acquisition criteria may focus on smaller acquisitions. Then locating low-cost or variable-cost sources of market and prospect information should be considered. Searching for candidates rather than markets and prospects can also reduce the cost of scanning by focusing resources on alternatives which can be selected and implemented. Intermediaries are one means because their services are usually free unless their candidate is acquired and they can provide some information for influencing selection. However, the information which intermediaries can provide is often incomplete or inaccurate and focused on the historical performance of the candidate rather than on the future potential of its markets.

The scope and extent of general management capabilities available within the firm at both the corporate and divisional levels also has an important influence on the scanning process. Market scope should be limited to a range of markets to which general management talents can be applied.[3] This is particularly important at the beginning of an acquisition scanning program when a firm does not have the experience of a successful acquisition program. If general management capability is limited, the firm should establish a criterion that only well managed companies will be acquired when the management is willing to remain after the acquisition and manage its business. To make this criterion operational, it must be stated in terms of information which is more easily available. For example, historical performance better than competitors in the market, proprietary position within its markets, or high price/earning ratios are all indicators of good management and can be stated as formal criteria. Translating historical performance into the future may be more difficult, but can be done after initial indicators are favorable.

General management availability may also limit the firm's ability to scan more directly. If managers are already overburdened with their responsibilities, they may not allocate adequate time to scanning for acquisitions, particularly if they have no experience in doing so. Hiring experienced scanners may not alleviate the problem unless top management will take the time to work with the scanners and develop a relationship with them. When diversifying acquisitions are an urgent issue, managerial resources may limit achievement of objectives. Attempting to acquire firms with excess managerial capability may not solve the problem, because of the time required for new executives to learn to work together. When general management capability is limited more in terms of post integration activity than scanning activity, the firm should use its financial resources to acquire a smaller number of larger companies.[4] This may facilitate integration without overburdening the firm's management.

The firm should also assess the major resources available to it or its division in terms of marketing, manufacturing, research, or other major business functions.[5] If the firm has an excess or shortage of these resources, then the scanning process may search for acquisition alternatives which complement them.[6] If operating synergy is to be sought through integration, the scanning process will require much more information gathering, but prospects may be available on more acceptable terms since both parties benefit from an acquisition. Also, some resources in excess or short supply, may suggest markets for entry which could utilize or provide similar resources.

Resolving the problem of resource assessment should provide an initial set of acquisition criteria which state the information to be obtained by the scanning process. They may be revised in light of other scanning problems. Scanners should clarify both objectives and criteria and obtain agreement, from top management and the board, that they are appropriate and supported. Since the board is the ultimate recipient of acquisition recommendations, its needs should be carefully considered, particularly when the firm does not have a record of successful acquisitions, and must consider proposals partially on their merit.

Information Sources

The second problem in designing the acquisition scanning process is to assess the firm's access to sources of information. This assessment should outline some of the feasible approaches to scanning process design in terms of the availability of information, the reliability of sources and accuracy of their information, and the cost of gathering their information.

Information Availability.   Availability of information about markets or candidates influences the choice of criteria and the sources from which prospects are identified and information is gathered.   If target markets for entry are specified as part of the acquisition criteria, then competitors in those markets may be easily identified as prospects. Gathering information about these markets or prospects is not difficult. Industry associations generally publish limited information which can provide rankings for the prospects relative to some acquisition criteria. Experts in the industry, including former executives, often can provide some additional information.   When markets are not specified, but criteria limit search to only a few markets or groups of markets, then sufficient information can be gathered from these sources to rank or select among them those which are more appropriate.

If target markets for entry are not specified or severely limited by the criteria, selecting markets may be difficult.   If information about markets are complete, comparable, and disaggregated, firms could systematically perform computerized searches to identify markets with acceptable performance characteristics.   However, with information about markets incomplete, incomparable, and aggregated, as it was during this study, systematic searches for markets are impossible.   Firms can either identify markets on an informal basis or identify candidates which compete in markets conforming to the criteria.

When identified markets are old and established, much information is published about them and information gathering is not difficult.   Fulfillment of criteria can be somewhat easily established. However, when identified markets are new or emerging, little information is usually published about them.   Gathering sufficient information to determine if they satisfy criteria is difficult and either requires fewer or less stringent market criteria or locating more expensive sources of information and increasing the amount of information processing.   Also, it is often difficult to identify the competitors, or potential competitors, in these markets.   Some of these companies can be identified by locating and communicating with sources of venture capital.   Also, these companies can be identified by managers within the firm when the markets relate to those of the firm.

Many firms rightfully establish maximum or minimum size criteria for prospects.   Size has a significant impact on the scanning process.   Small prospects are likely to be privately owned companies which publish no financial information and very little other information. The companies themselves, or their intermediaries, are the major source of this information.   Some nonfinancial information can be obtained from industry associations or industry experts.   Thus, when criteria require small prospects, the firm should establish communication with a prospect early in the scanning process. This communication will permit the firm to gather information about a prospect while simultaneously determining if it is interested in being acquired. If the market of the prospect is related to the firm, management should gather a sufficient amount of information about the market to be able to indicate the benefits of an acquisition to the prospect when it is first approached.

Larger prospects are likely to be publicly owned. They are required to publish financial information and other pertinent information for investors and prospective investors. In addition, larger companies usually receive more coverage in general business or industry publications. Although these companies are also more complex organizations, information gathering for some criteria is not difficult. The firm should begin by gathering this published information and should establish some criteria which can be determined using it. Also, the firm may obtain additional information from investment services and stock analysts which monitor publicly owned firms for investment purposes.

Information Sources. The reliability of various sources, the accuracy of their information, and the cost of gathering their information should be considered in resolving this problem. The sources explicitly assessed here include: primary sources, publications, industry experts, intermediaries, manager's associates, and investment analysts. The sequence in which they are discussed is not an indication of the sequence in which they should be preferred. The purpose of the discussion is to help a firm determine which sources to prefer for its scanning process.

The primary sources of information about markets and prospects include the managers, customers, and vendors of the companies in those markets. These sources may have the most accurate information, but may not be motivated to provide it. In some cases, gathering information from these sources requires formal market research procedures. The expense is often unjustified unless previously gathered information indicates that the market satisfies the criteria and that candidates are available in the market.

General periodicals, industry associations, and government agencies provide limited information about groups of markets for a minimal cost. Firms can utilize these sources to assess the accuracy of information gathered from other sources and to locate sources of additional information. At the industry level this information can highlight some historical or projective trends or identify markets or prospects. Information about prospects is more valuable when they are larger companies with broader product lines so that published information more accurately reflects their situation.

Consultants and other industry experts can provide more detailed information about a market after it is identified. The cost of obtaining this information is high and the accuracy usually good. Several large consulting firms maintain experts in almost every field and can often supply information on short notice. These sources should be used only after a firm has gathered some information from other sources which suggests that a market fulfills most of its criteria, and that the likelihood of identifying candidates is high.

Intermediaries can be useful sources of information when a firm knows how to use them effectively. Finders and brokers generally have little information about either acquiring firms or the candidates which they represent. Usually they can supply historical data on financial and market share performance, managerial backgrounds, and products market coverage. If this information indicates that a candidate does not fulfill the criteria, further scanning is generally not warranted. Commercial and investment bankers generally have more information about their candidates. This information is often gathered during a longer term association with both parties. Unlike brokers and finders, bankers will listen and respond to the firm's acquisition criteria if it is clearly and specifically stated to them. Banks are also a more useful source for identifying and providing information about larger candidates.

The personal and professional associates of the firm's managers often have access to useful and inexpensive information. They are more numerous and reliable when the firm seeks to enter related markets. It is important to distinguish between accurate information and rumors or heresay from these sources. Long term associations with these sources permit a manager to estimate their reliability in terms of the accuracy of information they provide and the areas in which they provide it. Access to these sources is considerably more limited when the firm seeks information about unrelated markets. These associations are not available to firms on short notice unless they were previously developed.

For large publicly owned companies, many investment analysts, research services, and stock brokers have or have had access to information. Since many of these sources use the information they provide for their own investment purposes, its accuracy is usually reasonable. In using this information, the firm must be careful to recognize that these decisions are for investment purposes, not management purposes. These sources are important because of the information upon which their recommendations are based.

When a firm seeks related acquisitions, personal and professional associates become an important source of information about markets and prospects. When a firm seeks large acquisitions, investment analysts are an important source of information. When the firm seeks small, unrelated acquisitions, both of these sources are inaccessible, as are primary sources and publications. This may partially explain why few firms seek small acquisitions in unrelated markets.

It is usually impossible to plan the major sources of information which will be located prior to the start of the scanning process. However, the firm can determine which types of sources are more likely to provide useful information and which are more worth the cost of the information they will provide in terms of timeliness and accuracy. Over time the firm can also assess the reliability of particular sources of information.

Sources of information may be particularly important when a firm first formulates a diversifying acquisition program and the board of directors cannot evaluate its appropriateness in terms of historical results. Furthermore, members of the board may not have the requisite knowledge, analytical skill, or time to consider proposals on their individual merit. Under these circumstances, they can be strongly influenced by the sources of information whose reliability they can assess from previous experience.[7] Many firms find external consultants particularly useful in this respect.

Organization

The final problem of design is assessing the managerial and technical resources available to and required for the acquisition scanning process. These resources can be described primarily in terms of people and the organization which facilitates or impedes their support and participation. Three types of resources appear important (1) access to source of information, (2) knowledge to comprehend information, and (3) analytical skills to process information.

Access to Sources. People with access to sources of information are important since they represent the means of gathering information. Resolution of the previous problem was concerned with identifying appropriate sources of information. Resolving this final problem of design concerns enlisting the support and participation of people who have or can develop the desired access.

For related acquisitions, managers of organizational units with which they will be combined represent an important access to sources of information. Their major access is to personal and professional associates who have information about markets of interest and prospects in those markets. To participate in the acquisition scanning process, these managers must find personal rewards from doing so. These rewards may be in terms of increased power or wealth from participation or a reduction in either from refusing to participate. The rewards must be structured in a way that encourages their participation on behalf of the best interest of the firm. In addition, for participants in the process, the organization must facilitate a working relationship between these unit managers and the corporate acquisition staff or acquisition scanning coordinator.[8] The organization also must provide them with adequate time for scanning without detriment to their other responsibilities. Explicitly recognizing acquisition alternatives in the formal planning process reinforces the desirability of scanning for acquisitions from the corporate point of view. Finally, these unit managers should be involved early in the acquisition decision process and should be made to feel they have important influence on the decision.

For unrelated acquisitions, business unit managers often have little access to sources of information, so the burden of the scanning task rests with corporate managers. Although there appears to be no one best way to distribute and motivate this burden, several approaches are useful. First, corporate managers can be encouraged to maintain wide interests in many fields other than those for which they are directly responsible. Second, corporate functional staff can be encouraged to maintain wide external contact not only to keep current within their specialities, but also to enlarge their access to sources of information. Third, acquisition scanning can be included as part of the duties of corporate managers so that they will appropriately communicate potentially useful information to the acquisition managers when they discover it. Finally, many of the corporate managers can be involved early in the acquisition scanning process so that they can be made aware of the information needs of the organization.

Knowledge. People within the organization may not only have access to sources of information, they may also be sources of information themselves. Prior experience or interests in a particular market or set of markets may equip them with knowledge necessary to determine the relevancy and usefulness of information gathered.   For related acquisitions, these may be the same people who would have access to sources of information. For unrelated acquisitions, these people may be more difficult to locate. Computerized personnel files can facilitate the location of these people. Also, widely disseminating information needs within the corporate management can elicit the participation of these people. The acquisitions manager can work closely with these people and facilitate their communication with other managers who have access to sources of information. Task groups or temporary committees may also facilitate the development of these kinds of relationships.

Occasionally, individual board members will have or have access to information about a particular alternative because of their personal or professional associates including other directorates. This information should be sought early in the scanning process and outside of the board room. If the director provides information and positive recommendation, then scanners can usually use his help to access additional sources of information and engender his support for the proposals. If the director opposes the alternative, then scanners must either look for other alternatives, or allocate a considerable amount of time and energy to convincing the director otherwise before presenting the proposal to the board.

Analytical Skills. People with the analytical skills necessary to process gathered information are important in the acquisition scanning process. Their role is to translate the gathered information into recommendations for action. Although primary responsibility for this task may rest with the acquisitions managers, he may have neither the time nor skill to do it all himself. For large scale acquisition programs, it is possible to provide the acquisition manager with a full time staff of analytical experts. However, in many organizations analytical skills are grouped together elsewhere and must be coordinated by the acquisition manager, as needed. Sometimes processing must be done outside the organization.

The availability of analytical skills influences the amount of information processing which the firm performs. When urgency is great, the firm may not have the time for extensive processing. In this case, the firm may gather information in a more processed form from recognized experts. The same may be true when the firm does not have adequate analytical skills within its organization. When urgency is not great, the firm may consider developing the required skills. However, utilizing either external or newly acquired internal analytical skills often will create problems. Analyzing acquisition alternatives not only requires information about markets and prospects, but also information about the firm which is part of the general knowledge available to people who have been associated with the firm for longer periods of time.

When related acquisitions are sought and are to be integrated with existing business units, more information of different types and more detailed information processing is required. Not only must the firm determine that it wants to be in a particular market and that the particular candidate can perform well in that market, but also, the firm must determine the feasibility and difficulty of achieving the integration required.

Analytical skills, knowledge, and access to sources of information are all important considerations in the design of an acquisition scanning process. The organization must facilitate the identification, development, and participation of people with these necessary resources. Well-defined criteria and good understanding of available sources of information help scanners consider the organizational needs and provide for them.

As the research findings indicate, the probability of designing a successful and fruitful acquisition scanning process is considerably greater for a firm which adequately resolves these design problems. Planning is important when a firm first begins an acquisition program because early unsuccessful acquisitions compound the problems and often create a negative attitude of both managers and the board of directors. Furthermore, the early involvement and continuing support of the chief executive officer appears to be necessary for sound planning and organizational commitment.

The Problems of Evaluating
The Acquisition Scanning Process

As the previous chapters indicate, scanning for acquisitions is a complex process and, as with any complex apparatus, is highly susceptible to inefficient operation and to breakdown. At times, some judicious tinkering can make a great difference in how well the scanning process performs. In other instances, the problem goes outside the scanning activity itself, and no amount of adjusting will suffice.

One of the necessary considerations for proper scanning is that the basic underlying decisions are consistent with the independent variables. For example, in a company where a management is highly focused in one business and inexperienced with diversification and where a board of directors is wary and timid and does exercise restraints on management, a diversification strategy to acquire large unrelated businesses would probably have very little chance of success, even with the best of information. Under these circumstances, scanning is not at issue, since the necessary conditions for a successful diversification program are lacking or at least seriously deficient.

The basic conditions also can and do vary over time. A new chief executive with a quite different approach from his predecessor, a considerable change in the pressures perceived for diversification, and successful or unsuccessful experience with diversification are all examples of changes which can affect the setting for scanning. This study would suggest that the scanning activities probably need to be changed accordingly.

The evaluation problems are related to the six characteristics of a scanning process described in Chapter II. For each characteristic, the evaluation problems are primarily concerned with consistency between the scanning process and the factors which influence it. The six characteristics are: (1) Types and amounts of information gathered, (2) sources of market information, (3) sources of prospect information, (4) types and amount of information processing, (5) the participants in the process, and (6) the sequencing of acquisition scanning activities.

Examining the Types of Information Gathered

Acquisition criteria should encourage searching a market scope with sufficient breadth to fulfill the urgency requirements of the acquisition program. Unless these requirements are modest, they will require several large or many small acquisitions. Since many companies are unwilling to be acquired, generally limiting search for candidates to a small number of markets is undesirable unless many companies compete within those markets.

The size criterion should be appropriate for financial and managerial resources. Small and large acquisitions alike require some integration. If managerial resources are limited, then many small acquisitions may be beyond the management's capability to successfully integrate even at the administrative level. However, large acquisitions also impose a strain on the financial resources of many firms, particularly if they are acquired in exchange for stock with low price/earnings ratio. Size criteria should balance these two requirements.

Markets or market characteristics should be specified for related market entry. When a firm plans to utilize or improve certain functional resources through acquisitions which will be integrated with existing operations to create synergy benefits, the nature of the benefits and the characteristics of markets or firms which have them must be carefully specified by the criteria. If they are not well specified, search may not provide them or many inappropriate alternatives will be investigated unnecessarily.

Criteria should identify antitrust problems. Generally an antitrust lawyer can provide some guidance with this problem. Related market acquisitions generally have a higher probability of causing antitrust problems than unrelated market acquisitions. This does not suggest avoiding related market acquisitions, but rather identifying antitrust problems early in the process.

Adequate information should be available to use criteria effectively. Criteria which are concerned with future performance are the most suspect since the future is uncertain. However, future performance is a major reason for most acquisitions. The problem is to state criteria in terms of factors which are likely to result in future performance based on current and historical evidence. If a firm states criteria in terms of future performance, it must be willing to support those criteria with substantial information and analysis.

Criteria should be acceptable to the board of directors. This is important since the board will finally ratify or reject any acquisition proposals. If the board has not approved criteria in advance, then scanners compound their problem by trying to determine what information to gather for each alternative as well as how the board will judge or use that information. Once criteria are approved, the board will usually be more concerned with whether or not they are met.

Examining Sources of Information

Sources should provide for use of functional resources if the scanning process is primarily concerned with related acquisitions. If markets for entry are identified by managers of related business units, then the resource requirements are easily ascertained. When only a few markets could satisfy the resource requirements, then broad searches for candidates may be inefficient unless they are simultaneously conducted to locate unrelated acquisitions, or related acquisitions for many different operating units.

Sources should recognize and respond to information availability patterns. If alternative markets are identified about which little information is available, developing markets for example, the scanning process should be able to develop unique and creative approaches to information gathering. If sources of market identification are also sources of prospect identification, then the problem is less significant.

Sources should identify a sufficient number of prospects to satisfy the urgency requirements. If sources identify candidates, then a problem is whether or not sources will identify a sufficient number of candidates which meet the criteria. If sources identify prospects, then the problem also concerns whether or not the sources will identify a sufficient number of prospects which both meet the criteria and are willing to be acquired on acceptable terms. In either case, the problem can usually be resolved by locating additional sources of prospect identification.

Sources should be able to respond adequately to requests. If the firm selects to identify candidates before identifying markets for entry, the ability to gather market information rapidly is important. Good acquisition alternatives generally do not remain available for long periods of time. If the firm does not respond quickly to them, it may need to forego attractive alternatives. Similarly, if the firm plans to achieve diversification quickly, it must gather information about many markets and therefore cannot usually afford much time allocated to any one.

Sources should provide indications of functional resource compatibility for related market acquisitions. If sources cannot provide sufficiently detailed information to determine if synergistic benefits can be derived from related acquisitions, then acquisition alternatives cannot be adequately evaluated in terms of the established criteria.

Sources should be sufficiently reliable to provide accurate information. This problem concerns the totality of information from all sources which are consulted, not each individual source. Multiple sourcing is one approach to insuring accuracy. However, if the aggregate reliability is inadequate, then there is cause for concern. Similarly, if some sources are unnecessary or excessively unreliable, then they can be eliminated from the scanning process.

Sources should be sufficiently motivated to provide the information which they possess. Sources of information must be evaluated in terms of the information they provide, not the information they possess. One way to determine in advance the likelihood that a source will provide information is to determine the motivations it has for doing so. Sometimes these motivations will also indicate the accuracy of the information which they will provide.

Sources should be credible to the board of directors. The problem here is whether or not the board will be willing to act on the information as though it were accurate and unbiased because of the sources from which it was obtained. This problem is particularly acute when a firm does not have the experience of successful acquisitions. When recognized experts are the source or when many sources have provided the same information, the board need be less concerned with the accuracy of information upon which a proposal is based. When the source has also provided a recommendation, it too may become more credible than a recommendation from the management, unless the management has a record of successful acquisitions.

The costs of using these sources should not be excessive. This is a difficult problem since the alternatives may not be known. The costs should reduce as the firm becomes more able to evaluate the reliability of sources.   Many firms hire consulting firms to gather information for their first few acquisitions and then learn that they can gather the information themselves for much lower cost.   Other firms utilize industry experts only after other information sources indicate the appropriateness of completing an acquisition.

Examining Information Processing

Information should be adequately processed for the urgency of decisions required.   Some forms of information processing, for example financial analysis, require little time to complete, whereas others require a considerable amount of time, for example long range forecasting.   The types and amounts of processing should not impede the acquisition scanning process, particularly if the firm urgently needs acquisitions.

Information sources should be able to process information to the extent required.   Consultants may present recommendations ready for the board of directors; primary sources may present historical statistics which have not been processed at all.   Between these extremes are many levels. When the firm does not have the internal capability to process information, then more must be done externally.   However, processing tends to aggregate information and eliminate distinctions which may be important to the firm.   The more processing is done internally the more it can fit the needs of the firm.   Also, external processors can bias information, intentionally or unintentionally.   Internal processors can do this also, but are less likely to do so unknowingly.

The skills required to process information should be available. Although resolving the previous problem suggests a preference for internal processing, the firm may not have the capacity or capability to process information.   In the short term, the firm must work with what it has available, but in the longer term, it can alter that availability to suit expected needs. If information processing capability is limited, then the firm should not establish criteria which require extensive processing. Criteria which require processing are often easier to state, but harder to determine.   The balance between the two is difficult to achieve.

Processors and types of processing should be acceptable to the board of directors.   This problem is best resolved by open discussion with the board at the time criteria for acquisition are proposed.   If the board is generally supportive of the diversifying acquisition program, then the problem will probably not be important. However, if the board is reluctant, then processors should have good reputations for their skills and some description of the processing should be included with the proposals submitted to the board to indicate the quality and depth of analysis behind them.

Examining Participants

Managers required for integration should participate in the scanning process. These managers are able to determine what information will have a significant impact on the ability to integrate an acquisition into the firm's organization. Furthermore, their support and cooperation will be essential to achieve integration.

Managers with access to information sources should participate in the scanning process. Similarly, managers with knowledge about particular alternatives or with analytical skills should participate in the process. For example, antitrust attorneys should be involved early in the process if antitrust enforcement is stringent and/or if the firm is seeking closely related market entry. This problem is difficult because it considers whether or not the firm has adequately assessed the availability of these skills within the firm. Shortages of manpower may result in missed opportunities, hasty decisions, and ill-conceived proposals. Considering the importance of diversifying acquisitions to a firm and the amounts of money and time invested in acquired companies, the firm should be sure that adequate manpower is provided for the task.

Board members with information or access to information should be involved in the scanning process. Including them not only seems politically expedient, but also functional. Board members are usually important people with broad contacts and rapid access to sources of some information on many topics. Scanners would do well to monitor the interests of board members to be sure they are fully utilized as sources of information.

Examining the Sequence of the Process

Sequencing should insure broad consideration of alternatives. This problem arises primarily with respect to the urgency of acquiring. When urgency is great, a sequence which identifies markets before it identifies prospects or that requires substantial processing for initial screening will detract from the purpose for which it was established. Similarly, when unrelated acquisitions are sought, but criteria are restrictive or focus on limited markets, appropriate alternatives may be eliminated unnecessarily.

Sequencing should utilize source characteristics effectively. Some sources can provide information quickly and inexpensively while others are slower, more expensive, but more reliable. Often less accurate sources are acceptable for initial screening purposes, particularly if they are biased toward presenting more favorable information. These same sources of information may be inadequate for final evaluation, but to permit rapid consideration of prospects or markets they may be considerably more valuable than sources which are expensive or which require months to provide information which leads to negative decisions.

Finally, sequencing should facilitate involvement of appropriate personnel. For related acquisitions, business unit managers should be involved early in the scanning process. If antitrust enforcement is stringent, attorneys should be involved early in the process. In most cases, there is no reason to involve accountants in the early stages of the process.

Epilog

This treatise set out to describe the process by which firms gather information for their domestic diversifying acquisition decisions. In Chapter VI the description was stated in the form of a model based on observations of the actual scanning processes of several firms. In Chapter VII, this description was used to develop a procedure for designing and evaluating the acquisition scanning system of a firm. In the author's opinion, this procedure represents a contribution to the managers of firms who want to begin or to improve their acquisition scanning processes. Heretofore, these managers did not have guidance of this type.

NOTES

[1]This concept of gap analysis is explained in more detail in H. Igor Ansoff, *Corporate Strategy* (McGraw-Hill, New York, NY, 1965); however, the emphasis on urgency is not considered as important in his treatment.

[2]This observation is generally consistent with Harry Lynch, *Financial Performance of Conglomerates* (Division of Research, Graduate School of Business Administration, Harvard University, Boston, MA, 1971), although the emphasis was strongly on the urgency perceived by conglomerate firms and the reasons for it.

[3]The concept of limited general management skill transference is discussed in Stanley S. Miller, *Management Problems of Diversification*, (John Wiley and Sons, New York, 1963).

[4]Problems of integrating acquired companies into a firm's organization are discussed by Richard E. Davis, "Compatability in Corporate Marriages," *Harvard Business Review*, July-August 1968, and Robert A. Howell, "Plan to Integrate Your Acquisitions," *Harvard Business Review*, November-December 1970, p. 66.

[5]For some insights on how to evaluate competitive resources within a market, see Howard H. Stevenson, *Defining Corporate Strengths and Weaknesses* (Unpublished doctoral dissertation deposited in Baker Library, Graduate School of Business Administration, Harvard University, Boston, MA, 1969).

[6]For a detailed discussion of the major advantages of alternative diversification strategies see H. Igor Ansoff, *Corporate Strategy*; and Norman Berg, "What's Different About Conglomerate Management," *Harvard Business Review*, November-December 1969, p. 119.

[7]For a more detailed understanding of the roles of boards of directors in major decisions, see Myles L. Mace, *Directors: Myth and Reality* (Division of Research, Graduate School of Business Administration, Harvard University, Boston, MA, 1971).

[8]See Warren J. Keegan, *Scanning the International Business Environment: A Study of the Information Acquisition Process* (Unpublished doctoral dissertation deposited in Baker Library, Graduate School of Business Administration, Harvard University, Boston, MA, 1967) for a more detailed discussion of roles and role sets in the scanning process.

INDEX